The Spirit of Oakland

An Anthology

Abby Wasserman, Editor ∞ Diane Curry, Photo Editor

First Edition
Copyright©2000
by Heritage Media Corporation
All rights reserved. No part of this book may be reproduced in any form or by any means, electronic or mechanical, including photocopying, without permission in writing from the publisher. All inquiries should be addressed to Heritage Media Corp.

ISBN: 1-886483-36-1

Library of Congress Card Catalog Number: 99-073077

Publisher: C.E. Parks

Editor-in-Chief: Lori M. Parks

Editor: Abby Wasserman

Photo Editor: Diane Curry

Contributing Photographer: Robert A. Eplett

VP/Sales: Jill DeLeary

VP/Corporate Development: Bart Barica

CFO: Randall Peterson

Production Manager: Deborah Sherwood

Managing Editor: Betsy Baxter Blondin

Art Director: Gina Mancini

Assistant Art Director: Susie Passons

Project Editor: Renee Kim

Coordinating Editors: Betsy Lelja, Elizabeth Lex, Sara Rufner, Mary Ann Stabile, Adriane Wessels, John Woodward

Production Staff: Astrit Bushi, Jeff Caton, Dave Hermstead, Jay Kennedy, Vincent Kornegay, John Leyva, Marianne Mackey, Gavin Rattmann, Charlie Silvia

Profile Writers: Sue Buchholz, Laura Bueno, Allen Gardiner, Stephanie Holland, Nora Horn, Stephen M. Kinney, Angela Kucherenko, Katherine Mehrer, Kent Streeb, Barbara Szerlip, Patrick Totty

Human Resources Manager: Ellen Ruby

Administration: Juan Diaz, Debbie Hunter, Azalea Maes, Majka Penner, Scott Reid, Patrick Rucker, Cory Sottek

Published by

Heritage Media Corp.
1954 Kellogg Avenue
Carlsbad, California 92008
www.heritagemedia.com

Printed in cooperation with the Oakland Museum of California (www.museumca.org)
Printed by Heritage Media Corp. in the United States of America

Richard Diebenkorn, *Figure on a Porch*, 1959, oil on canvas
Oakland Museum of California, Anonymous Donor Program of the American Federation of Arts

3

table of Contents

The Spirit of Oakland

5

FOREWORD

Wallace Stegner is credited with a phrase I have always liked: "California is America, only more so." I think in many ways Oakland is California, only more so — if not California now, certainly its future. No gold was found in its streams, no oil deep in the ground, no thousand-acre monocultures, no movie industry, and certainly no Disneyland by the freeway. With one border on San Francisco Bay and another in redwood-forested hills, Oakland has throughout its history served as a gateway for commerce as well as being one of California's best living environments. But what really makes Oakland an all-California city and certainly a bellwether of the future is the diversity of its people. In this lies the richness of Oakland and all it has done and will do.

In the chapters that follow you will find a variety of points of view reflecting Oakland's diversity, a richness of outlook we could not have captured had this book been written by an individual historian. You will also be introduced to the rich source of visual images housed and occasionally exhibited in the city's highly regarded museum: the Oakland Museum of California. In fact, one of the reasons we undertook this project was to share these images more widely. We are a resource for Oakland as well as for California, collecting, exhibiting, and interpreting the art, history and natural environment of the state. More recently, we have come to recognize we are also about the people of California, something to which I hope this book attests.

I acknowledge with deepest gratitude the people at Heritage Media Corporation who worked with us to make this book a reality and the financial support of the fine businesses who made the project possible. Diane Curry of the museum's staff served most admirably in selecting the images. Abby Wasserman, with whom I have had the pleasure of working for the last six years, did her usual magic as organizer and editor. She is the consummate professional. And finally, I thank the many authors who contributed their time, expertise, and knowledge. They represent, and have captured, the spirit of Oakland.

— DENNIS M. POWER, EXECUTIVE DIRECTOR, OAKLAND MUSEUM OF CALIFORNIA

ACKNOWLEDGMENTS

This book was a collaboration among many wonderful people. First, special thanks to our Historical Consultant, William Sturm, head of the Oakland History Room at the Oakland Public Library, for his astute guidance and careful research, and to L. Thomas Frye, who helped conceptualize the book and was a stalwart ally. Annalee Allen, Betsy Anders, Deborah Cooper, Harlan Kessel, Arabella Martinez, Mark Medeiros, Tony Molatore Photo Lab, Nicholas Petris, Margaret and Leo Saito, Mary Perry and Norvel Smith, Paul Takagi, Yasuko and Bob Utsumi and Charles M. Wollenberg read individual sections and made invaluable suggestions for incorporation. The staff and board of the Oakland Heritage Alliance furnished a complete set of their excellent newsletter and allowed us to quote from them. David Glover and OCCUR generously allowed the use of their neighborhood profiles series. Mary Ellen Butler, Carey Caldwell, Jo Ann Coleman, Kathleen DiGiovanni, Jack Foley, Meoy Gee, Warren and Elizabeth Hayashi, Susan Lobo, Helen Lore, Celia McCarthy, Woodruff Minor, Oakland Heritage Alliance, Dorothy Patterson, Frankie Rhodes, Christopher Richard, Floyd Salas, Joe Samberg, Sandra Sher, Richard Silberg, Helen Tryon, Jo Takata, Potter Wickware, Dean Yabuki, and Tony and Nowie Yokomizo extended kindnesses and material assistance. Thanks to Dennis M. Power, who furnished essential help and encouragement; to the Oakland Museum of California curators for placing their photographic collections at our disposal; to Gail Bernstein, who proofread the manuscript; and to Betsy Blondin and Renee Kim at Heritage Media, for their fine editorial eyes. Finally, our warm appreciation to the authors, whose intelligence, diligence and insight enliven these pages.

— ABBY WASSERMAN AND DIANE CURRY

Introduction

Oakland WILL CELEBRATE ITS SESQUICENTENNIAL IN 2002.
THE CITY HAS TRAVELED A LONG WAY IN 150 YEARS, YET TWO
FORCES AFFECTING THE ECONOMY AND DEMOGRAPHICS TODAY
ARE REMARKABLY SIMILAR TO THOSE AT WORK DURING THE CITY'S
CREATION: A RUSH FOR RICHES AND AN INFLUX OF IMMIGRANTS.
THE GOLD FEVER OF THE MID-19TH CENTURY, WHICH BROUGHT
THE WORLD TO CALIFORNIA, CREATED THE CITY OF OAKLAND JUST
AS IT CREATED HER SISTER ACROSS THE BAY, SAN FRANCISCO.

Oakland's history is one of power struggles and "firsts," of creativity and accomplishment, of high achievement and ignominious failures, of survival and triumph through earthquake, fire and flood. The good times have been many, and there have been dog years, too. The city has working-class roots and was for much of its history a prominent industrial center; it is equally rich in the culture of its people. Its politics tend to be progressive, its social innovations enlightened or at the very least well-intentioned, its politics often surprising.

Throughout its growth from village to metropolis, Oakland has been dubbed many things, often in the attempt to arrive at a definitive identity for outsiders. An early sobriquet, "Athens of the Pacific," expressed satisfaction with the city's cultural institutions and excellent private schools. "Hub of the West" described Oakland as an essential crossroads of air, rail and water transport. "Progressive City" made sense in the 1910s, during the progressive reign of Mayor Frank Mott, and would work today. "Eden of the Pacific: The Flower Garden of California" showed the city's pride in its horticulture. Oakland in the 1990s was honored as an All America City® for the cultural and racial diversity and social programs. I like "My Oakland," from the 1930s, for its settled, affectionate tone. The only phrase that captures all of Oakland for me, however, is "Oakland is California, only more so." This acknowledges both the city's complexity and its inextricable ties to California's own fortunes.

Oakland residents are puzzled when outsiders dismiss or belittle their city. They shake their heads as if to say, "They just don't understand, poor fellows." Oakland is not a tourist city, despite its many tourist attractions; it is a place to *live*. Throughout its history, Oakland has been thought a good place to live for many reasons: the climate, soil, air, space, architecture, parks, people, libraries, colleges, culture and small-city (currently 400,000) atmosphere. I've heard people say that if Oakland were anywhere else in the world rather than across the bay from San Francisco, it would be acknowledged as a city of the first rank. But then, Oakland anywhere else in the world wouldn't be Oakland.

What does the city look like? High, graceful hills crisscrossed with creeks and verdant with redwoods, bay and oak, descending into hilly lowlands, deep canyons and sloping meadows, and on to a great spreading plain with sparse greenery that reaches to the bay. Like all of the region, the topography is dramatic. The Hayward Fault runs through the hills from north to south, and there are smaller faults everywhere. The city is composed of neighborhoods or districts, most with their own small commercial centers. Oakland grew by annexation, so each district retains its own flavor and has a colorful history. Parks abound, some of them extensive and beautifully kept, others sparse and neglected. The city has a full spectrum of wealth and poverty, but most residents are situated between the two extremes. In a crisis, people come together. They come together in good times, too, at festivals or street fairs, where the feeling is overwhelmingly friendly and inclusive. Highways surround parts of the city, but commercial transport concentrates near the water. Planes take off next to the bay at Oakland International Airport, great container ships dock at the Port of Oakland, trains rumble into the station at Jack London Square and ferries, a couple of blocks away, start or finish their runs.

Ten books could not do justice to this city's intricate and multilayered past. Our book seeks rather to illuminate in distinct voices some aspects of Oakland's history from too seldom-heard perspectives. The organization is thematic rather than chronological, and the narrative moves back and forth in time. Each chapter is briefly introduced and the writer identified, but otherwise the whole can be read as a single narrative.

We begin at the city's beginnings with the "claims, characters and commerce" of the Oakland waterfront, then segue to Latino history, starting with the Peralta family, whose land grant comprised all of Oakland and much of the East Bay. A chapter on the inventive art of politics follows, then one on the inventive arts, which traces Oakland's history as a focus for artists and art schools. The story of Oakland Chinese and Japanese Americans comes next, then a chapter pairing Oakland's little-known automobile industry with the city's aviation "firsts" and airport. Highlights and struggles of African Americans in Oakland are the subject of the next chapter, followed by some remarkable athletes, teams and coaches. Then comes a chapter with a section on libraries and another on gardens and parks. Next we

City Hall Plaza, 2000
Photo by Robert A. Eplett

go back in history to find the original inhabitants of this area, the Ohlone, and look at how, during the last 60 years, Native Americans from around the country established an intertribal community here. Music and dance, from blues to classical, ballet to ethnic, comprise the next chapter. Finally, there are chapters on the growth of downtown in relation to two great earthquakes and on a spectrum of Oakland writers. And throughout the book there are neighborhood profiles rich in history. Historian Charles M. Wollenberg concludes with reflections on Oakland's "regional reality."

The Spirit of Oakland is dedicated to all of the men and women — sung and unsung heroes and heroines — whose labor, talent and vision created the city we know and love.

— Abby Wasserman, Oakland, California
May 25, 2000

9

Chapter 1

CLAIMS, CHARACTERS AND COMMERCE

Oakland's WATERFRONT, STRETCHING FOR MILES, IS THE CITY'S TRANSPORTATION HUB, HOUSING ITS SHIPPING AND AIRPORT FACILITIES. HISTORICALLY IT IS EVEN MORE, AS **MICHAEL DOBRIN** ILLUSTRATES: POLITICAL FOOTBALL, LITERARY INSPIRATION, CENTER OF INDUSTRY, RECREATIONAL PLAYGROUND AND A SYMBOL OF OAKLAND'S ECONOMIC HEALTH.

The boisterous 150-year history of Oakland's waterfront encompasses elements as diverse as the demise of the archaic Spanish empire, the momentous arrival of the transcontinental railroad, arctic whaling, two world wars, shipbuilding, political and commercial machinations, growth of the American labor movement, emergence of regional transportation systems, ascendancy of the city as a major manufacturing center and arrival of the Port of Oakland as a global port of call.

The story, too, is dominated by personality — individuals who left a distinct imprint on the waterfront legacy: the Spanish grantee Luis María Peralta, Yankee opportunists Horace Carpentier and Samuel Merritt, the rough-and-tumble young Jack London, legendary sailing captains such as Mike Healy; industrialists like shipbuilder Joseph Moore; and politicians of the stamp of Mayor Frank K. Mott.

As diarist and chaplain for the Juan Bautista de Anza exploratory Spanish expedition from Mexico to California in 1776, the Catalán friar Pedro Font led a scouting party around the south end of the great bay (technically an estuary) and up the eastern shore. Encamped at a knoll near present-day Mills College, he noted navigable waterways and observed a peninsula to the west, framed by two creeks and marked by an ample stand of trees. The two creeks, later to be named San Antonio and San Leandro, were like dozens of others transecting the entire region, each bearing clear, rushing waters down from the hills into the vast marshes.

Font's explorers encountered a marine environment far greater than that which we know today. Half tidal marsh and half open water, the entire bay — reaching north past Suisun Bay and into the San Joaquin Delta — was larger than Rhode Island. The marshes spread inland to the foothills of what are now the cities of Fremont and Milpitas, and over the flatlands of Berkeley, Emeryville, West Oakland and most of Alameda. This was the land of the Ohlone, and their permanent villages and temporary camps dotted the shores. They used tule reeds to create broad-beamed canoes in which they rowed the open waters and interstices of the marsh. These skilled swimmers and adept fishermen, hunters and gatherers built shelters from the same reeds. Their distinctive sweathouses were given the name *temescal* by the Spanish. It was a region of great beauty, fertility and bounty.

The Spanish military explorers-cum-colonists soon established Mission Dolores and the Presidio military garrison on the western side of the bay, which they called Yerba Buena. Its deep water access — while the eastern shore was awash in shallow tidal flats — would play a significant role in Spanish plans for the region, determining San Francisco's dominance as a shipping and commercial center into the 20th century.

Accompanying the Anza expedition was 16-year-old Luis María Peralta, who was destined to own much of the East Bay. Born in 1759 in Sonora, Mexico, he enlisted as a soldier, serving at both Monterey and San Francisco presidios. In 1821, when he was 62 years old, Don Luis was granted a 45,000-acre estate as a reward for his fealty to the Spanish crown. His land stretched from San Leandro Creek north to present-day El Cerrito. Along with his wife, four sons and five daughters, Peralta lived the sweet life of a Californio, raising cattle and conducting a subsistence trade in hides and tallow. The Peralta rancho embraced tidal waters of San Antonio Creek, but in order to transship hides and tallow to deep water vessels anchored across the bay, Don Luis built a small wharf at the end of what is now 14th Avenue.

The discovery of gold at Sutter's Mill on the American River in 1848 changed life in California forever. The world poured in overland and through the Golden Gate, and soon both sides of the bay teemed with speculators and adventurers. The rancho, by this time, was divided among Don Luis's four sons, and all of them had to contend with squatters who rustled Peralta cattle, set up sawmills and hauled virgin redwoods out of Peralta hills. These renegade entrepreneurs were so efficient (they had a ready market over in notoriously combustible San Francisco) that by 1860 they had completely denuded the crestline forests.

The Peraltas had displaced the Ohlones, and they were, in turn, to be slowly, relentlessly and ruthlessly displaced by the newcomers, among whose numbers were Oakland's future founders.

Horace Walpole Carpentier, an attorney from New York, and two other attorneys, Edson Adams and Andrew J. Moon, crossed over from San Francisco in 1850 and staked out adjoining tracts among other squatters near present-day Jack London Square. The 24-year-old Carpentier, educated at Columbia University, came West as a forty-niner, eschewing life in the gold fields in favor of managing a lucrative practice in San Francisco with his brother, Edward. Pious, self-righteous, ascetic and reserved, he let few obstacles impede his well-oiled plans to acquire land and power. He made an early career of wresting Peralta land from the family, acting alternately as counselor and confiscator. He is rumored to have dressed as a priest and performed bogus rituals at the Peralta rancho. He once covered a debt for Domingo Peralta, then took part of his lands in payment. He was accused of rustling cattle. Filing exhaustive and endless appeals, claims and litigation, he kept courts, cohorts and correspondents at arm's length for years.

His most impressive and outrageous act was manipulating ownership of Oakland's entire waterfront. He did this by promising to build two wharves and a schoolhouse. "The exclusive right and privilege of constructing wharves, piers and docks at any points within the corporate limits of the town of Oakland, with the right of collecting wharfage and dockage at such rates as he may deem reasonable, is hereby granted and confirmed into Horace W. Carpentier and his legal representatives, for the period of thirty-seven years," read the Act of Incorporation in 1852. Oakland would suffer bitterly for this ill-conceived largesse. But at first, the ramifications weren't clear. In addition to his wharves, piers and a toll bridge across the eastern reaches of San Antonio Creek, Carpentier, with Moon, operated a ferry between San Antonio Township and San Francisco. Carpentier later formed the Contra Costa Steam Navigation Company with an early ferryboat competitor, Charles Minturn, securing a 20-year monopoly for service to San Francisco.

Oakland was incorporated again, this time as a city, in March 1854. Carpentier became its first mayor that year, calling for, among other things, saving shade trees, outlawing prostitution and gambling, ending bull and bear fighting — and, prophetically, advocating Oakland as the terminus of the transcontinental railroad.

Oakland did become the western terminus, not through Carpentier's efforts but to his profit. After considerable negotiation between the Central Pacific Railroad's Big Four — Charles Crocker, Collis P. Huntington, Mark Hopkins and Leland Stanford — the agreement to bring the railroad to Oakland was actually brokered by Dr. Samuel Merritt, who, as the city's mayor in 1868, helped create the "Oakland Water Front Company" to which Carpentier transferred a small portion of his waterside holdings. Merritt, Carpentier and Stanford, among others, were financial beneficiaries of the transaction, which provided the railroad with substantial land adjacent to San Antonio Creek. Merritt played prominent roles in the civic, cultural, commercial and political life of Oakland. Surgeon, ship builder, lumber baron, developer, philanthropist, politician, yachtsman and banker, he was the very embodiment of Yankee certitude when he arrived in San Francisco in 1850. Within two years he had purchased property in Oakland, where he built a wharf and warehouse on a brackish branch of San Antonio Creek.

The railroad brought immense, immediate change to California and Oakland. The rail bed ran west along Seventh Street to its waterfront end, where in 1871 the Central Pacific built the two-mile Oakland Long Wharf into the bay, allowing freight and passengers to move more rapidly to San Francisco. Shops, yards and attendant commerce along the corridor created jobs for hundreds; by 1880, Oakland's population had soared to 35,000. An

Samuel Merritt, c. 1867
Oakland Museum of California, Oakland Tribune Collection, gift of ANG Newspapers

Pencil sketch of Lower Broadway, May 1854, about the time Oakland was incorporated as a city
Oakland Museum of California, gift of Mr. Joseph R. Knowland

13

Looking TOWARD OAKLAND FROM THE TOP OF THE SOUTHERN PACIFIC RAILROAD DEPOT AT THE END OF THE OAKLAND MOLE, C. 1880. THE OAKLAND LONG WHARF IS TO THE LEFT.

Oakland Museum of California, Oakland Tribune Collection, gift of ANG Newspapers

adjacent bay extension, the Oakland Mole, was completed in 1882 and dedicated to the movement of passengers. The Central Pacific and its successor, Southern Pacific, operated transbay ferry service. Businesses grew up along the waterway: shipfitters and shipbuilders, jute factories, breweries, flour mills, pottery and tile manufacturers, lumber mills, wagon builders and ore crushers.

An ambitious dredging plan, kept on course by Col. George Mendell of the Army Corps of Engineers, deepened and widened the tidal canal. A cut was made between Brooklyn Basin and San Leandro Bay, making Alameda an island. Dredge spoils were used to fill nearby marshlands. But in spite of these commercial developments, the legacy of Carpentier's deal, now subsumed by the railroads, kept the city from controlling its waterfront. Citizens became increasingly outraged with the state of affairs. By 1880 a disgruntled Carpentier had returned to New York, where he continued to amass his fortune (estimated at his death in 1918 at $3.5 million) and direct protracted litigation over his California holdings. In 1894 Oaklanders tore down a fence erected by the Southern Pacific to keep them from the waterfront.

Young Jack London, ghosting out of Oakland on the night tide at the helm of *Razzle Dazzle*, found escape and adventure raiding the oyster pens off Bay Farm Island. *Ostrea lurida*, a silver dollar-sized oyster, was the prize. "My reputation grew," he later wrote. "There were the times I brought the *Razzle Dazzle* in with a bigger load of oysters than any other two-man craft; there was the time when we raided far down in Lower Bay and mine was the only craft back at daylight

to the anchorage off Asparagus Island…. What completed everything and won for me the title of 'Prince of the Oyster Beds,' was that I was a good fellow ashore with my money, buying drinks like a man. I little dreamed that the time would come when the Oakland water-front, which had shocked me at first, would be shocked and annoyed by the deviltry of the things I did."

As deep-draft oceanic vessels made their way further into the dredged Oakland Estuary, shipbuilders proliferated along the waterfront. The yards of Charles G. White, Hay & Wright, Dickie Brothers, William A.

William T. Shorey and his family, 1900. Shorey was a prominent member of Oakland's African-American community and a successful ship's captain, one of the only captains on the West Coast of African descent.
Oakland Museum of California, gift of Mrs. Victoria Francis

The Ferry *Piedmont* was one of the ferries that carried passengers from Oakland to San Francisco, c. 1897.
Oakland Museum of California, gift of Mr. Linwood L. Clark

Boole, and Barnes & Tibbetts flourished at the end of the 19th century. The oldest working boat yard in California is the Stone Boat Yard, which was founded in 1853, when Englishman William F. Stone set up works in San Francisco. By 1912 his son, Frank, had moved the operation to Oakland; and *his* son, Lester, continued the business until the late 1970s. The Stones built more than 220 wooden vessels, from five-masted schooners to tugs, tenders and elegant yachts.

15

The exigencies of commerce and catastrophe collided to bring to the Oakland waterfront what was to become its most influential shipbuilding firm. Founded in 1905 after acquisition of San Francisco's Union Iron Works, the Moore & Scott Iron Works had begun expansion into marine repair when the great fire and earthquake struck one year later. Although relatively unscathed in the holocaust, the company was unable to secure permanent dry dock facilities in San Francisco and moved in 1909 to the expansive Boole yards in Oakland at the foot of Adeline Street. In 1918 the company became the Moore Shipbuilding Company, and with the advent of World War I it boomed with government contracts. Employing up to 13,000, the firm turned out 30 freighters and oil tankers. After the war, the company diversified into ship repair, dry dock, dredge, structural steel and bridge construction. The company built the Park Street (1935) and High Street (1939) bridges from Oakland into Alameda.

World War II brought dramatic expansion to Moore Dry Dock. More than 37,000 workers labored around the clock to build some 200 cargo ships, submarine tenders, landing craft and floating dry docks. The war accelerated change all along the waterway. The Outer Harbor terminals were developed and vast westerly tracts given over to the Oakland Naval Supply

The FIRST TRAIN COMING THROUGH THE NEWLY LAID TRACKS AT THE OAKLAND ARMY BASE, DECEMBER 1941. THE BASE AND THE U.S. NAVAL SUPPLY DEPOT PLAYED MAJOR ROLES IN MOVING TROOPS AND SUPPLIES TO THE PACIFIC THEATER THROUGHOUT WORLD WAR II, KOREA AND VIETNAM.

Oakland Museum of California, Oakland Tribune Collection, gift of ANG Newspapers

Depot and the Oakland Army Base. Hundreds of acres were filled to create Alameda Naval Air Station.

For 35 years, from 1893 to 1928, the Oakland Estuary was home to the Alaska Packers fleet. Every spring the tall ships went north to the Aleutians to catch salmon for processing and canning — and when the old windjammers died, their hulks settled in along Brooklyn Basin's "Rotten Row." Skeletal remains of these ships can be seen today at low tide around Government Island. Seasoned Arctic hands like Oakland skipper Christian Theodore Pedersen and John Justus "Johnny the Painter" Bertonccini, who painted primitive views of Arctic whaling life, sailed on Packers vessels. When Pedersen abandoned his Canalaska trading outpost on remote Herschel Island in 1936, it signaled the end of a vibrant 70-year relationship between the Oakland waterfront and the Arctic.

When America purchased Alaska in 1867, one of the first resources to be plundered were the Pribilof seal herds. The government collected substantial taxes from the sealing trade and assigned vessels of the Revenue Cutter Service to protect its interests. The best-known of these was the steam cutter *Bear*, and the most famous of its early captains was "Hell Roaring" Mike Healy, the light-skinned son of a Georgia plantation owner and a slave woman. He was educated in Massachusetts and passed for white all his life; to do otherwise would have cost him his command. A fearless and deft skipper, his word was American law over 30,000 miles of Bering Sea coastline between 1885 and 1895. *Bear* was sold to Adm. Richard E. Byrd in 1932.

The Arctic fishing trade, commercial shipbuilding and ancillary businesses all contributed to the waterfront's economic life. But until the 1920s, Oakland lost lucrative shipping to new wharves and piers all along the San Francisco waterfront. The railroad, and the ghost of Carpentier's waterfront deal, effectively kept the city from developing its own waterfront for many years. In 1897 the California Supreme Court ratified Carpentier's original grant — but at the 1852 low-tide line, which was far inland by then (thus in effect nullifying what it had just ratified). Facing the loss of control over the land, the Southern Pacific countered with more litigation. In 1909 Mayor Frank K. Mott, along

18

with a Progressive Movement coalition, went directly to the railroad and drew up a compromise whereby Oakland finally gained access to its waterfront and the railroad won a 50-year lease. In 1925, Oakland voters approved a $10 million bond issue for waterfront development and one year later approved the creation of an independent Port Commission, with its own budget and the oversight to guard against the graft and corruption that had plagued Eastern cities.

Piers, wharves and handling terminals went up from outer to inner harbors. By the mid-1930s, Oakland was a port of call for 40 world shipping lines. Outbound cargoes included dried and canned foods, ores, glass products, cotton, salt, sugar, walnuts, almonds — some of these goods a boon to Central Valley farming — as well as buses, tractors, cars, engines, batteries, tires and beer from Oakland's industrial and manufacturing engine.

The boom in postwar global trade changed shipping profoundly. By the 1960s cargo transfers were being made by faster and more efficient intermodal systems. One operator in an overhead crane was able to offload stacked containers from one vessel in one day, transferring the cargo directly either to truck or rail car, a task formerly taking up to three days with stevedores and primitive cargo winches. Through the leadership and vision of Port Executive Director Ben Nutter, Oakland's waterfront site became one of the world's premier container and intermodal shipping operations; in fact, for some years it was the leading such port in the world. In a reversal of fortune, the working port of San Francisco withered and died during the same period for lack of interest and forward motion. During Nutter's 15-year tenure, which ended in 1977, the Port enjoyed tremendous expansion. He was influential in securing reciprocal port and trade operations in Japan, which further solidified Oakland's powerful trading stature.

Today small wooden day sailors, carbon fiber racing sloops, motor yachts, speedboats and kayaks ride the Oakland Estuary tides, tacking between shores, boosted by filling westerlies. As they sail, motor or row under the lee of huge ocean cargo ships, and slip by wharves and piers, their helmsmen may be unaware of the tumultuous history surrounding them — a history of claims, characters and commerce that spills over the narrow confines of this bustling world waterway.

Boxes of canned Hawaiian pineapple sit on the dock at the Grove Street Pier, c. 1910.
Oakland Museum of California, gift of Herrington and Olson

In the winter of 1932-1933, 200 homeless men took up residence in surplus sewer pipes in a storage yard at the foot of Nineteenth Avenue on the estuary. The mayor of this "Pipe City" was Dutch Jensen. To qualify for a pipe the potential resident had to be jobless, homeless, hungry and scruffy — but absolutely not helpless.
Oakland Museum of California, gift of Martin J. Cooney

19

THE

NEigHbORHOOds

West Oakland

An area of marshland and oak groves before the mid-1800s, West Oakland is one of the oldest districts in the city and a transportation hub, housing the terminus of the transcontinental railroad, ferry dock and the port facility. Elegant Victorian homes, built between the dock and downtown to house the growing population, were converted into multi-unit apartments beginning in the late 1890s. West Oakland was home to one of California's oldest black middle-class communities, railroad workers who settled there in the 1870s. Important black charities and self-improvement societies were founded, and for a long time the First AME Church was the center of activity. Following the 1906 earthquake, many more African Americans settled in the district.

During World War I, West Oakland shipbuilding drew new waves of migrants who contributed to the already strong working-class neighborhood. The neighborhood had a highly diverse population, with large numbers of black, Irish, Italian, Dutch, Mexican and Portuguese Americans working and living side by side. During the second world war, African Americans — many of whom worked in the shipyards — became the most prominent ethnic group. Their presence encouraged cultural activity; jazz musician Horace Silver once referred to West Oakland as "the Harlem in California." Rail service along Seventh Street terminated in 1941, and the year 1945 marked the end of the shipyard boom. Many people lost their jobs, and West Oakland's economy began to decline drastically.

Federal urban renewal programs in the late 1950s and 60s — new projects such as the Grove-Shafter and Cypress freeways, BART, the Acorn Housing project and the new Main Post Office — brought further significant economic and social change. The Cypress freeway structure physically split the community in two. Historic homes were demolished and commercial activity weakened. Hundreds of residents were displaced, and the community organized in opposition. Seventh Street, once the busy center of the neighborhood, is a multilane divided thoroughfare.

The Loma Prieta earthquake of 1989 hit West Oakland hard, destroying housing and causing the collapse of the double-decker Cypress freeway. When the city planned to rebuild it in the same location, the neighborhood was adamant against being divided it once again. Local organizations demanded an alternate route to inspire the reconnection of the community, preserve the accessibility of the convenient Mandela Parkway and promote commercial development. A compromise was reached that answered some of the community's concerns.

Today West Oakland is armed with strong visionary leadership and renewed dedication to its cultural legacy. Among the many active community-based organizations are the West Oakland District Council and the Coalition for West Oakland. Although many of the issues that confronted it in the past still exist, great strides have been made towards revitalizing this historic neighborhood. ■

Chapter 2

There WAS A TIME WHEN ALL THE LAND ON THE EAST SIDE OF SAN FRANCISCO BAY WAS OWNED BY CALIFORNIOS — SPANISH-SPEAKING CITIZENS OF MEXICO. THE GOLD RUSH AND OTHER SOCIAL FORCES DISPLACED THE CALIFORNIOS — BUT, AS **CHIORI SANTIAGO** WRITES, THEIR SPIRIT NEVER LEFT.

Luis María Peralta's original land grant from the King of Spain stretched from present-day Albany to San Leandro Creek, from the bay to the crest of the hills. When he was 83 years old, in 1842, he divided his land among his four sons. The eastern portion, from San Leandro Creek to the area of Seminary Avenue, went to Ignacio, the eldest. The acreage from Seminary Avenue to Lake Merritt was Antonio's, the second son. The land north and west of Lake Merritt, following the bayshore from the lake to present-day Alcatraz Avenue, went to Vicente; all the original town of Oakland was contained in his acreage. Domingo, the youngest son, received the portion where Berkeley, Albany and a small section of North Oakland are now located. The sons had little time to enjoy their land; six years later gold was discovered in the Sierra foothills and an "American invasion" began.

Oakland's modern Latino history began some 25 years later, in 1869, with the wail of a train whistle floating over West Oakland. Over the years, laborers from Mexico came to work in the railroad freight yards, the canneries and garment factories of the bustling city. They stepped off the train at the western terminus building of the transcontinental railroad on Seventh Street, which until three years ago housed the Mi Rancho grocery store — one of the earliest East Bay groceries selling Latin American products.

The next wave came after the Mexican Revolution broke out in 1910. Nearly 10 percent of Mexico's population fled their homes to relocate in the American Southwest and in California. Among them was a young man named Javier Macias, whose story was typical of what the refugees to California had endured. As he recalled in 1999, the fighting brought first government soldiers, then revolutionaries sweeping through his village, each demanding supplies, each with a distinct brand of terror. Macias' town was destroyed. At the age of 10, he went to work selling

A rare tintype of one of the sons of Luis María Peralta, the grantee of Rancho San Antonio, c. 1860
Oakland Museum of California, gift of Mrs. M.E. Schlichtmann

fruit to help his family. The music of his *pregones* — the melodies he sang to hawk his wares — attracted a circus owner, who recruited the boy as an announcer. He traveled with the circus as far as Arizona, then, all of 14 years old, took off for Los Angeles. He followed the harvest to Sacramento, finally settling in Oakland. He later helped build the city's first soccer field at Raimondi Park in West Oakland, where the soccer teams of Club Guadalajara — organized in 1952 by Manuel and Alberto Valle — reigned supreme.

Soccer was just one of the traditions that held the Mexican-American community together in its West

Oakland neighborhood. There were *tardeadas* (afternoon dances) at Sweet's Ballroom downtown, baptisms, *quinceaños* (debutante parties), and communal suppers at The New Century Recreation Center at Fourth and Peralta streets. Shared values and language allowed Spanish-speaking newcomers — who eventually included immigrants from Central and South America and the Caribbean — to bond, despite radical differences in culture. The "barrioization" of California, a result of the desire for community as well as prevailing discriminatory housing practices, historian Albert Camarillo writes, was as much "a help to the new arrival as it was a stamp of one's alien status." Before World War II, "the segregation of Mexican residents in their communities reinforced the use of the Spanish language, religious practices, cultural and social activities and family ties."

By the 1920s St. Mary's Church, on Eighth and Jefferson in West Oakland, boasted a predominantly Mexican-American congregation. Seventh Street, a thoroughfare of shops and restaurants catering to a Spanish-speaking clientele, was a neighborhood focal point. La Borinqueña grocery store and bakery survives to this day, a tribute to four generations of determined women. Rosa Lopez, an enterprising *mexicana*, purchased La Borinqueña on credit after making a deal with her Puerto Rican husband: he'd sanction her endeavor if he could name the business (*la borinqueña* means a woman from the island). But inside the shop the flavor was *puro mexicano*. Despite her maternal duties — the couple had nine children — Rosa Lopez was up at dawn every morning to bake fragrant, sweet *pan dulce*. At noon, working men stepped in for a plate of

Oakland's oldest train station, photographed about 1939. It later was the home of the Mi Rancho grocery store, which operated until the late 1990s.
Oakland History Room, Oakland Public Library

George (Guadalupe) Carlos, the promoter and emcee for Latino acts at Sweet's Ballroom, c. 1945
Oakland Museum of California, gift of Mr. Charles Hector Carlos

24

Children FROM LA ESCUELITA SCHOOL PERFORM AT LANEY COLLEGE DURING CINCO DE MAYO CELEBRATIONS, MAY 5, 1982.

Oakland Museum of California, Oakland Tribune Collection, gift of ANG Newspapers

25

The sorting tables at Del Monte Plant No. 6. The predominately female work force is grading the asparagus for size and color, c. 1925. *Oakland Museum of California, gift of Del Monte Corporation*

Anti-Latino sentiment permeates the caption of this news photo in the *Oakland Tribune* on February 18, 1949: "Smirking for benefit of the camera are four of the 'pachucos' picked up by police last night during a wholesale arrest of hoodlums." *Oakland Museum of California, Oakland Tribune Collection, gift of ANG Newspapers*

tamales or that newfangled California invention known as the "burrito." Unfamiliar with the assemblage of beans, rice and meat rolled into a flour tortilla, Lopez bought several from a lunch truck in the neighborhood and dissected them to figure out how they were made, recounts her granddaughter, Natividad Ramos.

Secure in their neighborhood and among friends, barrio residents celebrated Cinco de Mayo and other holidays, organized political clubs and mutual aid societies and published Spanish-language newspapers that "were… central to the psychological well-being of their readership," Camarillo notes. "They expressed pride in Mexican-American ethnicity, presented minority viewpoints and denounced the discrimination and racism faced daily by Spanish-speaking citizens."

That discrimination was rooted in deep ambivalence on the

part of employers who increasingly depended upon immigrant labor to harvest, process and ship California's produce. In 1928 Mexican Americans made up eight percent of

The Spirit of Oakland

Alameda County's cannery work force. Between 1920 and 1950, when California was packing more produce than any state in the nation, growers, packers and the Southern Pacific Railroad alternately lobbied for more Mexican workers and argued for their deportation.

The situation was particularly acute during World War II, when efforts to bring in American laborers from the South apparently failed. The shortage led to the creation of the Bracero Program in 1942, instituted by agreement with the Mexican government. Five thousand Mexican nationals were sent to Oakland under the Bracero Program to work in the shipyards. With the help of the Pan American Association, the New Century Recreation Center opened to serve them in 1944. Yet often when the season was over, the welcome mat was quickly removed. "Mexicans were viewed alternatively as foreign usurpers of American jobs and as unworthy burdens on local relief rolls," writes historian Vicki L. Ruiz.

Tensions between citizens and those perceived as "deportable aliens" led to an echo of the infamous Los Angeles zoot suit riots in June 1943. Two shipyard workers out on the town, nattily attired in wide-brim hats and pegged pants, clashed with two sailors and an Army corporal near Eighth and Washington streets. The "pachucos," the *Oakland Tribune* reported, were detained, and police declared West Oakland out-of-bounds to servicemen. Spats between zoot-suiters and military personnel continued throughout the fall of that year; in November a "riot" between East Oakland youths and "Okies" in Alameda underscored the notion that whatever their social position, "aliens" knew that turf wars were a fact of life in the United States.

Not all Spanish-speaking immigrants, of course, were underpaid workers from Mexico. Luisa Moreno had been born into a wealthy Guatemalan family. In the 1920s she was enjoying a life of privilege as a boarding school student at Convent of the Holy

Braceros, who were brought to Oakland to work on the Southern Pacific Railroad Lines, pose on the tracks, 1944. *Oakland Museum of California, gift of Mr. Jose Cruz*

27

Names near Lake Merritt. She embraced, with some zeal, the flapper's creed of independence and returned to Guatemala to fight for educational rights for women. By 1928 she had married a Mexican artist and relocated to the United States. She worked as a sweatshop seamstress in New York during the Depression to support her husband and baby, and this experience, combined with confidence and persuasive powers, led her to become an organizer with the American Federation of Labor in 1935 and a pivotal figure in the organization of Oakland's cannery workers in the 1940s. Known as "the California Whirlwind," Moreno also helped found El Congreso de Pueblos de Habla Española (Congress of Spanish-speaking People), a civil rights organization dedicated to the cause of Mexican American, Puerto Rican, Cuban, Central American and other Latino workers — one of the first cross-national service groups in California.

The efforts of Moreno and her colleagues set the stage for the rise of Unity Leagues, grassroots groups that fought for the civil rights of Spanish speakers, and the statewide Community Service Organization, founded in Los Angeles and spearheaded in Oakland by James Delgadillo with Evelio Grillo, Edward Reyes, Elvira Rose and Herman Gallegos, among others. In 1963 Arabella Martinez became a member of the Oakland CSO, using a talent for mobilization to help establish the Spanish Speaking Unity Council of Alameda County and other advocacy organizations that continue

Labor leader César Chávez and John George, an Alameda County supervisor, at the Safeway store on Broadway encouraging a boycott on grapes, July 22, 1985
Oakland Museum of California, Oakland Tribune Collection, gift of ANG Newspapers

to serve Oakland's Latino community today. The Unity Council created the East Bay Spanish Speaking Citizens Foundation as its program arm.

César Chávez, who later would head the United Farmworkers, was a CSO organizer, working from a base at St. Elizabeth's Catholic Church in the heart of the Fruitvale and focusing on issues of police brutality and the difficulties for Spanish-speaking residents in securing burial insurance. He and Father Bill O'Donnell of St. Joseph the Worker Church in Berkeley became lifelong friends after meeting in an organizing course. In those days, O'Donnell said in an interview with Brenda Payton, Chávez was so shy that he would drive around the block several times before getting up the nerve to go into a house meeting. He described his friend as a man of "an almost frightening strong moral power."

In 1949 physical changes in West Oakland's landscape had helped to fracture the community. The city's redevelopment agency announced plans for "a first class freeway," an extension of Highway 80 along Cypress Street, with a double-decker "Cypress Structure" that would cut through the neighborhood and require the relocation of many of its citizens. As construction forced residents from their homes, many relocated to the Fruitvale district near East 14th Street, but many more were scattered around the city, leaving "no concentration of Mexican-Americans in any one area of Oakland," points out Amory Bradford in his book *Oakland's Not For Burning.* As the Latino population dispersed, churches and social associations continued to be centers of information exchange in Spanish-speaking communities. Los Hijos de Puerto Rico, founded in 1965, held dances and social events. At St. Elizabeth's Church on 34th Avenue, Father Oliver Lynch ran a recreation program for youth and helped families obtain basic employment, legal and family services. These were the seeds of larger, established nonprofits such as Centro Legal de la Raza, the Spanish Speaking Unity Council and the Spanish Speaking Citizens Foundation, all of which Father Lynch helped found. Father Valdivia at St. Mary's also had a hand in establishing both the Unity Council and Citizens Foundation in the mid-1960s.

Arabella Martinez says of those days, "We organized because we wanted to enhance communication among

28

the various Latino organizations and wanted to be more effective politically in terms of addressing issues of major concerns. Now we have this incredible network of agencies that give the political, economic and social viability and power of the Latino community today."

José Arredondo, director of the Spanish Speaking Citizens Foundation, recalls, "We opened in a brown shingle house on Fruitvale Avenue as El Centro de Información in 1971. Many people still refer to us by that name." The agency works to advance its constituency by providing scholarships and citizenship classes and offering employment training and placement to more than 500 youths each summer.

A core of activists went on to establish Centro Legal de la Raza in 1970 and La Clínica de la Raza the following year. "La Clínica is the Kaiser Hospital of the Fruitvale," Arredondo says, comparing the clinic to Oakland's largest medical facility. "It started out grassroots and now has 400 employees, a $15 million budget, and provides a full range of services."

It is an example, he notes, of how Latinos have capitalized on the resources available to them. "As people learn the processes you need to survive in this country, they become more acculturated. Our job is to get people to participate in these processes, to advocate and represent them, to create a safety net for those in our community. As a result, you can see that put together, Latinos have a stronghold in Oakland, and their presence has been a big part of the recovery of the city's depressed areas. They have taken what they've learned and used it to improve the quality of life in their communities."

There are traces of the Peraltas throughout Oakland today — a creek, a park, street names, the Peralta Community College system, small businesses, and the Peralta Hacienda in Fruitvale, which is in the process of being restored and made into a community museum and education center. The Latino community itself has become increasingly pluralistic and representative of the more than 40 nations that share the Spanish language. "At one time, we used the words 'Mexican' or 'Chicano' to describe ourselves," Arredondo says. "Now we use 'Latino.' That's very reflective of the changes that have taken place: today probably 40 percent of the Spanish-speaking population in Oakland comes from non-Mexican countries. And Latino influence is more prominent than ever. Even the Allen Temple Baptist Church in the barrio, which used to be predominantly African American, offers a Spanish service and has a Latino youth choir," illustrating that, although the Peraltas lost their land, Oakland retains a proud Californio spirit.

The strength and optimism of Oakland's ethnic diversity shines in the faces of children at the DeColores child care center, 1989. *Oakland Museum of California, Oakland Tribune Collection, gift of ANG Newspapers*

29

THE neighborHOOds

San Antonio

In 1850 Moses Chase and the Patten brothers purchased a portion of Antonio Peralta's land, reaching from Lake Merritt to 14th Avenue, and developed it as Clinton Park. The principal industry of the area in the 1850s and 60s was logging. Old-growth redwood harvested in the hills of Oakland was hauled down Park Boulevard onto 13th Avenue and into San Antonio Creek. The majority of the wood was transported across the bay to San Francisco, where it was used to build and rebuild the fire-prone city numerous times. A commercial district formed near the timber loading site in Oakland.

In 1870 all districts in this area were incorporated as the town of Brooklyn; and two years later Brooklyn was annexed to the city of Oakland. Through the 1920s it was a desirable suburban community. In the years leading up to World War II, a number of single-family homes were converted into apartments to accommodate newcomers drawn to the area for defense-related job opportunities.

In the late 1940s, the construction of the MacArthur and Nimitz freeways separated San Antonio residents from the hills neighborhoods. By stripping San Antonio's traditional commercial streets of traffic, the freeways disabled the district's commerce.

Many people of color moved into San Antonio in 1948 after the Supreme Court ruled that racially exclusive neighborhood covenants were unconstitutional. Many African-American and Latino residents, displaced by huge construction projects in West Oakland, settled in San Antonio in the mid-1960s.

Clinton Park, the Chase-Pattens' original development, was selected as the first western site of the Federal Urban Renewal Project in 1955. One thousand new units of housing in 57 apartment buildings were constructed. By 1990, 98 of Oakland's 291 Federal Housing Authority Projects were located in San Antonio. Unfortunately, the government's efforts to provide low-income housing were not matched with efforts to spark economic growth. The result was continuing physical, cultural and commercial isolation from the surrounding neighborhoods, high concentrations of low-income housing and economic stagnation.

The San Antonio Community Development Corporation and the District Council have taken steps towards building a housing, commercial and service infrastructure for the future. Emerging commercial strips along Foothill Boulevard and East 18th, East 14th and East 12th streets and are testing the blend of old and new revitalization strategies.

The neighborhood is a true blend of cultures, with rows of Spanish-style bungalows standing next to Victorian homes. Thirty-four different languages are spoken there, and Thai, Latino, African-American, Chinese and Native American children play together. Women and men walk through town in native dress, and on festival days neighbors gather to celebrate one another's cultural heritage. ■

Chapter 3

THE POLITICS OF INVENTION

Innovative SOLUTIONS AND THE STRUGGLE FOR INCLUSION ARE THEMES THAT RUN THROUGHOUT OAKLAND'S HISTORY. **BRENDA PAYTON** DESCRIBES THE COMPLEX AND INTRIGUING MACHINERY OF THE CITY'S POLITICS.

Oakland has been a hotbed of political invention from its earliest days, when the city's first mayor stole the waterfront, to the election of a former California governor as mayor. Struggle for inclusion is the theme running through the city's political history, manifested in fights for women's suffrage, decent working conditions and political representation of racial and other minority groups in city government. The issues that emerged in Oakland often mirrored and sometimes led the national debate. The city's diverse population and openness to change came to define its unique character. In an interesting illustration that history is not so distant, many of the challenges that will face Oakland in 2002, its sesquicentennial year — the quality of public school education, control of the waterfront and the pros and cons of a strong mayor vs. city manager form of government — were debated in the early days of the city.

Horace Carpentier, Oakland's first mayor, combined talents of political networking and legal savvy with less-than-savory tactics of trickery to secure the acreage where the city would later flourish and to appropriate its waterfront rights for himself. Carpentier was also charged by detractors with fraud after he was elected to the state assembly in 1853 by more votes than the total number cast in the election. Despite this, he was seated anyway.

During those scrappy early days, a local licensing issue served as a starting point for the involvement of women in electoral politics. In 1874 a fight heated up over whether a town should decide by vote to permit the sale of liquor under a license. Women took the lead in Oakland in opposition to the licensing plan, and 1,000 signatures were collected to put the issue on the ballot. Women, clergymen, church members and some city officials held nightly meetings in a large tent while saloon owners and their backers registered voters and raised

campaign funds. In the end "The Drys" won with a vote of 1,291 to 1,038, but the Pendegast Act, which enabled municipalities to pass by-laws, repealed the vote, ending the first attempt to abolish the sale of alcohol in California.

The next year, Oakland women appealed to the Republican state convention to nominate two women for the state board of education. They were turned down, but the flames of political activism had been ignited and would develop into a significant movement for women's suffrage. Marietta Stow, an Oakland property owner and fierce defender of women's economic rights, ran for governor of California in 1882. She helped organize the first political convention called by a woman, the National Equal Rights Party convention in 1884, which nominated the well-known Eastern suffragist Belva Ann Lockwood for president and Stow for vice president, making Stow the first woman candidate for that office. She lived her last years in a house in the Temescal district, continuing her progressive work in the form of a combined kindergarten and youth recreation center where the children formed a "Congress" with an upper and lower elected house. In alternating years, girls and boys ran for president.

In 1907, Oakland was the site of California's first parade in favor of women's suffrage, with supporters packing Broadway. The next year, women again appealed to the Republican Convention for political recognition. Headed by Lillian Harris Coffin, 300 women marched under a silk embroidered banner displaying the word "Eureka." The convention thanked them for their attendance and interest but denied their appeal. Over the next years, Oakland vigorously argued the issue of suffrage. In 1911, when California voted on the Fourth Amendment, a state amendment for women's suffrage, a huge billboard in a central location in the city read: "Justice to California Women. Vote Yes on Amendment Four." Another prominently displayed sign argued the other side: "Vote No as Home-Loving Women Do Not Want the Ballot." In Oakland many of the prominent Catholic clergy supported women's suffrage. However, when the votes were counted and California women won the right to vote, Oakland itself had turned it down.

On the uglier side of Oakland's political scene, a strong and virulent anti-Chinese immigrant sentiment had long festered. On May 27, 1876, a mass meeting opposing further Chinese immigration was held in front of Oakland City Hall. The so-called Anti-Coolie Club fanned the flames of resentment that nearly boiled over into mob violence against Chinese residents. Threats to burn down Chinatown and kill its residents were crushed by police officers. The worst of the violence was averted, but extreme anti-Chinese propaganda continued for the next 20 years.

For some 15 years, city mayors served for one year only and are, for the most part, forgettable. A new stamp of leader arrived in the late 1860s in the person of Samuel Merritt, who during his single term nevertheless began to usher Oakland into the modern age. He supported the establishment of the first municipal water supply, public health department and subscription library. With his own money he built structures that would turn the shallow tidal basin in the middle of Oakland into a lake. Lake Peralta, renamed Lake Merritt, would become the jewel of the city. In 1870

34

The wildfowl sanctuary at Lake Merritt, c. 1925, a legacy of Mayor Samuel Merritt
Oakland Museum of California, Oakland Tribune Collection, gift of ANG Newspapers

Brooklyn fire station, 1885. The neighborhood of Brooklyn near Lake Merritt was one of the city's oldest. During his mayoral term, Frank Mott reorganized the fire department and made fire and earthquake safety a priority.
Oakland Museum of California, Oakland Tribune Collection, gift of ANG Newspapers

Merritt persuaded the state Legislature to declare the lake a wildfowl refuge, the first one in North America.

With hardware merchant and city councilman Frank Mott's mayoral election in 1905, a new era dawned in Oakland politics. Mott would serve as executive officer for 10 years, transforming a rough-and-tumble Oakland into a model of progressive city government. He ended the six decades-long waterfront controversy. He reorganized the police and fire departments, established the civil service system and oversaw the adoption of a new city charter. Mindful of what we would call quality-of-life issues, Mott established the Oakland Public Museum in 1910 and a park commission that set up a system of parks and playgrounds throughout the city. Lake Merritt was dredged and landscaped and street lighting was modernized. After witnessing the destruction of San Francisco in 1906, he saw to it that fire and earthquake safety were considered in the design of all new buildings. It is little wonder Mott gained the moniker, "The Man Who Built Oakland."

Following Mott, the mayor's office was occupied by a very different personality, the flamboyant John L. Davie, who served four consecutive terms, surviving numerous attempts to recall him. Davie always wore a red carnation in his lapel and coined the

phrase "My City Oakland." He oversaw the development of the harbor, the construction of the airport and the industrialization of the city, finally retiring at the age of 80.

During Davie's tenure, Joseph R. Knowland emerged as a formidable power broker after serving five terms in the U.S. House of Representatives and assuming the leadership of the Oakland Tribune in 1915. From his post as publisher of the newspaper, Knowland used his influence to control city politics. He functioned as a kingmaker — no one could be elected as mayor of Oakland without the Tribune's endorsement. He is credited with launching and nurturing the career of Earl Warren from California's attorney general to governor and even influencing his appointment to the U.S. Supreme Court. With extensive political connections in Washington, D.C. and Sacramento, Knowland, known as "The Old Man," was able to attract much-needed capital to Oakland. He brought in millions of federal dollars for crucial improvements to the Oakland Harbor and fought to bring the Panama Pacific International Exposition to San Francisco; he knew a world's fair so close to home would spur Oakland's growth. Knowland used his Washington

36

Under THE LEADERSHIP OF DISTRICT ATTORNEY EARL WARREN, A PROTÉGÉ OF JOSEPH R. KNOWLAND, OAKLAND'S POLICE DEPARTMENT ENFORCED PROHIBITION DURING THE 1920S.

Oakland Museum of California, Oakland Tribune Collection, gift of ANG Newspapers

37

connections to help break a deadlock over the proposed San Francisco-Oakland Bay Bridge and secured the loan that made its construction possible.

The Knowland family influence continued with his son, William Fife Knowland, who officially became publisher upon the death of his father in 1966. Along with key industrialists such as Henry J. Kaiser and Stephen Bechtel, Knowland formed an oligarchy of power and influence, merging business and city government in an ironclad alliance that controlled nearly every aspect of the city's life. While that centralization of power spurred the growth of business in the city, it also gave rise to a resistance by those locked outside of the power circle, including African Americans, workers and neighborhood activists. That tension would later mature into another important phase of the city's development.

In 1930, Oakland was engaged in a major battle over how the city was to be governed. The choice was between the pervasive strong mayor form of government, with the mayor overseeing the departments of the city, and a city manager form, in which the city manager ran operations and the city council made law. A plan that year to change to a city manager form of government was vigorously opposed by those in power in City Hall. Lawsuits were filed over the petitions to vote on the measure and opponents attempted to confuse voters with amendments and candidates on the same ballot. But in July 1931 the city council-manager form of government was adopted. Foreshadowing future battles, the first city manager, Ossian Elmer Carr, immediately

set out to shake up city government, asking for a voluntary pay cut from fire and police department employees. However, the police and fire department employees had political clout with the elected council members, and in June 1933 the city's first city manager was ousted by a council vote.

The virtual stranglehold the Knowlands had on city officials and agencies sparked one of America's few successful general strikes. Under "The Old Man," the Tribune had been a dogged and virulent opponent of organized labor; his son went to the U.S. Senate as a "right-to-work senator." In October 1946, when Kahn's department store fired a clerk for signing a union card, an estimated 80 percent of the clerks at the Kahn's and Hastings department stores in downtown Oakland walked off the job. The picket line was honored by the Teamsters and deliveries to the stores were stopped

during the busy Christmas shopping season. The city's power brokers would not tolerate the disruption of business and hired a strike-breaking trucking firm to make the deliveries. Oakland police officers were used to protect the strike breakers, wielding their billy clubs to move the picketers and make way for the trucks.

It was the role of the police force, supported by taxpayers' money, in protecting the strike breakers that touched off the 1946 General Strike. Two days later, more than 100,000 workers from 142 unions walked off their jobs in Alameda County, and for two days downtown Oakland was at a standstill. Stores, restaurants, bars, factories, shipyards, even streetcars, buses and gas stations were shut down. A settlement

An INFLUENTIAL GROUP OF OAKLAND AFRICAN-AMERICAN LEADERS WITH CALIFORNIA POLITICOS, MAY 1959.
(LEFT TO RIGHT) D.G. GIBSON, LIONEL WILSON, GOV. PAT BROWN, SEN. STUART SYMINGTON,
AND ELSIE AND WILLIAM BYRON RUMFORD.
Oakland Museum of California, Oakland Tribune Collection, gift of ANG Newspapers

Chapter Three

Black Panther leader Bobby Seale campaigned door-to-door during the Oakland mayoral race in 1973. John Reading won the election. *Oakland Museum of California, Oakland Tribune Collection, gift of ANG Newspapers*

promising the police would stay out of the department store labor dispute ended the strike. Although the settlement was promptly violated, the organization and experience of the strike led to the formation of the Oakland Voters League, a coalition of labor, minority and community groups that ran candidates for office and began setting into motion major shifts in the power equation in the city.

One shift had its earliest beginnings in the mid-1930s over a pharmacy counter in Berkeley, where pharmacist William Byron Rumford and businessman D.G. Gibson began discussing politics. They started by protesting the blatant racial discrimination in Oakland and Berkeley, picketing businesses that refused to hire Negro employees, and then turned toward local electoral politics by backing candidates. They proved to be an effective team, recognizing the political potential of Oakland's black population, which had grown tenfold with the migration of Southerners to work in the shipyards during World War II. When Rumford ran for the California State Assembly in 1948, Gibson managed his campaign. It was a close race, requiring a recount,

but Rumford won, launching the emergence of black political power. While Rumford was in Sacramento, Gibson continued to act as his political strategist. As a state legislator, Rumford would establish the Fair Employment Practices Commission and win passage of the landmark Fair Housing Act, which together codified into state law their early fight against job and housing discrimination. Their formation of the East Bay Democratic Club would carve out a niche for black politicians in the Democratic Party, paving the way for Mayor Lionel Wilson, Supreme Court Justice Allen Broussard, Judge Donald McCullum and Rep. Ron Dellums, among others, to create the base for a powerful black political establishment in the East Bay.

The Black Panther Party was started in 1966 in Oakland by Bobby Seale and Huey Newton, who met as students at Merritt College's Grove Street campus, and David Hilliard. The Panthers first organized neighborhood patrols in African-American neighborhoods to observe and document police behavior. Their black berets, black leather jackets and militant defiance gained national attention when they demonstrated against gun control, brandishing weapons on the steps of the state capitol. They captured the imagination of a generation of young black Americans frustrated by the seemingly slow pace of civil rights reforms. Panther chapters sprang up in cities across the country. In Oakland, the group expanded its work to set up a Free Breakfast for Children program, free clinics and a school. Panther leaders such as Elaine Brown and Ericka Huggins began to move into the political mainstream, gaining appointments to city and state commissions; Seale ran for mayor in 1973, winning enough votes to force a runoff. As organizers and precinct workers, the Panthers were among the instrumental groups behind the 1977 election of Oakland's first black mayor, which opened doors for the election of other black and Latino candidates. Divisions between leaders, fueled by government infiltrators and a program of FBI sabotage, eventually would destroy the Black Panther Party.

Lionel J. Wilson's mayoral election win marked the beginning of a new day in Oakland and in the East Bay in terms of racial inclusion. During his three terms, the city council, school board and offices throughout the city and county would change complexion, with African

Americans serving and working at every level of government. Henry Gardner, the city's first black city manager, appointed several African Americans to key positions, including Jayne W. Williams as Oakland's first woman city attorney. Minority representation on the police force increased from 26 percent to 43 percent, more closely reflecting the city's population. For much of the two decades that Wilson and his successor, Elihu Harris, controlled City Hall, Oakland's key political institutions were headed by African Americans. Even the *Oakland Tribune* — in former times the bastion of the conservative status quo — was published and edited by Robert Maynard, formerly of the *Washington Post* and the first African-American editor and publisher of a mainstream daily newspaper in the country. "The Old Man" wouldn't have recognized his town.

The emergence of Latinos in Oakland politics came about through a coalition with African-American leaders that developed in the mid-1960s. The first Latino political organization was the Mexican American Political Association, a statewide association headed in Oakland by Bert Corona. A coalition of Latinos, blacks and Asians, with strong white support, elected Joe Coto as the first Latino on the city council in 1972 — a big win, since the election was citywide and Coto's opponent was an eight-year incumbent who had the endorsement of the Oakland Tribune. The strong coalition of Latinos and African Americans has since elected numerous candidates, including Noel Gallo to the board of education and Ignacio de la Fuente to the city council.

In another branch of political action, the Oakland Community Organizations (OCO), established in 1977, formed an impressive church-based coalition of more than 180 neighborhood groups. This umbrella group developed out of meetings of neighborhood leaders and quickly became a voice with which city officials had to reckon. The group tackled intractable urban problems such as street prostitution, drug dealing, blight and traffic safety. It represented a different kind of coalition, cutting across racial and neighborhood divisions and based on common concerns about issues that impacted daily life in the city's neighborhoods. By pulling such a range of smaller community organizations together, OCO amplified the grassroots voice, making the neighborhoods a major player in city decision-making.

The Oakland of the late 1970s and 80s was a far cry, indeed, from the tightly controlled city of the 1940s and 50s.

As yet another example of the city's openness, Oaklanders overwhelmingly elected former California governor Jerry Brown as their mayor in 1998, also handing him a strong mayor charter amendment that ended nearly 60 years of the city manager form of government. Some viewed Brown's support across racial and geographic lines as an indication citizens had moved away from the politics of racial and community allegiance. Echoing far earlier days, the relationship between the Port of Oakland and the city was one of the first issues Brown tackled as he attempted to gain more control over decisions relating to commercial development on the city's waterfront. His plans to revitalize downtown with new housing developments, while refueling the age-old debate about who will be included in future benefits, have the potential of transforming the core of the city.

Since its founding, Oakland has been a laboratory for political innovation. It has served as a stage for the struggle to amass power and the struggle to make sure it is shared. The city continues its interrelated traditions of embracing its challenging diversity and remaining open to change.

Mayor Jerry Brown, 2000
Photo by Janet Orsi

THE

nEigHbOrHOOds

Central Oakland and Chinatown

Central Oakland has experienced constant growth since the mid-1800s, when commercial and housing development began at the foot of Broadway. The downtown business district had begun as a wholesale produce market by the 1890s, based between 11th Street and Washington. Chinatown began concurrently near Eighth Street and Webster.

Oakland became the seat of Alameda County in 1873, after the San Leandro county courthouse was destroyed by earthquake. Oakland's first courthouse was erected in 1875. In 1914, when the new city hall was completed, 14th and Broadway had evolved into the center of business and civic activity.

The slough that ran through Oakland into the central district was dammed to create Lake Merritt in 1869. Today Laney College stands on what was once the arm of the marsh stretching to the bay.

Chinese immigrants first came to California to mine gold beginning in 1848; a second wave, in 1861, arrived to work on the transcontinental railroad, specifically to build tunnels through the Sierra Nevada mountains. Opportunities for Chinese Oaklanders were limited by laws that restricted choices of employment, education and residence. Segregated to one area, a designated "exclusion zone," Chinese Americans developed a self-sufficient community. In 1943 they became eligible for U.S. citizenship, and racially restrictive covenants were struck down in 1948.

Adams Point, originating from a tract of land claimed by Oakland co-founder Edson Adams, is one of the district's residential areas. The majority of the land was undeveloped until after the 1906 earthquake, when earthquake victims streamed into Oakland and Adams Point became the largest refugee camp in the area. Many refugees settled in Oakland afterwards and built homes in this area. During the 1930s and 40s some of the larger estates were subdivided into apartment buildings and during the 1960s, 70s and 80s, Adams Point was one of the more popular communities for apartment and condominium living. Richmond Boulevard, with its attractive rows of cabin-like homes along the banks of Glen Echo Creek, is another distinctive early neighborhood in the Central District.

Since World War II, Kaiser Industries, steel manufacturers, were major employers in Oakland. In recent decades the company's contribution to the work force in Oakland has gradually declined. Originally from New York, Henry J. Kaiser settled in Oakland in 1921. He started the Kaiser Permanente Health Plan in 1942, initially for his shipyard employees. The low-cost, comprehensive, prepaid service was eventually opened to outside subscribers. Kaiser Permanente is now the biggest nongovernmental health service in the country. ■

Chapter 4

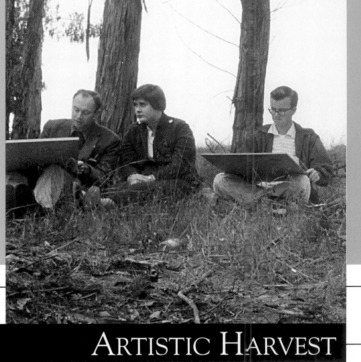

ARTISTIC HARVEST

Oakland LONG HAS BEEN HOME TO A VIBRANT ART COMMUNITY. **KAREN TSUJIMOTO** DETAILS SOME OF THE ARTISTS, ART SCHOOLS AND MOVEMENTS THE CITY HAS NURTURED.

In the history and growth of all important cities, the visual arts play a vital role. Once the streets have been laid, water and transportation systems established, schools built and stores opened, a cluster of culturally minded individuals will see the need to plant and nurture the seeds of artistic creativity within their community. This may be prompted by civic pride: we all want to believe that our home towns are prosperous and sophisticated. But more important, the creative arts are an undeniable expression of our shared humanity.

So it is with Oakland. Its colleges, museum and artists have reached heights of achievement and made important collective contributions to the visual arts. In fact, nearly all significant art in the state until well into the 1920s came principally from Oakland and San Francisco, the two cities forming the heart of cosmopolitan California. The arts in Oakland have continued to flourish.

The earliest artists to settle in the city were European painters following the westward expansion. The English-born Thomas Hill, known for his paintings that captured the virgin beauty of California's wilderness, maintained a studio in Yosemite Valley and produced hundreds of works that helped establish Yosemite as a tourist attraction. Hill moved with his family from San Francisco to Oakland in 1879, where he lived for the next seven years on a grand 10-acre estate on Seminary Drive. It was during these years that he worked on his mammoth painting, *The Driving of the Last Spike* (1881), commissioned by Leland Stanford to commemorate the completion of the Transcontinental Railroad. Those seeking out the famous painter easily found him listed in the Oakland city directory under "Artist."

Another landscape painter, Joachim Ferdinand Richardt, a native of Denmark, settled in California late in his life to paint the sublime beauty of the state. His last studio was in Oakland, where he died in 1895. Helen Tanner Brodt, a nationally celebrated artist known for her paintings on china, was art director of the Oakland public schools for many years and, in 1867, became the first art instructor of a young Oakland high school student, Arthur F. Mathews, who was destined to lead the California decorative arts and craft movement.

When these 19th-century painters sought collegial support and lively artistic discussion, they could call upon the small art faculty at Mills College, an all-women's school known as Mills Seminary when it was established in Oakland in 1871. The school's art program, one of the first in the Bay Area, initially consisted of classes taught by Juan Wandesforde, an English painter of portraits and landscapes who was also active in San Francisco. In 1888, a four-year program in studio art was established at Mills, with noted landscape painter Raymond Dabb Yelland joining the faculty. Like Hill and Richardt, Yelland was enamored with California's natural wonders and sought to depict the beauty of the changing light and weather patterns on its landscape and coast.

The calamity of the 1906 earthquake and fire left an indelible imprint on Oakland. Although damage to the city was relatively light, the social impact was huge. San Francisco's tragic misfortunes proved a key event affecting Oakland's growth, as thousands settled

in the city that sheltered them following the disaster. Many artists were among them. After losing everything in San Francisco, Giuseppe Cadenasso relocated to Oakland in 1906, where he headed the art department at Mills until 1918. Xavier Martinez moved to Piedmont after his San Francisco studio was similarly razed. Both men, highly admired for their landscape and figure paintings rendered in softly contoured forms and muted tonal color harmonies, were part of a circle known as "tonalists," whose work set the artistic standard of the day.

Oakland was also the home of Anne Brigman, one of California's most important early photographers. Known for dreamy, softly-focused images of female nudes in landscapes, Brigman was the only California member of the New York group known as the Photo-Secession, an elite association of invited pictorialists presided over by Alfred Stieglitz.

Notable among the 1906 transplants was Frederick H. Meyer, a faculty member at the University of California, Berkeley, and Mark Hopkins Institute of Art, and president of the San Francisco Guild of Arts and Crafts. His elegantly designed and handcrafted furniture significantly contributed to the California decorative arts aesthetic. After his home and business were destroyed in the quake, Meyer moved to the East Bay. In 1907 he

46

Xavier Martinez painting Jack London's portrait, c. 1900

Oakland History Room, Oakland Public Library

47

Anne BRIGMAN, *THE BUBBLE*, 1906, GELATIN SILVER PRINT

Oakland Museum of California, gift of Mr. and Mrs. Willard S. Nott

Panama-Pacific International Exposition (PPIE). a grand and colorful world's fair in San Francisco commemorating the 1914 opening of the Panama Canal. The exposition was an opulent and optimistic extravaganza shining through the deepening shadow of World War I. It not only recognized the completion of the canal, but celebrated the rebuilding of San Francisco after the earthquake. Moreover, it affirmed the new importance of California and the American West and their vital economic connections to South America and the Pacific Rim.

The exposition abounded in art. Sculptor-in-chief A. Stirling Calder — whose work graces the portals and doorways of the Kaiser Convention Center (formerly the Oakland Auditorium) — ensured that sculpture was amply displayed. On view in the Palace of Fine Arts were over 11,400 artworks, including examples by modern Europeans little seen beyond the East Coast (the Italian futurists, impressionists and post-impressionists) and paintings by well-known Californians, including William Keith, Arthur Mathews and Xavier Martinez.

Exposure to progressive new European art excited and influenced many in the Bay Area art community, including a group of Oakland-based landscape painters who became known as the Society of Six. William H. Clapp, August F. Gay, Selden Connor Gile, Maurice Logan, Louis Siegriest and Bernard von Eichman banded together in 1917 to form an association that lasted almost 15 years. Inspired by the French impressionism they had seen at the PPIE, the

opened the School of the California Guild of Arts and Crafts in Berkeley, which later changed its name to California College of Arts and Crafts (CCAC) and relocated to Oakland.

At the time, Meyer's school was one of but a handful in the United States that taught industrial and applied arts and art education. His ultimate goal, through his newly formed institution and curriculum, was to enable his students to earn, as he put it, "a comfortable living" by their craft work, which he believed was as important as painting and sculpture. Putting theory into practice, he also served as director of art for the Oakland public school system (c. 1913-1919). Meyer's school acquired the James Treadwell estate in Oakland in 1922 and spent the next few years converting its facilities. When the new CCAC opened for classes in 1926, faculty, students and alumni had transformed the rundown four-acre property into an intimate and casual campus. Meyer landscaped the grounds himself, adding many rare varieties of plants.

Meyer's tenure lasted until 1944. During this time the position of craft artisans gradually shifted from its secondary status and emphasis on manual training and occupational therapy to a field of professional artists and teachers pursuing fine crafts and arts. A selection of early faculty members confirms the school's important role in disseminating this artistic philosophy: William Bragdon and Chauncey Thomas, who formed the California Faience tile shop in 1924; ceramists F. Carlton Ball, Antonio Prieto and Marguerite Wildenhain; weaver and bookbinder Ilse Schulz Hiller; and metal artist Harry St. John Dixon.

Another important historical event that helped shape Oakland's early cultural life was the 1915

William H. Clapp,
Bird-nesting, c. 1909,
oil on canvas
*Oakland Museum
of California,
gift of Mr. and
Mrs. Donn Schroder*

house on Chabot Road for group critiques and a shared meal peppered with spicy conversation. At the time, the art establishment and critics found their work crude and unrefined, but as art historian Nancy Boas has observed, today their paintings represent some of the most important and lasting contributions to modern art created in the western United States at the time.

The exposition sparked unprecedented cultural awareness not only among Oakland's artists, but its general citizens as well. The infectious sense of civic pride and celebration that spread throughout Oakland as overflow visitors discovered the city's charms resulted in the 1916 establishment of the Oakland Art Gallery, the first public institution in the Bay Area devoted solely to the fine arts. The gallery was sponsored by a newly formed Oakland Art Association with Dr. William S. Porter as president and was housed in the Oakland Auditorium, renamed the Henry J. Kaiser Convention Center in 1984. Robert Harshe, who had been the assistant director of fine arts at the PPIE, was appointed the art gallery's first director, although it was a position he held only briefly. With American entry into World War I in 1917, the gallery went through tenuous times, but was soon stabilized by two key events: the donation of Porter's private collection, with the city's guarantee that an exhibition space would be provided, and the 1918 appointment of Society of Six artist William Clapp as its director and curator.

group shared an adventuresome aesthetic distinguished by their vivid use of color and bold, energetic brushwork. Together they hiked Oakland's hills and bayfront to paint the brilliant, sun-drenched color and beauty of the natural environment. After working outdoors all day, they would often convene at Gile's small

During three decades, Clapp played a crucial role not only in Oakland but throughout Northern California as a passionate advocate for the arts, particularly the modern and the new. Among his East Bay cohorts he was one of the most worldly and accomplished, having studied abroad and arrived in California as a recognized artist in Europe and his native Canada. Drawing upon his international experiences as well as his strong advocacy for local artists, Clapp quickly established a lively and diverse program. Indeed,

Bernard von Eichman,
Eighth Street, 1928,
watercolor
*Oakland Museum
of California,
gift of Bernard von Eichman*

50

Peter Stackpole,
Catwalk and Marin Tower,
Golden Gate Bridge, 1936,
gelatin silver print
*Oakland Museum
of California, The Oakland
Museum of California
Founders Fund*

until the San Francisco Museum of Modern Art opened in 1935, the Oakland Art Gallery was the most adventurous institution in the area. The series of annual exhibitions Clapp initiated in 1922 became one of the most important venues in northern California for contemporary artists to exhibit their work. He also organized the first public exhibitions of the Society of Six, which received laudatory reviews. Clapp's vision of art was in the vanguard for his time, and the gallery offered a remarkable array of significant exhibitions, hosting some of the earliest presentations in the state to feature the work of modern Europeans and initiating regular exhibitions of photographers and African-American artists. A singularly progressive force, the Oakland Art Gallery contributed to the cultural vitality of the East Bay and communities well beyond its borders.

Oakland's reputation as a place for lively encounters with art was bolstered by new programs initiated at Mills College during this same period. In 1925 the Mills College Art Gallery was opened, with Roi Partridge as its first director and curator. A nationally regarded printmaker who had moved to Oakland in 1920 to join the art faculty of the college, Partridge was married to Imogen Cunningham, who was establishing her own reputation as a photographer. Under Partridge's leadership, the gallery presented innovative

exhibitions on contemporary crafts and design, photography and the work of important American, European and Latin American artists. In the 1930s and 40s, Mills was a pioneer in offering regular courses on American and Latin American art, and was one of the few schools on the West Coast to hire German emigré art historians and scholars. An important figure was Dr. Alfred Neumeyer, who arrived in 1935 to teach and subsequently direct the art gallery. He taught one of the earliest courses offered in the United States on museum studies, and through his important European connections, he initiated a lively visiting-artist program that brought to the Bay Area international figures such as Max Beckmann, Fernand Léger and Lazlo Moholy-Nagy, who influenced many local artists.

During this period, Oakland artists experimented with new directions. Particularly important was the photographic Group f.64, whose founding members included Ansel Adams, Imogen Cunningham, John Paul Edwards, Sonya Noskowiak, Willard Van Dyke, Edward Weston and Henry Swift, the only amateur among them. Others associated with the group were Brett Weston, Consuelo Kanaga, Dorothea Lange, Alma Lavenson, Preston Holder, William Simpson and Peter Stackpole, one of the youngest members. Stackpole, the son of sculptor Ralph Stackpole,

51

Peter Voulkos, *Mr. Ishi*, 1969. This cast bronze sculpture resides at the Oak Street entrance to the Oakland Museum of California.

Oakland Museum of California, gift of Concours d' Antiques, Art Guild and the National Endowment for the Arts

became known for his daring photographs of the construction of the Golden Gate and Bay bridges, taken from their towers and cables with one of the earliest 35mm cameras. Meeting regularly at Van Dyke's Oakland gallery, 683 Brockhurst, Group f.64's modern vision contributed in a major way to the course of photographic history. In contrast to the hazy romanticism of pictorialism, the stunning clarity and precision of their work was revolutionary. Although the lifespan of Group f.64 was short (1932-35), its accomplishments have influenced generations of photographers.

Following World War II and the Korean War, Oakland's art community experienced a surge of activity as war veterans, supported by the G.I. Bill of Rights and its educational benefits, and European emigrés flooded the art schools of the Bay Area. Older, more mature and worldly in their perspective, these new students and faculty infused the field with energy and vision. F. Carlton Ball, a ceramist who began teaching at Mills in 1939 after two years on the faculty at CCAC, was a consummate educator, a pioneer on the West Coast in the use of the potter's wheel and known for his elegantly thrown vases and bottle forms. By the time he left Mills in 1950, the ceramics department had been transformed into one of the most active in the western United States. Antonio Prieto, a master potter influenced by the work of Joan Miró and Max Ernst, succeeded Ball and actively championed the achievements of West Coast ceramists.

Of the many fine ceramic artists with ties to Oakland, perhaps the most significant is Peter Voulkos. A war veteran and national award-winning potter when he did graduate work at CCAC (1951-52), the Montana-born artist went on to create an astounding body of large-scale abstract work that vaulted ceramics into heroic sculpture. Working with the improvisational energy of the abstract expressionist painters he admired, Voulkos' audacious clay sculptures, animated by unorthodox applications of color, were unprecedented in their vigor and size. Voulkos continues, in his Oakland studio, to create some of the most intellectually and visually challenging sculpture ever done in clay.

Since the pioneering work of these artists, others have created new vistas for ceramic art as well — Robert Arneson, who received degrees from both CCAC and

Mills in the 1950s; Viola Frey, an alumna of CCAC who joined its faculty in 1965; Ron Nagle, a professor at Mills College since 1978; and Oakland artists Marilyn Levine, James Melchert and John Roloff.

Other disciplines at CCAC experienced a similar charge of energy and change. In textiles, the teaching and work of immigrant German artist Trude Guermonprez introduced concepts of technique and design that helped revolutionize the field of textile and fiber arts. Her creative view of the relationship between tapestry and painting led her to invent her own textile graphics, and she freely introduced photographic and printed stencils into her work. In the area of jewelry, Margaret De Patta's Bauhaus-inspired geometric designs set new standards in her field, and she is considered by many to be the progenetrix of the contemporary jewelry movement in the United States. In the 1960s Marvin Lipofsky, a key figure in studio glass work, came to the school to head its new glass department. Known for looping abstract forms, variously flocked in bright red fuzz, electroplated or sandblasted, Lipofsky established one of the most respected studio glass departments in the country at CCAC.

Beginning in the late 1950s the school's painting department served as an important alternative to the Bay Area's other major art school, the California School of Fine Arts in San Francisco, eventually renamed the San Francisco Art Institute. While the CSFA championed the tenets of abstraction, those associated with

Ceremonial groundbreaking for the new Oakland Museum, 1964, at the corner of Oak and 12th streets. (Left to right) Mayor John C. Houlihan, Oakland Museum Commission Chairman William J. Hayes and Oakland Chamber of Commerce President Nils Ekland
Oakland Museum of California

53

CCAC helped introduce a new style of painting known as Bay Area figurative art, one of the most distinctive expressions to emerge from northern California and attain national attention. This movement was a pointed reaction to the dominant school of abstract expressionism that championed nonobjective painting. Five of the painters in the figurative movement — Richard Diebenkorn, Bruce McGaw, Manuel Neri, Nathan Oliveira and James Weeks — had strong ties to the East Bay and CCAC. Diebenkorn, for example, was on the college's faculty from 1955 to 1957, when he was formulating his unique figurative style. While all of these men had been strongly influenced by abstract expressionism and its gestural handling of paint, what set their new work apart was the emphatic introduction of recognizable figurative imagery, which they saw as a way to infuse the state of painting with new direction and vitality. By all accounts, the Bay Area figurative artists formed a tightly intertwined community of kindred spirits whose collective accomplishments broke new ground and helped gain critical and national attention for the region.

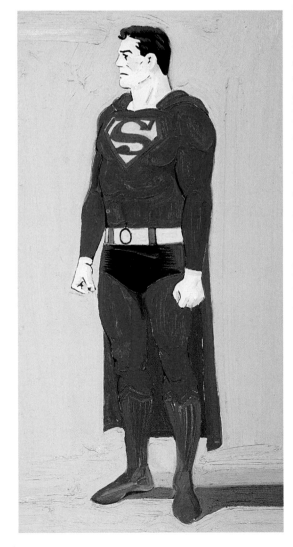

Mel Ramos, *Superman,* 1961, oil on canvas *Oakland Museum of California,* extended loan of Scot Ramos

Other painters associated with Oakland or its schools continued to participate in the national discourse on art. In the early 1960s Oaklander Mel Ramos and his paintings of popular icons, such as Superman and Wonder Woman, contributed an important West Coast perspective to the national pop art movement. Soon thereafter, in the late 1960s a small circle of CCAC alumni gained national attention for the uncanny realism of their paintings — Ralph Goings, Richard McLean and Robert Bechtle, who maintained an Alameda studio and taught at the school through the mid-1960s. Later, Jack Mendenhall, another CCAC alumni and Oakland resident, became associated with this movement. Looking at these artists' paintings, depicting ordinary scenes of parked cars and trucks, riders on horseback or flamboyant middle-class interiors, was almost like looking at photographs, so detailed and realistic was their work.

The Oakland Art Gallery, still located in the Oakland Auditorium, continued to play a strong role during this fertile period. Paul C. Mills, who assumed curatorial leadership in 1953, deserved much of the credit. Under his leadership, the institution's name was changed to the Oakland Art Museum (OAM) and its focus settled on the theme of California art and artists. Mills' wide-ranging artistic vision was reflected in shows he presented, which included paintings by Diebenkorn, Sabro Hasegawa, Chiura Obata and David Park, furniture by Sam Maloof, ceramics by Arneson and Wildenhain and sculpture by Claire Falkenstein.

An important turning point for the art museum came in 1961, when Oakland residents approved a bond issue to build a large new complex to house their three museums — the Oakland Public Museum, the OAM and the Snow Museum of Natural History. Their disparate collections form the base of the history, art and natural science departments of the Oakland Museum of California, one of the world's distinguished regional museums. Situated on four city blocks adjacent to Lake Merritt, the museum was designed by Kevin Roche as his first major commission. Construction began in February 1964 and in September 1969, citizens turned out in force to celebrate the opening of their grand new museum. Among its highlights are the Dorothea Lange photographic archive, arts and crafts, 19th-century California landscapes and the Arthur and Lucia Mathews decorative arts collection.

Oakland has seen a burgeoning of its arts community since the museum opened, not only in population but in creative expression and cultural diversity. The city has offered many attractions to working artists — stimulating college and museum programs, the amenities of an urban center coupled with beautiful open spaces and temperate weather, and perhaps most importantly, what was once easily affordable studio space. Many artists who moved to the East Bay for college decided to stay, including painters

54

Squeak Carnwath, Tom Holland and Raymond Saunders, each of whom enjoys a distinguished reputation far beyond the Bay Area.

In the early 1970s artists assumed the lead in establishing Oakland as a desirable place to live and work. Peter Voulkos and sculptor Bruce Beasley developed live/work spaces and rental studios in neglected old warehouses scattered throughout the city. Small artist-run businesses followed. In 1972 Kathan Brown moved her printmaking business, Crown Point Press, from Richmond to an old factory in downtown Oakland. During her 15-year stay, she worked with a prestigious group of nationally and internationally known artists. Other fine art presses — Don Farnsworth and David Kimball's Magnolia Editions and David Kelso's Made in California — have added to the city's cultural richness.

Richard Diebenkorn, *Figure on a Porch*, 1959, oil on canvas
Oakland Museum of California, Anonymous Donor Program of the American Federation of Arts

Community-based arts organizations also established a foothold in the city's cultural landscape. Pro Arts, founded in 1974, is an artist-based nonprofit organization that mounts regular changing exhibitions of local and regional artists and provides practical workshops and networking opportunities for artists of all disciplines. Established in 1980, Creative Growth Art Center, a nonprofit arts organization, is known for its innovative programs and advocacy for the disabled.

In 1985, recognizing that the visual arts have played a vital part in Oakland's economic base and quality of life, the city established a Cultural Affairs Commission and Cultural Arts Division to encourage and publicly fund the arts. Noteworthy among its achievements was the 1989 creation of a percent-for-art ordinance that funds the installation of public art throughout the city, from community-derived pieces in residential neighborhoods to large works in downtown civic spaces.

With the tremendous population growth of Oakland's art community, there has been a flourishing of different perspectives. Artists now work in broader arenas not strictly defined by movements, schools or 'isms." The diversity of the art community mirrors the multiplicity of viewpoints that contemporary art, on a national level, now enjoys. From Rupert Garcia's politically sensitized work and the paintings of immigrant artist Hung Liu to Jo Whaley's photographs exploring issues of beauty and decay, and Alan Rath's electronic sculptures, the range of art to be found in Oakland is inspiring. In the arena of crafts, artists similarly have expanded the boundaries through their art and teaching. The jewelry of Florence Resnikoff, handcrafted glass designs of John Lewis, furniture of Gary Knox Bennett and Gail Fredell Smith, and contemporary fiber work by Nance O'Banion and Ellen Oppenheimer, to name a handful, have enhanced the region's artistic environment.

Oakland has contributed significantly to the positive reputation and mainstream accomplishments that California art and artists have enjoyed over the course of the state's long and rich history. As a new century unfolds, the possibilities for even greater artistic opportunities and achievements seem boundless.

Chapter 5

The PULSE OF DAILY LIFE BEATS STRONG IN OAKLAND'S CHINATOWN, WHERE SO MANY ASIAN IMMIGRANTS SETTLED AND PROSPERED. **WILLIAM WONG** HIGHLIGHTS STRUGGLE AND ACHIEVEMENT IN THE LIVES OF CHINESE AND JAPANESE AMERICANS.

An easy eight-block walk from City Hall, the corner of Eighth and Webster streets at first glance appears to be a world apart from the center of city government or ordinary American life. In some ways, it is. Looking in all four directions, one observes crowds, mostly of Asian descent, strolling into stores, restaurants, banks and offices. The languages one hears are Cantonese, Mandarin, Vietnamese, Tagalog and English. Business and street signs are bilingual, in English and Chinese. Motor vehicle traffic along both corridors is usually heavy, with double-parked vehicles a common sight.

This busy corner is the epicenter of Oakland's Chinese and Asian communities. It has been so for at least 130 years. Today's Oakland Chinatown is a thriving economic, social, residential and cultural center and is generally well-regarded by government officials and residents outside of Chinatown. Such an accepting attitude has not always been the case.

The discovery of gold in the California foothills spurred the first migration to California of large numbers of Chinese, mostly from impoverished and disaster-prone Guangdong province. Some found gold, often working mines that were abandoned by others. But many never achieved their dreams, because other miners and the state government discriminated against them. Looking for refuge, they settled in developing cities, particularly San Francisco. Oakland became a viable alternative because of jobs, fertile land, good climate and easy proximity to the Chinese community across the bay.

Until about 1870, Chinese lived all over the city — 14th Street between Washington and Clay, Telegraph Avenue between 16th and 17th streets, San Pablo between 19th and 20th streets, and First Street between Castro and Brush. A small number settled in Oakland in the 1850s along the estuary. These Chinese settlements were frequently under siege. One, made up of tents and shacks, was set on fire by anti-Chinese Oaklanders. City leaders forced the residents of two other settlements to relocate. Finally, they settled at Eighth and Webster.

Chinese Oaklanders of this era mostly took low-paying jobs unwanted by white residents. Laborers built Temescal and Lake Chabot dams. They worked for a cannery, a cotton mill and an explosives factory. They worked as cooks, gardeners, houseboys and laundrymen. They made cigars, helped develop the

Servants, including a Chinese gardener, on the Delger family estate, located on extensive grounds between Telegraph and San Pablo, c. 1900
Oakland Museum of California, gift of Frank Moller

Chinese vegetable peddlers, balancing long poles with baskets suspended from either end, sold fresh produce in East Bay neighborhoods, c. 1890.
Oakland Museum of California, gift of the Berkeley Firefighter Association, Historical Commission

shrimp and fishery industries and labored in the city's thriving railroad-building industry in the 1860s and 70s. Traveling throughout Oakland and into Berkeley, vendors peddled fresh fruits and vegetables from baskets hung from a long pole. One of the innovations of Chinese farmers was growing two compatible crops on the same land at the same time. They introduced asparagus to commercial farming.

The treatment of the Chinese in California was sometimes benign but more often hostile, with local officials passing anti-Chinese legislation of one sort or another. Virulent sentiments broke out in the early 1870s as the general economy soured. The Workingmen's (also "Sand Lot") Party, dominated by an Irish immigrant drayman, Denis Kearney, was victorious in Oakland in 1878. W.R. Andrus was elected mayor and other anti-Chinese candidates won election as police judge, city attorney and city councilmen. The movement gradually moved to Washington, D.C., where Congress passed the Chinese Exclusion Act of 1882, suspending the legal entry of new Chinese laborers. Through attrition this reduced the Chinese population in America, particularly in California,

58

where most resided. The shrimp camp along the Oakland Estuary closed, as did the First Street Chinese settlement. Only the Eighth and Webster Chinatown survived.

Then came 1906 and the tragic San Francisco earthquake and fire. Many thousands of refugees fled to Oakland and were sheltered there, including about 4,000 Chinese, who were cared for in a segregated camp called The Willows along the shores of Lake Merritt. As San Francisco began its recovery, some 2,000 Chinese refugees chose to stay in Oakland. Chinatown's expansion didn't come without opposition. Some whites put pressure on the city to restrict the growing population to the Eighth and Webster neighborhood. Chinatown grew nonetheless, from the waterfront up to 10th Street along the Webster corridor.

Some noteworthy Chinese made names for themselves in Oakland in the post-quake era. Fung Joe Guey, the first Chinese aviator, was an earthquake refugee who set up an airplane manufacturing operation in Oakland. He tested his planes twice (1908-9) over Oakland skies, the first a failure, the second a 20-minute ride before it too crashed. He was invited to China, where he built that country's first airplane. He died there in 1912 in an air crash. Ng Poon Chew was also a San Francisco refugee, a Presbyterian minister who founded the first Chinese language newspaper in the United States, *Chung Sai Yat Po*. He bought a home outside of Chinatown, using a white friend's name, and lived there until he died in 1931. One of his daughters, Effie Bailey Chew, was Oakland's first teacher of Chinese ancestry. Lew Hing was a prominent Chinese businessmen early in the 20th century. He started Pacific Coast Canning Company, one of the country's largest canneries, located at 12th and Pine streets. The Depression hurt his business badly; he died in 1934 after his cannery failed.

Until 1890 the Chinese were virtually the only Asian group living in Oakland. A small number of Japanese immigrated to California in 1869, according to Dean Yabuki, but large-scale immigration didn't come until the 1890s. Filipinos began arriving in Oakland in the 1920s, settling at the outskirts of Chinatown.

Oakland's first generation of Japanese citizens (Issei) settled in West Oakland around Market Street.

Chinese dragon parade in Oakland's Chinatown, c. 1910
Oakland Museum of California, gift of Martin J. Cooney

Delivery truck from the Chew Hing produce company, c. 1915
Oakland Museum of California, gift of Martin J. Cooney

They worked in jobs similar to the Chinese — domestic services, laundries, dry-cleaning, gardening and nurseries. They established small retail shops in and around Chinatown, and businesses like the A-1 Fish Market on Eighth Street. Horticulture became a specialty on the rural outskirts of the city.

Japanese laundry, c. 1900
Oakland History Room, Oakland Public Library

H. Hayashi Nursery, founded 1906, and its owners' homes (at right) in the Eastmont district. The Chevrolet plant can be seen at rear, left. Brothers Hirokichi Hayashi, Tomoichi Kitano and Kunitaro Minami were forced to sell the nursery for back taxes during their enforced internment at Topaz Relocation Camp during World War II. Reopened after the war in Fremont, the business operated successfully until the early 1990s.

Collection of Warren and Elisabeth Hayashi

60

學汉 撮影

十九白二十四年四月

Even as Chinatown grew in the decades following the earthquake, it became more isolated, but its mostly Chinese residents developed a complex society. There were organized men's and women's sports teams (baseball, football, basketball, volleyball, softball, and track and field). The Wa Sung Service Club, an established Oakland-based Chinese American organization, began as a baseball team in the 1920s. The Japanese community organized athletic teams that afforded young people leadership training and travel opportunities. Many facilities were de facto segregated: for a long time, no Asians — or Jews or African Americans — were allowed to swim at Oakland public pools. They had to travel to Hayward or Richmond, where at least two public "natatoriums" welcomed their business.

Japanese Independent Congregational Church, 1927
Oakland History Room, Oakland Public Library

Chinese and Japanese organizations of all kinds evolved in Oakland. There were Chinese family associations, groupings of like-named families from specific areas of Guangdong Province. Tongs were another type of organization whose members were not necessarily related, but who shared common social and employment status. Some engaged in criminal activities. Several patriotic organizations had strong ties to Oakland's Chinatown. One was the Kuomintang, the political movement founded by Sun Yat-Sen, leader of the Chinese Republic. Another was the Chinese American Citizens Alliance, which fought for the civil rights of Chinese Americans during a period of intense anti-Chinese sentiments. The Oakland branch, located at Eighth and Harrison streets, was the third branch formed. Japanese immigrants organized *ken* associations based on prefecture origins. The Japanese

American Citizens League and the Japanese Association of Oakland offered help to new immigrants and served as focal points for the community, which was increasingly spread throughout the city.

As family life developed in Chinatown, a process of Americanization began. Lincoln Elementary School was the principal vehicle of acculturation. Chinatown children began their American educations there. They also went to privately operated Chinese schools, founded in the 1910s and 20s. By the early 1930s there were as many as 13 such schools scattered throughout Chinatown. In 1953 the Oakland Chinese Community Center and its Chinese school opened at Ninth and Harrison streets, to great fanfare.

Chinese refugees from the San Francisco earthquake brought their church affiliations to Oakland with them. In fact, the growing number of Christians in the Oakland Chinese population acted to reduce attendance at the Buddhist temple on Harrison Street. Chinese churches — Presbyterian, Methodist, Episcopal and Baptist, some tracing their roots to the 1870s — were well-established in Chinatown by the 1940s and continue to be viable institutions today.

Among Japanese Christian churches were West 10th Methodist and Sycamore Congregational. There were also Roman Catholic, Presbyterian, Episcopal, Seventh-day Adventist and Mormon churches for Oakland's Japanese community. The first permanent building of the Japanese Buddhist Church of Oakland was in Chinatown at Sixth and Jackson streets. When the new Nimitz Freeway was being built in 1950, they were forced to relocate. Buddhist leaders and Caltrans brokered a deal in which the new church was physically moved to an empty lot at Ninth and Jackson and settled there. Japanese-American churches in Oakland served major social functions, such as incubating Boy Scout and Girl Scout troops, women's auxiliaries and youth clubs. The Buddhist Church of Oakland had a Japanese language school, SHOWA GAKUEN. Oakland's first sister-city relationship, with Fukuoka, Japan (the city of origin for many Oakland Issei), was given strong support by members of this church.

Among Chinatown's distinguished sons and daughters is the late watercolorist Dong Kingman, born in Oakland in 1911. A restaurateur for a while, he preferred painting. In the 1930s his paintings began to get

62

creation of a new Chinese-American middle class. The notorious Chinese Exclusion Act was repealed in 1943, a reflection of China's status as a U.S. ally. Shipyards hummed in Oakland, employing thousands of people, including many Asians. Chinatown businesses saw profits soar. The Oakland Chinese population grew 37.5 percent to 5,500 in the 1940s. Many Oakland Asians fought in the war, while others raised funds to help China battle the invading Japanese army.

noticed. He abandoned the restaurant business and moved to San Francisco to nurture his art career, which made him famous. A wisp of a woman, Fong Git Mo, the California-born daughter of a gold miner, was the only woman barber in Chinatown, and many youngsters sat for trims in her venerable shop at Eighth and Harrison streets. She died at the age of 97 in 1989. Fong Wan, an herbalist and businessmen, was a flamboyant character who operated a nightclub called Club Shanghai in the 1930s and 40s. Fong's herbal medicine business, based at a colorful, pagoda-style building on 10th Street near Clay, was investigated by local and federal governments and the mainstream pharmaceutical industry. He prevailed in many suits filed against him, in large part because of supportive testimony from his white patients. Even though millionaire businessman Joe Shoong wasn't based in Oakland, he had an impact on Chinatown. He founded the National Dollar Store chain in Vallejo and opened several branches in Oakland. His greatest contribution was establishing the Milton Shoong Foundation, which financed the construction of the Oakland Chinese Community Center.

The cataclysm of World War II accounted for Chinatown's greater integration in Oakland and the

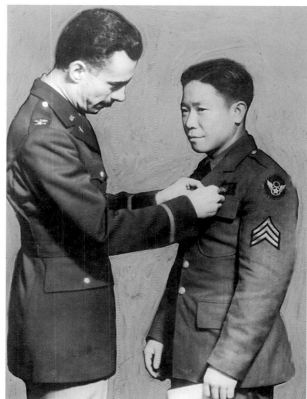

63

If World War II meant better times for the Chinese, at least in the short run, it was nightmarish for all ethnic Japanese along the Pacific coast. After the 1941 Pearl Harbor bombing, war hysteria and racial prejudice prevailed. Japanese living throughout Oakland received notice on April 30, 1942, that they

would be removed by May 7. Extended families quickly gathered at one address, fearful they would be separated. People sold their property at distressed prices, unable to find tenants on such short notice and fearing to leave their homes empty. Of the non-Japanese friends who stepped in to help at this distressing time, Cos Loustalot, a former Chevrolet salesman and insurance agent, deserves notice. A French American, he took care of the Buddhist Church of Oakland building during the war years and extended many kindnesses after.

Japanese Oaklanders were transported to the Tanforan Assembly Center, a racetrack in San Mateo County where stables had been hastily "prepared" for habitation, and forced to live there for five months, until Topaz internment camp in Utah was ready. In all, more than 9,000 people from Alameda County lived in Topaz during the war. After their release, many families

returned to Oakland but others, including community leaders among the Issei who felt betrayed by the country they had so heartily embraced, never came back. For a long time, life for Japanese Americans in Oakland remained difficult.

In the postwar years housing biases were gradually dropped, and Asians, including second-generation Chinese Americans, moved out of Chinatown to buy homes in parts of Oakland that once forbade racial minorities from owning property. This movement by the American-born children of immigrants mirrored a much larger American trend of middle-class families abandoning cities for the growing suburbs.

Ironically, the World War II prosperity was relatively short-lived for Chinatown itself. With the shipyards shut down and its younger generation moving out, businesses and quality of life suffered. In addition, major public projects — the Nimitz Freeway, the Bay Area Rapid Transit District (BART), Laney College and the new Oakland Museum of California — began absorbing Chinatown housing. The vibrancy of Chinatown, evident in the 1930s and 40s, began to be muted in the 50s.

During this relatively quiet period of Chinatown's history, several Oakland Asians emerged as citywide political players. Dr. Raymond Eng, an optometrist, became the first Chinese American elected to the Oakland City Council in 1967, where he served for 16 years. Frank Ogawa, who owned a wholesale nursery business on 73rd Avenue for many years, was elected to

64

the city council at about the same time and served 28 years until his death in 1994. Perhaps the most famous Chinese-American politician to emerge from Oakland is March Fong Eu. She served on the Alameda County Board of Education, Alamedy County Board of Supervisors, the California Assembly and, for five terms, was California Secretary of State, the first Chinese American elected to a statewide office. She then became U.S. Ambassador to the Trust Territories during the Clinton administration. Henry Chang Jr., an architect and developer who was born in China, emerged as a political figure in the 1990s. Active in Chinatown and other civic endeavors, such as the Oakland Port Commission and Bay Conservation and Development Commission (BCDC), Chang was appointed to fill Ogawa's at-large city council seat, and won the seat in the 1996 election.

Chinatown's dormant state lasted well into the 1960s, until Congress liberalized federal immigration laws allowing more immigrants from Asia and Latin America. Oakland Chinatown, among other ethnic communities, experienced a renaissance in the 1970s, accelerated as the end of the Vietnam War brought thousands of refugees from Southeast Asia.

Starting in the 1980s, Oakland's Chinatown started growing again, both inward and outward. Shuttered storefronts became restaurants and shops. Several gasoline stations were transformed into multi-use buildings. Banks opened Oakland Chinatown branches. Redevelopment, a dream of leaders since the somnambulant 1950s, was epitomized by the construction of the multipurpose Pacific Renaissance Plaza. This project attracted Hong Kong money, as have other smaller developments. The injection of capital has helped sustain a robust economic life.

The resurgence of the traditional Chinatown and the creation of a new Asian district east of Lake Merritt is attributable in part to southeast Asians, including ethnic Chinese from Vietnam, Cambodia and Laos. Korean immigrants in the 1980s and 90s have revitalized businesses along 14th Street and Telegraph Avenue.

Perhaps Chinatown is now a misnomer, because the district at Eighth and Webster, while still very Chinese, is much more than that today. The ebb and flow in Oakland will continue to be influenced by immigration policies and geopolitical and geo-economic trends. With multiple generations of Chinese, Japanese, Filipinos, Koreans and southeast Asians living all over the city and a population of at least 60,000, the Asian-American presence in Oakland is deeply rooted.

Attorney Gen. William A. Norris, Secretary of State March Fong Eu and Sen. Ted Kennedy at a rally for Democratic candidate for Congress George Miller, 1974
Oakland Museum of California, Oakland Tribune Collection, gift of ANG Newspapers

Several generations of Oakland's Asian community watch a Columbus Day Parade, October 1981.
Oakland Museum of California, Oakland Tribune Collection, gift of ANG Newspapers

65

CHapter 6

WHEELS AND WINGS

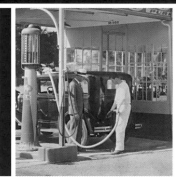

Oakland's HISTORICAL ROLE AS A TRANSPORTATION HUB WAS UNMATCHED IN THE WEST THROUGH WORLD WAR II. CATHERINE DOBRIN EVOKES OAKLAND'S INVOLVEMENT WITH CAR PRODUCTION AND RECREATION IN "THE AUTOMOBILE AGE," AND BOB MIDDLETON DETAILS FLYING FEATS AND AIRPORT BONA FIDES IN "CEILING UNLIMITED."

The Automobile Age

One hundred years ago Oakland, like other cities in the United States, was moving from an agricultural to an industrial economy, and automobiles were a major force in that change.

These self-propelled harbingers of a new age captured the imagination of local inventors, investors and innovators. The earliest vehicles to navigate Oakland's streets were built behind livery stables or cycle shops. Backyard mechanics experimented with gasoline, steam and electric motors, attaching them to anything with wheels — carriages, wagons, bicycles, even tractors. One of the first horseless carriages in Oakland was built by the manager of a Telegraph Avenue cycle shop. William Elliot, following drawings published in a French technical journal, devised a single-cylinder two-horsepower engine and attached it to a two-passenger buggy.

Centrally located on the Pacific coast, Oakland was closer to Western population centers and Asian ports than either Los Angeles or Seattle. As the western terminus of the transcontinental railroad and home to a thriving shipbuilding industry, skilled labor and industrial suppliers were already in place. Additionally, the automobile was welcomed by the progressive government in place during Oakland's early years — men who looked to new technology to solve the problems of a growing city. Far-sighted county supervisors began a road-building program in 1895 to provide access into Oakland from the outlying areas. In 1906, Oakland became the first city west of the Mississippi to use a police patrol car. The department quickly added motorcycles and other vehicles and had completely converted to all motorized vehicles by 1917.

A White Stanhope steam-powered car built by the White Motor Steam Car Company of Oakland, 1901
Oakland Museum of California, gift of Louis L. Stein

Paving 13th Avenue in East Oakland, 1892
Oakland Museum of California, gift of Edwin R. Jackson

(Far right) New automobiles in the yard at the Chevrolet plant in the Eastmont district, c. 1918. The plant opened in 1916.
Oakland Museum of California, gift of Herrington and Olson

The traffic squad of the Oakland Police Department showing off their new Indian motorcycles, May 1926
Oakland Museum of California, gift of the Oakland Police Museum

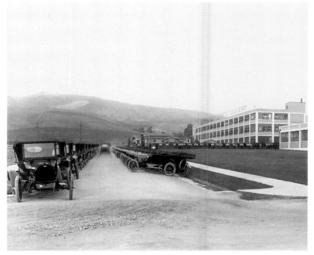

figure in American industry. In 1910, when he lost control of General Motors, he promptly started Chevrolet and by 1914 was selling every car his Flint, Michigan, plant could produce.

He raised capital for distribution and assembly plants by convincing local investors to put up the cash and he would provide the management. Durant was by all accounts a super salesman, but he met his match in Oakland's Mayor John Davie. With former Oakland Buick distributor Norman deVaux, Durant and Davie forged a plan that began Oakland's growth as an automotive center.

The Chevrolet plant was built on a seven-acre site at Foothill Boulevard and 69th Avenue in Elmhurst. In September 1916 the first vehicles came off the line. The $250,000 plant originally produced 20 cars per day. By the end of 1919, 1,000 workers in four large buildings were assembling 100 touring cars, roadsters and trucks a day. Suppliers of parts and accessories quickly established operations here to service the Chevrolet plant. In the 1920s the Chamber of Commerce proclaimed Oakland as the "Detroit of the West."

Fageol Motors, founded in 1916, initially built one of the largest and most expensive passenger cars ever produced in the United States. With high-quality materials in short supply during World War I, Fageol shifted production to heavy-duty trucks at its plant at

For these and other reasons, William C. Durant chose Oakland for a sales and distribution center and, later, for an assembly plant for his new Chevrolet Motor Company. Durant was an important and engaging

107th and Hollywood (now MacArthur). In 1921 it initiated what would become its most successful product — a passenger bus called the Fageol Safety Coach. Fageol trucks and buses were built in Oakland

68

Mayor John L. Davie handing over a letter to be delivered to the mayor of Los Angeles on the first Fageol bus run from Oakland to Los Angeles, January 1922

Oakland Museum of California

Chapter Six

until the early 1930s. In 1939 lumberman T.A. Peterman bought the plant and began producing heavy-duty trucks under the Peterbilt name.

Durant and Chevrolet had rejoined General Motors, but by 1920 Durant was again in the midst of a financial crisis. Forced to resign the presidency of General Motors in 1920, he took his remaining assets and started a new venture, the Durant Motor Company. Along with his son, R.C., and Norman deVaux, he created Durant Motors of California to produce and distribute Durant, Star and Flint automobiles in the West. By March 1921, automobiles were being produced at an 18-acre site at East 14th Street and Durant Avenue for delivery to the western states, Hawaii, the Philippines and other Pacific nations.

The industry continued to grow, and by 1928 Oakland was the largest automobile producer on the West Coast. Major manufacturers included Chevrolet, Fisher Body, Durant, Caterpillar and Fageol, plus the scores of suppliers and accessory manufacturers who serviced these plants and those of Chrysler in San Leandro and Ford in Richmond.

Durant Motors, however, did not survive the Depression. GM purchased the Oakland plant in 1935 for truck assembly and a parts warehouse. In 1936 *The Oakland Tribune* reported that General Motors had the highest industrial payroll in the city. The Oakland facility was the largest assembly plant west of the Mississippi, producing 118,000 Chevrolets that year and employing 1,600 workers. In 1958, when General Motors celebrated its 50th anniversary, it had over 19 different corporate headquarters in the East Bay.

The automobile affected many areas of life in Oakland. From the earliest days of motoring, newspapers ran pages of auto news with information on the latest models, tips on driving and even suggestions for an appropriate touring wardrobe. Auto racing also started early in Oakland. The first race track, the Oakland Motordrome, was built in 1911. Families rode the streetcar to the outlying Elmhurst area to watch Pope-Hartfords, Nationals and Simplexes compete on the half-mile banked track.

In 1931 the Oakland Speedway was built in the unincorporated Ashland district. The one-mile oiled-dirt track was designed for speeds up to 110 mph. The track was demolished in 1940, and after World War II, a new Oakland Stadium racetrack was built on the old Speedway site. Many national records were set by stock cars, track roadsters, hardtops and midgets on this

The 1924 Oakland Auto Show, held in an annex of the Oakland Auditorium, promoted local auto manufacturers. *Oakland Museum of California, gift of Martin J. Cooney*

(Far right) A crack-up during an auto race at the Oakland Speedway in 1952. This photograph won the photographer, Russ Reed, Sports Photo of the Year from *LIFE* magazine. *Oakland Museum of California, gift of Randy Reed*

New businesses developed between 1910 and 1930 to support Oaklanders' love affair with the automobile. Car accessory stores, mechanics and gas stations joined the car manufacturers in the area to make Oakland the "Detroit of the West," c. 1925. *Oakland Museum of California, gift of Martin J. Cooney*

70

The Grand National Roadster Auto Show, 1996

Photo by Tom Mullins

Chapter Six

five-eighth mile track. There was even a match race between Mayor Clifford Rishell of Oakland and Mayor William Swift of San Leandro in 1950. The track was torn down in 1954 when Bay Fair Shopping Center was built.

In 1948 a small one-twelfth mile oval track was laid out inside Oakland's Exposition Building, where Laney College now stands, for winter-season midget racing. In spite of noise and fumes, it was a popular social and spectator event for nearly 20 years.

Like other California cities, Oakland was swept up in the hot rod craze that roared across America after 1945. Car clubs with names like the Idlers, Rod Reckers, Swanx, Knights and Nomads were formed to build, race and show off their creations. In 1949 promoter Al Slonaker and his wife, Mary, visited the drive-ins, gas stations and race tracks favored by the local hot rodders and convinced them to bring their cars to the Exposition Building for a special car show. The first Grand National Roadster Show was held in 1950 and returned to Oakland each year until 1998.

As the automobile took a stronger hold on society, many things began to change for Oakland. Its fine transit system of streetcars and electric trains became a casualty of the automobile's success and the industry's growing dominance. General Motors, Standard Oil, Firestone Tires and others formed National City Lines to acquire local transit companies for the sole purpose of eliminating streetcars in favor of motorized buses and automobiles. National City Lines took over Oakland's Key System in 1946 and replaced its streetcars with buses in 1948. The train tracks were removed from the Bay Bridge in 1958.

Automobiles and buses eclipsed the efficient Key Route streetcar system, which ran to all parts of Oakland, by 1948. The streetcars stopped running completely by 1958. *Oakland Museum of California, gift of Enid Walsh*

The roads linking outlying areas to the township for business, commerce and community, led out as well as in, and as urban flight and suburban migration took hold in the 1970s, the center of the city began to decline.

Except for a brief interruption during World War II, automobiles were manufactured in Oakland from 1916 until 1963, when General Motors shifted manufacturing to its new Fremont plant. In 1978 GM officials broke the news that the big parts warehouse occupying the original Durant Motors facility would move operations to Sparks, Nevada. This announcement was met by a loud outcry from city and union officials. "A lot of people depend on us," United Auto Workers representative Clarence Robinson told the *East Bay Voice*. "We support almost the entire community, from the Eastmont Mall on down. A lot of small businesses, many of which are minority-owned, will fold if GM leaves town. The ripple effects will be overwhelming. It will turn the area into a no-man's land." Protests were unsuccessful and GM followed the 35 manufacturing and wholesale firms that abandoned Oakland between 1970 and 76. East Oakland has never fully recovered.

Today the only automobiles built in Oakland are one-of-a-kind creations handbuilt by craftsman like Steve Moal, a third-generation Oakland artisan and heir to its automotive history. He learned his art through his grandfather, William, who came to Oakland in 1911, a time when both the city and the motorcar were young.

Ceiling Unlimited

In the exuberant early days of civil aviation, there was no Federal Aviation Administration or Civil Aeronautics Board, no Mission Control. Flights were not remotely controlled by computers on board and bureaucrats on the ground. Flight was the incredible made real, humanity's universal dream come true, more miracle than science. It was the essence of modernism, and the Oakland Airport — both destination and take-off point — was on the cutting edge.

Consider the airport's legendary origins. In 1926 Truby Davidson, the nation's war secretary, embarked on a hurried tour of West Coast cities. His mission was to ordain a site for a new "aerodrome," a facility from which to demonstrate the mainland's access to the Hawaiian islands by plane. In a confidential White House memo

72

the secretary wrote, "I can think of no other site so thoroughly suited for modern aviation than Oakland." Less than a year later, bulldozers carved a 7,020-foot log runway out of the lettuce fields on the shoreline of San Leandro Bay — the longest airfield in the world. In rapid succession came the significant first flights.

On June 18, 1927, Army Air Corps Lts. Lester Maitland and Albert F. Hegenberger took off in a Fokker C-2 bomber, *Bird of Paradise,* bound for Hawaii. It was the longest flight yet over water, exceeding by 600 miles the over-water portion of Charles Lindbergh's Atlantic journey a few months before. *Bird of Paradise* reached Wheeler Field in Oahu in 25 hours, 50 minutes. Less than a month later, on July 14, pilot Ernie Smith and navigator Emory A. Bronte made the first civilian flight to Hawaii in the Travel Air monoplane *City of Oakland.* They got there faster, in 25 hours, 36 minutes, but landed in the trees of Molokai rather than on Wheeler Field.

Lester Maitland and Albert Hegenberger's plane, the *Bird of Paradise,* June 28, 1927. The pair and their Fokker tri-motor plane were the first to fly from California to Hawaii, making the trip in 25 hours and 49 minutes. *Oakland Museum of California, Oakland Tribune Collection, gift of ANG Newspapers*

Lts. Hegenberger and Maitland upon their return from Hawaii, July 12, 1927 *Oakland Museum of California, Oakland Tribune Collection, gift of ANG Newspapers*

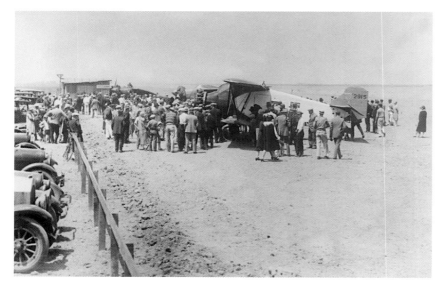

An "air race" from Oakland to Hawaii was all the rage that summer, with few regulations governing entry and lucrative prizes for the winners. Pineapple magnate James Dole offered a purse of $25,000 for first place and $10,000 for second, but of 15 entrants, only two finished. The competition resulted in 10 deaths, including two would-be rescuers who crashed at sea. The tragedy led to stricter rules governing qualifications of aviators and fitness of planes.

During the 1920s, California led the 48 states in number of airports,

Some of the entries in the Dole Race at the Oakland Airport, August 1927. The only building at the airport was a shack that served as a restaurant and office. *Oakland Museum of California, Oakland Tribune Collection, gift of ANG Newspapers*

Paul Mantz, Amelia Earhart, Harry Manning and Fred Noonan at the Oakland Airport in March 1937 before Earhart's first attempt to fly around the world at the equator

Oakland Museum of California, Oakland Tribune Collection, gift of ANG Newspapers

and the Oakland Municipal Airport was the finest of these. In September 1927 the airport was formally dedicated. Charles A. Lindbergh flew into Oakland in a replica of the *Spirit of St. Louis* to preside at the ceremonies.

At the end of 1927 Boeing Air Transport (the predecessor of United Air Lines) inaugurated U.S. transcontinental passenger and air mail services between Oakland and New York. In May 1928 Australian World War I ace Sir Charles Kingsford-Smith departed from Oakland with a crew of three bound for Australia via Hawaii. The 7,300-mile trip took seven days and was the first flight between the two continents.

On July 30, 1929, the Oakland Airport Inn, touted as the nation's first airport hotel, was dedicated. In 1931 Amelia Earhart guided an autogiro (a hybrid airplane/helicopter) into Oakland, the first-ever transcontinental flight in this aircraft. Then, in January 1935, after an 18-hour, 15-minute flight from Honolulu — the first trans-Pacific solo venture — Amelia Earhart landed at Oakland, where she was greeted by 15,000 aviation enthusiasts. In May 1937 the celebrated aviatrix and navigator Fred Noonan took off from Oakland to begin their ill-fated around-the-world journey.

A month later, in June 1937, United Air Lines introduced the Douglas DC-3 aircraft for its Oakland-New York service. The plane carried 14 passengers and made the trip in a little over 15 hours, with stops in Salt Lake City, Cheyenne and Chicago.

After Pearl Harbor, Oakland became the marshaling point for all planes bound for the U.S. forces in the Pacific. In 1943 all of Oakland's commercial flights were diverted for the duration of the war to San Francisco Municipal Airport. The interruption of service at Oakland was a boon to San Francisco's absentee airfield on the mud flats east of Millbrae, 20 miles outside the city. In 1946, Oakland quickly doffed its uniform and resumed civilian business. Western Airlines began scheduled service between Oakland and Los Angeles, a harbinger of traffic in what is now the highest-volume air traffic corridor in the world. In 1954 the name of the airport was changed to

An aerial view of the Oakland Airport, c. 1955
Oakland Museum of California, gift of Herrington and Olson

World AIRWAYS WAS ONE OF THE AIRLINES THAT PARTICIPATED IN OPERATION BABYLIFT FROM VIETNAM IN APRIL 1975. MORE THAN 2,000 ORPHANED CHILDREN WERE EVACUATED. THEY RECEIVED MEDICAL TREATMENT UPON ARRIVING IN THE STATES AND WERE ADOPTED BY AMERICAN FAMILIES.

Oakland Museum of California, Oakland Tribune Collection, gift of ANG Newspapers

Metropolitan Oakland International Airport. A 10,000-foot runway and a $5.2 million passenger terminal were added to welcome jets in 1962. The original airport, now known as North Field, is used mainly for cargo operations.

Two charter airlines had important Oakland histories, Woodruff Minor writes in his history of the Port of Oakland, *Pacific Gateway*. Transocean, founded in 1946 by Orvis M. Nelson, was the airport's principal tenant in the late 1940s and 50s and the world's largest nonscheduled carrier. World Airways, founded in New Jersey in 1948 and later bought by Edward J. Daly, was moved to Oakland in 1956. World took over many of Transocean's facilities and became the world's leading charter carrier by the mid-1960s, when it began passenger service between the coasts.

World Airways was the main airline contracted by the U.S. military to transport troops to and from Vietnam during the war. Thousands of soldiers embarked from Oakland and if they were fortunate, returned there. World Airways was also a major carrier during the Vietnam airlift for orphans. The airline relocated to the East Coast in the 1980s.

In one of the last of the "firsts" for the venerable airport, the first Concorde (Supersonic Transport, or SST) flight between North America and Asia took off from Oakland in 1985.

Today Oakland International Airport, with expansion plans on the drawing board, annually handles about 15 percent of the Bay Area's airline travelers and 48 percent of the region's air cargo. It is many people's favorite airport, for its easy access and relatively infrequent weather problems. The airport continues to be one of the city's sterling assets. If flight is the stuff of soul, Oakland's laurels are unmatched, bona fide and evergreen.

Terminal 1 at the Oakland International Airport, c. 1965. The airport now encompasses two terminals, with massive expansion plans in the works. *Oakland Museum of California*

THE

neigHbOrHOOds

Central East Oakland

Henry Fitch, an explorer, was sailing to Marin County when he lost his way and docked in the Oakland estuary in 1850. Enchanted by the beauty of the land, he decided against continuing his journey north. He remained in the area and soon purchased a parcel of land near the present-day Oakland Coliseum. There he created the small rural district of Fitchburg, home to many early settlers of East Oakland. A short distance to the north, local cattlemen founded the village of Melrose. This location was ideal for raising cattle because of its proximity to the railroad line. Manufacturing operations and factories moved into the area, followed by residents attracted by the employment opportunities and the surrounding environment of orchards and flowers.

Mills Seminary was established by Cyrus Taggart Mills in Central East Oakland in 1871. It lent its name to Seminary Avenue before becoming Mills College in 1885. Mills' interest in horticulture led to the development of the campus into a landscaped, park-like island. Mills became the largest women's college in the west, and has established a reputation as one of America's finest liberal arts colleges.

Melrose and Fitchburg were annexed to the city of Oakland in 1909. In 1916 General Motors built a Chevrolet automobile plant at 69th Avenue and Foothill Boulevard. This factory helped promote Oakland's reputation as an industrial center. Other car companies followed Chevrolet into Oakland, attracted by the convenience of the railroads and the Pacific Coast market. The large influx of factory workers led to rapid home construction in the late 1920s. Between 1920 and 1924 alone, 13,000 new homes were built in Oakland, many of which were built along Havenscourt, 55th Avenue and Seminary Avenue. In the early 1920s,

planning began for the Maxwell Park development, a model project for innovative urban housing and planning. By the 1950s there were hundreds of homes in the hilly area surrounding Mills College.

Throughout the 1930s, World War II and the 1950s, industry continued to flourish. Soon after, however, things took a downturn. Plants and factories moved out of Oakland into new locations where work and production could be done faster and for less expense. By 1963 the Chevrolet plant was obsolete, and in 1965 it was demolished and replaced with the Eastmont Mall, now Eastmont Town Center.

Without an industrial base, this once-thriving community now struggles against high unemployment, crime, homelessness and drugs, while also remaining the proud home of Mills College, the Oakland Coliseum sports complex, a charming row of antique shops and some of the most beautifully kept residential blocks in the city. Above all, it is characterized by the strength of its working-class politics and activism. The celebrated Community School of the Black Panthers was formed there in the 1970s. Fremont High School, the only high school in the nation with a full-service health clinic, is located there, as is Frick Middle High, the host of an array of nationally recognized demonstration projects. The Midnight Basketball program and meaningful public housing safety patrols were initiated there. The district's Community Development District Board and Community Development Corporation are pursuing a joint vision of revitalization and new development. In Central East Oakland a bold combination of citizens, youth centers, employment projects, women's organizations, churches and men's groups are diligently working to find a new direction and maintain a viable and proud community. ■

Chapter 7

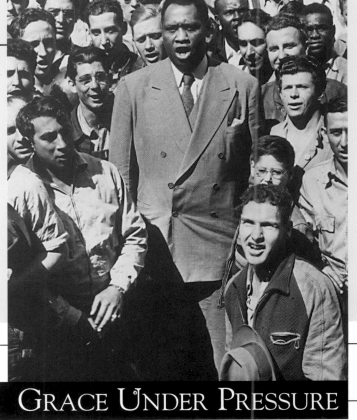

GRACE UNDER PRESSURE

The HISTORY OF AFRICAN AMERICANS IN OAKLAND, MARY ELLEN BUTLER WRITES, IS INEXTRICABLY LINKED TO THREE GREAT CATALYSTS: THE GOLD RUSH, THE RAILROAD AND THE WAR.

Oakland has nurtured achievers of African descent since its earliest days. Many have either joined or come out of the solid working and middle-class African-American communities that have been among the city's assets. African Americans continue to be attracted from other parts of the nation and world to the artistically vibrant, socially wide-open city. Their choice of residence benefits not only the black community but Oakland as a whole. The presence of a critical mass of stable families, for example, enabled the city to stay cool through the troubled second half of the 20th century. While other urban areas exploded into violence after the assassination of Dr. Martin Luther King Jr. in 1968 and the acquittal of four Los Angeles police officers in the beating of motorist Rodney King in 1992, Oaklanders strongly protested the crimes but declined to destroy their own city in the process.

To be sure, the path to equal opportunity has not been smooth. Until the mid-1940s, discriminatory practices in housing, employment and law enforcement prevailed in Oakland as they did throughout the United States. It took the determined efforts of activists from that decade through the 1950s to outlaw these practices, or at least to drive them underground, where they occasionally fester. But the battle did not end there. No sooner was equal opportunity achieved than the nation's economy began to shift from heavy manufacturing to computer-based service industries. At that point, in the 1960s and 70s, as blue-collar jobs gradually gave way to white-collar office employment, many black households began to lose ground. Today, 30 years later, young black people are starting to understand that in order to survive in the new digital world they must become skilled in high technology.

The continuous struggle to attain and maintain economic security has not prevented African Americans from joyfully expressing themselves in the artistic, intellectual, athletic and spiritual realms. Whether in church, on stage, in school

Mary Sanderson and her
students at the Brooklyn
Colored School, 1870.
Oakland's schools became
integrated by 1872.
*Oakland History Room,
Oakland Public Library*

or studio, black folks have added immeasurably to the social, cultural and spiritual life of the city. And they've done so with the help of at least three great catalysts: the Gold Rush, the Railroad and the War.

African Americans made their living in early Oakland as skilled craftsmen, blacksmiths, livery men, laundry women, cooks and house servants, restaurateurs, barbers and free-lance providers of other goods and services. They were met with bigotry outside these occupations — firms advertised for white workers, home builders sold to white buyers, and unions reserved memberships for white apprentices. In the public sector, African Americans were excluded from holding civil service jobs until well into the 1920s. Determined not to submit to second-class citizenship, they created their own institutions. During the 1850s and 60s, African Americans started churches, schools, charities, newspapers, and civic and social clubs for personal and group advancement. In 1857 they helped organize a meeting in Sacramento of the first Colored Convention in California. The first black church in Oakland, First African Methodist Episcopal (AME), was created in 1852 at the home of Isaac and Elizabeth Flood in West Oakland. It became a center of activity for the city's large black middle class.

The first public schools in Oakland admitted only whites. Elizabeth Flood conducted a private school for black children from 1857 until her death in 1867. The

Oakland Board of Education agreed to provide education, but in a segregated setting. The first public school for minority children, according to Donald Hausler, was established in 1867. It was taught by Mary Jane Sanderson, who, although only 16, had completed rigorous teacher training. Her one-room school was distinguished for high achievement. Later, education became integrated, at least on paper. During the 1890s and early decades of the 20th century, the black community established an old folks' home, a children's home, the Watts Sanitarium, a YWCA and YMCA. The YWCA, Hausler writes, functioned as a job placement and welfare agency during the Depression. The YMCA promoted competitive sports, sponsored classes and maintained free beds for men seeking shelter.

In the early 1900s the Oakland chapter of Marcus Garvey's Universal Negro Improvement Association was considered one of the three strongest such units in the West. The first Bay Area chapter of the National Association for the Advancement of Colored People was founded in 1913 in Oakland. With attorney John D. Drake as president, the chapter blocked repeat showings in 1915 of the D.W. Griffith film, *The Clansman* (renamed *Birth of a Nation*), protested the presence of KKK

Easter Sunday at
Beth Eden Baptist Church
on West Filbert Street,
1901. The church,
established in 1889,
was an important gathering
center for Oakland's
African-American
community.
*Oakland History Room,
Oakland Public Library*

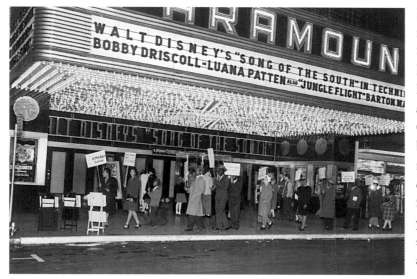

Pullman Company "sleeping cars" that ran between Chicago and Oakland. Starting in 1870 the company began to hire black men as porters. Because of housing segregation in Oakland, virtually all African Americans lived in West Oakland. A new railroad station had been built at 16th and Wood, and all railroad operating employees on 24-hour call were required to live west of Adeline Street for quick access. For the next 50 years, work for sleeping car porters was steady but pay was low, hours grueling and job protections few.

In 1925 the Brotherhood of Sleeping Car Porters was formed in Chicago. A. Phillip Randolph asked union co-founder Cotrell Lawrence (C.L.) Dellums, an Oakland porter, to form an Oakland branch. Dellums, fired for his organizing activity, persevered until the union won a contract in 1937. Higher pay allowed the porters to better support their families, purchase homes and educate their children. Another railroad-based union, the International Brotherhood of the Redcaps, was also formed in 1937. Its primarily black membership, along with the unionized cooks and dining car waiters, added more depth to the growing black middle class.

sympathizers in the East Bay, and threatened legal action after Ida Louise Jackson, a charter member of the chapter, was passed over for a teaching post in the Oakland public schools. She was subsequently hired in 1925. From 1923 until 1934 Delilah L. Beasley, the first African-American woman on the staff of a major metropolitan daily, recorded many of these activities in her *Oakland Tribune* column.

This early tradition of civic participation remains vigorous today. "They were strong black people, independently minded," wrote Lawrence Crouchett, the late director of Oakland's Center for Afro-American History and Life (now the African American Museum and Library in Oakland). "You could see it in their day-to-day life. They were entrepreneurs, running their own businesses. In their letters and newspapers they didn't write about slavery. They talked about themselves as U.S. citizens."

With its strategic location on the continental side of the bay, the new city quickly developed into a major manufacturing, shipping, transportation and distribution hub. In 1869 the Central Pacific Railroad decided to make Oakland its transcontinental terminus, cementing the city's brawny identity while tangentially providing a major boost for its African-American community. Among the services the railroad provided were luxurious

83

Their families formed a well-established presence in the city and left a proud legacy that continues today.

Not only did this solid, wage-earning base foster "continued political and social organizing," writes *Tribune* columnist Brenda Payton, but "the railroad connected Oakland to the rest of black America. Porters traveling back and forth across the country kept Oakland abreast of developments in the Eastern and Southern black communities and transported Oakland's ideas and innovations to those areas. Oakland's African-American community was small and distant, but its strong foundation, determination for racial equality and key location made it a town that would greatly influence and shape African-American history." When Oakland's new train depot in Jack London Square was dedicated in 1995, it was named the C.L. Dellums Amtrak Station, in honor of the longtime resident and equal-rights activist and, by association, the men he represented in their fight for better treatment.

Hearing about Oakland from the men who "ran the railroad," many African-American families migrated west during the 1920s and 30s to pursue professional goals in comparative freedom. In 1921, for example, Dr. William Douglas Wilson moved his wife and sons from Shreveport, Louisiana. "My father would tell people that he chose to live in the East Bay because there were so many wonderful educational opportunities here," said Dr. Clay Wilson, the youngest son. The three brothers became a dentist, insurance agent and physician, and their wives were among the first black public schoolteachers in Oakland and Berkeley. Other black professionals came from points east, attracted by the promise of superior, low-cost, state supported education for their children. The Berkeley campus of the University of California, which had its beginnings in Oakland, became a magnet for such families from around the country.

During World War II Oakland's strategic location and well-established industrial might catapulted it to the forefront of the defense effort. The federal government established several military installations, including the Oak Knoll Navy Hospital and Alameda Naval Air Base. Shipyards built by Oakland industrialist Henry J. Kaiser and others cranked up production. Hundreds of thousands of workers were recruited to the Bay Area for the war effort, including tens of thousands of black southerners who were eager for a better life.

Many went to work at the military bases, but black applicants to privately owned plants faced whites-only hiring policies. In 1941, after C.L. Dellums, John Drake and other activists threatened a mass protest march on Washington, D.C., President Roosevelt issued Executive Order No. 8802, requiring defense contractors to offer equal employment opportunities to all. Still, major unions refused full membership to minority workers, shunting them into "auxiliary" chapters or assigning them to segregated work units.

When the war ended, most of the migrants stayed in the Bay Area. Oakland's black population jumped from 8,462 in 1940 to 47,562 in 1950, a nearly sixfold increase. The newest southern migrants "were as well-educated, more highly skilled, more likely to live in

(Far right)
Oakland street scene, 1952
*Oakland Museum
of California,*
© *Dorothea Lange Collection,*
gift of Paul S. Taylor

The great Paul Robeson sings "The Star Spangled Banner" with workers at Moore Dry Dock, September 21, 1942. Like many performers during World War II, Robeson visited the shipyards to encourage the employees to work harder and faster constructing ships to help defeat the nation's enemies.
*Oakland Museum
of California,
Oakland Tribune Collection,
gift of ANG Newspapers*

84

Shoppers EXIT THE 10TH STREET MARKET, C. 1942. OAKLAND'S ECONOMY BOOMED DURING THE WAR YEARS. THE MAN'S CLOTHING SUGGESTS THAT HE WORKS FOR THE RAILROAD.

Oakland Museum of California, © Dorothea Lange Collection,
gift of Paul S. Taylor

Chapter Seven

Yet for all these successes, discrimination in Oakland was persistent. A group of bright young men and women, armed with law degrees earned from U.C. Berkeley and other schools through the G.I. Bill, took up the cudgel once again, with more ringing results. Starting in the late 1940s, lawyers such as Thomas L. Berkley, Allen E. Broussard, Donald P. McCullum, Wilmont Sweeney, Clinton White and Lionel J. Wilson led a renewed charge against racial bias. Joining forces with the Democratic Party and the more receptive labor unions, they helped the East Bay black community gain political power. State Assemblyman William Byron Rumford's fair employment and housing bills dealt body blows to institutional racism statewide. In the late 1940s Joshua Rose, director of the Northwest Branch YMCA, became the first African American to sit on a City of Oakland board or commission, the Board of Playground Directors, while civic activist Barney Hilburn broke the color barrier on the Oakland Board of Education.

two-parent households, and more active in churches and labor unions than members of the non-migrant black population," writes Gretchen Lemke-Santangelo in *Abiding Courage: African American Migrant Women and the East Bay Community*. Like those who had come before, the newcomers were "ambitious, determined to buy homes, start businesses and obtain more training and education."

Not only that, they introduced a little soul to what had been a fairly strait-laced social set.

From the 1940s to the 60s, West Oakland's Seventh Street teemed with nightlife, led by Slim Jenkins' Supper Club and Esther's Orbit Room. When Duke Ellington, Count Basie and Lionel Hampton played downtown Oakland, they'd go to Seventh Street for after-hours relaxation. Jazz pianist Earl "Fatha" Hines lived in Oakland when he wasn't on the road. Migrants from Texas, Louisiana, Mississippi and Arkansas developed the Oakland Blues sound and enriched jazz and church music, too. In the past five decades, Oakland-born Edwin Hawkins' recording of "Oh Happy Day" became the best-selling gospel single of all time. Oakland artists in rhythm and blues (the Pointer Sisters), blues (Jesse "Lone Cat" Fuller) and rap (Hammer, Digital Underground) have influenced those genres nationwide. Symphony orchestra conductors — Michael Morgan and the late Calvin Simmons — have underscored the strong presence of African Americans in classical music nationwide as well.

African Americans began competing successfully for school boards, city council, county board of supervisors, state assembly, state senate and U.S. congressional seats. In 1964, Rose became the first black member of the Oakland City Council. The crusading lawyers — Broussard, McCullum, Sweeney, White and Wilson — were eventually appointed judges of the Alameda County municipal and superior courts, and Broussard went on to become a member of the California Supreme Court.

It was in this context of social change in the late 1960s that cross-cultural exchanges among different ethnic groups in the city flowered. Three programs serve as illustration.

Pressured by community groups to hire qualified minorities as professional staff, the Oakland Museum's leadership created a department of special exhibits and education and hired an African-American curator, Ben Hazard. He immediately formed the Cultural and Ethnic Affairs Guild, with a steering committee composed of

86

representatives from Asian, Native American, African-American and Latino community organizations. Dr. Norvel Smith, former director of Oakland's Department of Human Resources and Merritt College president, became chairman. The guild presented cultural and ethnic programs to attract new museum audiences from ethnic neighborhoods and to foster awareness across racial and ethnic lines. In 1970 MESA, or Mathematics, Engineering, Science Achievement program, was created at Oakland Technical High School. This national pilot program was designed to encourage students from minority groups to enter the mathematics and science professions. Professor Wilbur Somerton of the College of Engineering, U.C. Berkeley, worked with mathematics teacher Mary Perry Smith to implement and refine the concept into a workable set of academic support activities. MESA was expanded throughout California and eventually replicated in more than 10 other states. The Black Filmmakers Hall of Fame (BFHF) was created at the Oakland Museum in 1973, also by the Cultural and Ethnic Affairs Guild. It focused public attention on the history of African-American achievements in film and television and countered negative media images. Incorporated since 1977 as a nonprofit organization, it is recognized as an important resource for dissemination of information to educational institutions, Hollywood, libraries, film festivals and community organizations.

In 1970, in what seemed to bring history full circle, Ron Dellums, nephew of C.L. Dellums, was elected to represent Oakland and Berkeley in the U.S. House of Representatives. During the decades of the 1970s and 80s, black Oaklanders served as mayor, city manager, police chief, fire chief and chamber of commerce director, as well as council members. Oakland continues to be represented in Congress by an African American, Barbara Lee, while the positions of police chief (Richard Word) and city manager (Robert R. Bobb) are held by highly accomplished black civil servants.

Yet the same postwar decades brought grief to other families. Thousands of workers, black and white, lost their jobs as defense industries and military bases shut down or cut back. Manufacturing plants closed or relocated to areas offering nonunionized labor. So while black achievers were leading the way, their less fortunate counterparts were bringing up the rear. In the 1960s and 70s, as blue-collar jobs gradually gave way to white-color office employment, more black households began to lose ground. Today, 30 years later, young people are starting to understand that in order to survive in the new digital world they must become familiar with high technology.

Today African Americans in Oakland face new challenges. The age of dominant black political power has given way to a more multicultural establishment. The public school system is under great pressure to raise low levels of student achievement. And local commerce, long based on secure government jobs, is adapting to the burgeoning but unstable high-tech economy. It is estimated that as high as a quarter of Oakland's population lives in or near poverty. Poverty has led to the development of underground economies. One of the most destructive was the illicit crack cocaine trade of the 1980s, leading to high black-on-black crime rates which, thankfully, have abated. Now, immigrants from east, northeast and west Africa are bringing new vitality to old neighborhoods, finding in Oakland a place where they are free to work toward the American dream of educational attainment, home ownership and career pursuits.

As the 21st century spins off epochs yet to be named, there is every reason to hope that black Oaklanders will continue to achieve the timeless goals of equal opportunity and accomplishment in the city they have chosen to grace.

Dorothy Patterson contributed to this essay.

The Soul Vibrations Festival at the Oakland Museum of California, sponsored by the museum's Cultural and Ethnic Affairs Guild, c. 1975
Oakland Museum of California

THE

nEigHbORHOOds

In the late 1880s this area was made up of farmhouses scattered among groves of elm trees. In 1877, when the Southern Pacific rail service began, this small country village was one of the last stops on the line. In 1892, Oakland, San Leandro and Hayward's Electric Railway Company began service on what is now East 14th Street. A major power plant and roundhouse were built there near the corner of 98th Avenue, and the area grew rapidly. With the train station as its nucleus, Elmhurst received a constant stream of newcomers.

Real estate in the village was considerably less expensive than in the central parts of Oakland, enabling laborers who worked in canneries and factories to purchase homes and raise families away from the hustle and bustle of the central district. Elmhurst was annexed to the city of Oakland in 1909.

During World War II, in response to the wave of blue-collar workers streaming into Oakland to work in the defense plants and shipyards, large, multi-family housing units were built in Elmhurst. Longtime residents remember working in die-casting businesses, glass manufacturing plants and canneries that thrived from the 1940s through the 1960s. After the war these plants shut down or relocated to more cost-effective areas. As a result, Elmhurst experienced a long period of debilitating unemployment, poverty and increased crime.

Between the 1960s and 80s the district became the center for new housing and new populations. Many of West Oakland's residents moved there after being displaced by urban renewal projects, resulting in a dramatic increase in Elmhurst's African-American population.

Today Elmhurst, Oakland's most eastern district, remains a close-knit community, with many neighborhood associations and block clubs. Once solidly middle-class, it is challenged by a high level of persistent unemployment and its byproducts. These issues are being tackled head-on by organizations such as the Sobrante Park Neighborhood Collaborative, the Elmhurst Community District Board and the Brookfield Neighborhood Association, just a few of the district's active community groups. Elmhurst is the home of Elmhurst Pride Day, the East Oakland Youth Development Center and Allen Temple Baptist Church. The work of such organizations indicates a positive outlook for this community.

Chapter 8

SAFE AT HOME

Oakland's ATHLETIC HERITAGE IS UNSURPASSED FOR A CITY OF ITS SIZE. **PHIL MUMMA** DESCRIBES EARLY SPORTS IN THE CITY, AND BRINGS FORWARD SOME GREAT COACHES, INDIVIDUAL ATHLETES AND TEAMS — INCLUDING SOME UNSUNG HEROES.

When it was time to choose sides at DeFremery or Bushrod parks in the late 1940s and 1950s, pick-up games were often composed of kids from the neighborhood who were destined for stardom. Frank Robinson, Bill Russell, Curt Flood and Vada Pinson all lived nearby. John Brodie would occasionally arrive from North Oakland to make the competition even tougher.

Athletes have argued for years about why Oakland has produced so many superior performers. Champion sprinter Ray Norton believes that it is attributable to the values of the men and women who settled in Oakland, many of them blue-collar workers who came for jobs, worked hard and passed that ethic on to their children. Others would add a superior park system and excellent coaches who chose to work with youth. Joe Morgan, who grew up in the late 1950s in East Oakland, credits coaches Al Ferrara, Nick Garedakis, Stan Corich and George Powles with preparing him for professional baseball and giving him an early advantage over other players. Frank Robinson thought so much of Powles that he had his former high school coach introduce him at Robinson's Bay Area Sports Hall of Fame induction. John Brodie, later to be an MVP and All-Pro for the San Francisco 49ers, says simply, "All I ever wanted to be was a ballplayer, and my dad found Oakland. Thank God."

Long before big-time sports came to the city, Oakland's athletic heritage was unsurpassed by any town of similar size in the nation. There were Olympic champions such as diver Al White (1924) and 400-meter runner Archie Williams (1936); ballplayers Ernie Lombardi, Ferris Fain and Cookie Lavagetto; basketball Hall of Famers Jim Pollard and Bill Russell; multisports stars such as Jackie Jensen; youth national championship baseball teams in 1928, 1949, 1950 and 1959; the Pacific Coast League Oakland Oaks; the AAU basketball Oakland Bittners and countless others. By 1871 there were sports facilities around the

Sprinter Archie Williams crosses the finish line, 1936. Oakland Museum of California, Oakland Tribune Collection, gift of ANG Newspapers

The Pinehust Park bike race, between the Oakland and San Francisco chapters of the French Athletic Club, at the starting line on Franklin Street, July 1928 Oakland Museum of California

(Far right, below) The successful Greenhood & Moran amateur baseball team, c. 1884 Oakland Museum of California, Oakland Tribune Collection, gift of ANG Newspapers

The Estuary Hellcats beat out Golden Gate in a Raimondi League play-off game, 1948. Oakland's schools and amateur leagues encouraged young athletes. Oakland Museum of California, Oakland Tribune Collection, gift of ANG Newspapers

burgeoning city. Badger Park, in the Brooklyn district, featured a running track for men and boys and a 20,000-square-foot skating and dancing pavilion. Fencing was a popular sport at the Oakland Athletic Club. "Wheeling," first on velocipedes and later on roller skates, had many enthusiasts, as did sailing on Lake Merritt. There were swimming baths on Alameda's south shore. The Oakland Trotting Park was a leading horse racing facility where St. Julian set the world trotting record for the mile at two minutes, 12.5 seconds. An ice skating rink was added in the 1930s at 14th and Grove.

But it was baseball that really took hold in Oakland. In 1867 there were approximately 100 teams statewide, 25 of them from Oakland and San Francisco. In 1871 the Oakland Wide Awakes won the championship of the Convention of Base Ball Players for the Pacific Coast. The team, renamed the Grand Centrals, was considered by 1874 to be the best in California. The California League was formed in 1879. While most of the teams in the circuit were from the West Bay, its games were played at Center Street Park in West Oakland, sometimes before crowds of 5,000 people.

In 1886 the new California State League was created, four teams strong. The Greenhood & Moran, sponsored by an Oakland clothing store, were the local entry. The biggest draw was George Van Haltren, who became the first major league star to come from the Bay Area. In 1893 the team boasted a 23-year-old pitcher, Clark Griffith, who in the course of his long career won 240 big league games and owned the American League Washington Senators. Most legendary, perhaps, was Harry Hooper, who in 1907 stepped off the St. Mary's College campus, then in Oakland, into the state league's professional ranks before joining the Boston Red Sox.

The memorable Pacific Coast League formed in 1903. The Oakland Oaks were a charter member, along with San Francisco, Sacramento, Los Angeles, Portland and Seattle. The Oaks clinched their first PCL title at the end of the 1912 season with wins in a home-and-away doubleheader before 11,000 people in Oakland

92

and 18,000 fans in San Francisco. Pitcher Harry Ables was league co-leader in wins with 25, and Bert Coy won the home run title with 19. Former reserve third baseman Gus Hetling hit .297 and won the league's Most Valuable Player award, receiving a new Chalmers convertible.

The cozy Freeman Park at Fifth Street and San Pablo Avenue was the Oaks' home park for the last time that year, because Oakland built its champions a new stadium. Oaks Ball Park, at 1120 Park Avenue at San Pablo Avenue, Emeryville, was finished for the home opener against Portland in 1913. The primarily wooden structure was built at a cost of $80,000 and had an original seating capacity of 10,000.

The Oaks won their second PCL title in 1927, when pitcher George Boehler won a league-leading 22 games, as the Oaks finished 14 1/2 games ahead of second-place San Francisco. The man of the hour was Russell "Buzz" Arlett, the "Babe Ruth of the PCL." He hit .351, with 54 doubles, 30 home runs and 123 RBIs. Arlett would ulti-

mately become the PCL all-time leader in home runs (251) and RBIs (1,888) and would later be voted by the Society for American Baseball Research as the most outstanding player in minor league history.

In 1948 Oaks manager Casey Stengel assembled a veteran team known as

his "Nine Old Men." Six players were 34 years old or older. They included Ernie Lombardi, Cookie Lavagetto, Bill Raimondi, George "Catfish" Metkovich and Dario Lodigiani. Lombardi, despite being slow afoot, became a Hall of Famer by being the only catcher to win two batting titles. Billy Martin, a 19-year-old who had honed his skills on the diamonds of Berkeley

93

Chapter Eight

The OAKLAND LARKS, A WEST COAST BASEBALL ASSOCIATION NEGRO LEAGUE TEAM, SHOW OFF THEIR PITCHING STAFF IN 1946. (LEFT TO RIGHT) WADE JAMES, WEE WILLIE JONES, CHARLES "SPECK" ROBERTS AND MARION "SUGAR" CAIN

Oakland Museum of California, gift of Mr. Dick Dobbins

The Spirit of Oakland

and Oakland, was the team's only player with limited pro experience. In 1949 Chuck Dressen replaced Stengel as manager and in 1950, led by Artie Wilson at shortstop, the Oaks' first openly hired African-American player, the Oaks won the PCL championship again. Despite their popularity, in 1955 the Oaks moved to Vancouver.

The phalanx of Oakland stars marched on uninterrupted. The versatile Jackie Jensen, a 1948 college football All-American, became the 1958 American League MVP. Ferris Fain was a two-time American League batting champion. Frank Robinson became the first African-American major league manager in baseball. Joe Morgan was inducted to the Hall of Fame. Curt Flood's legal challenge of baseball's reserve clause in 1969 helped create player free agency. Dave Stewart was a 20-game winner in four consecutive seasons for the Oakland A's, and Rickey Henderson became major league baseball's all-time single season and career stolen base leader, primarily as a member of the Oakland A's.

In tennis Don Budge emerged from University High School and Oakland public courts to become an international champion. In 1937 he won the U.S. singles championship, led America to a Davis Cup win over England and was named both Associated Press Athlete of the Year and Sullivan Award winner, making him the nation's best amateur athlete. In 1938 the redhead with perhaps the finest backhand the game has known became the first player to win the Grand Slam by capturing the Wimbledon, Australian, French and U.S. championships. "Playing tennis against him was like playing against a concrete wall," opponent Sidney Wood remarked.

Oakland sprinters left their imprint on the track world record books. Archie Williams of University High, one of track's greatest stars of the 1930s, was the gold medalist in the 400 meters at the 1936 Olympics in Berlin. Oakland produced two "world's fastest humans" — Ray Norton and Jim Hines. In April 1959 Norton set the world 100-meter mark at 10.1 seconds. In 1960 he equaled

95

in 1935 when he defeated Bob Olin. One of the best fighters of his era, he defended his title five times and ultimately moved up in weight to unsuccessfully challenge the legendary Joe Louis for the heavyweight crown. Johnny Gonsalves was one of Oakland's most popular fighters during his 1948 to 1962 career. A lightweight title contender for 11 years, he fought five world champions.

While basketball generally may not be thought of as a West Coast game, it has a strong tradition in Oakland. Jim Pollard, an NBA all-star with the Minneapolis Lakers, was known as the "Kangaroo Kid" for his remarkable jumping ability. He later coached the NBA Chicago Packers and Minneapolis Lakers and is a member of the Basketball Hall of Fame. Bill Russell, who graduated from McClymonds High, led the United States to the 1956 Olympics gold medal and became an 11-time all-star, five-time MVP and 11-time world champion with the Boston Celtics. Russell went on to become the man "who made the biggest impact of any player who ever lived," in the words of Boston coach Red Auerbach. He was also America's first black professional basketball coach.

the 220-yard record of 20.6 seconds in Sweden and set the 200-meter world record of 20.5 at the 1960 Olympic Trials at Stanford University. Jim Hines rose to international stardom in 1967 when he tied the 100-yard dash world mark at 9.1. A co-world record holder in the 100 meters, Hines shattered the world and Olympic records with a 9.9 clocking at the Mexico City games in 1968, earning a gold medal. He also paced the U.S. 400-meter relay team to a gold medal, again in world-record time.

In swimming and diving, Oakland's major figure was Zoe Ann Olsen, national three-meter diving champion in the late 40s. She trained at the Athens Athletic Club downtown. By the time she was 18, the Oakland High School student had won 14 national titles and a silver medal in the 1948 Olympics. She was a member of the 1952 Olympic team as well.

Oakland was always known as a good fight town, and during some periods, matches were held in the city as often as 50 weeks a year. *San Francisco Chronicle* boxing writer Jack Fiske called Oakland "a factory for professional fighters." John Henry Lewis, one of a family of Oakland boxers, captured the light heavyweight title

Paul Silas was, Auerbach claimed, "the best power forward in basketball." Silas won many honors, two world titles with Boston and one with Seattle. For eight years he was president of the NBA Players Association and coached the San Diego Clippers and Charlotte Hornets. Joe Ellis, from McClymonds, had a stellar NBA career. Gary Payton, from Skyline High, and Jason Kidd, from St. Joseph's High, are current NBA all-stars.

The Oakland Oaks of the American Basketball Association were another of Oakland's great teams. While they lasted only two years in Oakland, because of direct competition with the nearby NBA Warriors, they captured the ABA title in their second year playing at the Oakland Auditorium. Owned by pop singer and film star Pat Boone and led by Hall of Famer Rick Barry, who had jumped to Oakland from the Warriors, the Oaks moved to Washington, D.C., in 1969.

The major league era of Oakland sports began in 1960, when a new American Football League franchise, first known as the Señors and later the Raiders, was established. Oakland originally had not been slated to join the new league, but was awarded a franchise when Minneapolis became an NFL expansion city. As a late addition, the Raiders had last pick of players and no Oakland venue, playing their home games at Kezar Stadium in San Francisco. The Raiders' first home stadium in 1962 was Frank Youell Field, 23,000 capacity, hard by the Nimitz Freeway near present-day Laney College. After three desultory years, Raiders management hired the young San Diego Chargers assistant coach, Al Davis, a hiring that over succeeding decades would be both a blessing and a curse for

Oakland fans. Davis immediately began to build an AFL power, as Oakland improved to 10-4, good for second place in the western division. Even if the AFL was seen by most observers to be inferior to the older National Football League, it was big league to Oakland, and the city and county guaranteed $25.5 million in bonds to build a 54,000-seat multipurpose stadium and a 14,000-capacity arena, complete with parking for 10,000 cars. Designed by Skidmore, Owings & Merrill, Architects, the spectacular Oakland-Alameda County Coliseum Complex would be the site of many of Oakland's greatest sports triumphs and most complex legal wranglings.

The 1967 season brought a championship of a different kind to Oakland, that of the National Professional Soccer League, an early attempt at establishing major league professional soccer in America. Oakland's franchise, the Clippers, was an instant playing success, finishing 19-8-5 and winning the NPSL crown. Plagued by poor attendance, the league folded the next year.

Oakland took to the ice as well. Figure skater Charlie Tickner, one of the most creative and elegant male competitors of the 1980s, was born in Oakland. In ice hockey, the Oakland Seals, later known as the California Golden Seals, played in the NHL from 1967 to 1976. A second-tier team that only made the playoffs once in their existence, they drew small but loyal crowds in Oakland and later relocated to Denver.

In 1968 Charles O. Finley, a contentious, self-promoting insurance executive from Indiana, moved his Kansas City Athletics into the Coliseum. Finley had been anything but beloved in Kansas City.

The stadium and arena at the Oakland Coliseum, 1969
Oakland History Room, Oakland Public Library

Victory PARADE DOWN BROADWAY IN CELEBRATION OF THE OAKLAND A'S 1972 WORLD SERIES WIN

Oakland Museum of California, Oakland Tribune Collection, gift of ANG Newspapers

Hearing of the team's move, Missouri Sen. Stuart Symington, in a verbal slap at Finley, called Oakland "the luckiest city since Hiroshima." He brought with him future Hall of Famers Reggie Jackson, Jim "Catfish" Hunter and Rollie Fingers, as well as Sal Bando and Bert Campaneris. Under the management of Dick Williams, the A's won Oakland's first world championship in 1972, downing the Cincinnati Reds in a seven-game

Golden State Warriors owner Frank Mieuli (center) and Oakland City Councilman Frank Ogawa congratulate Nate Thurmond on his 10,000th rebound, 1972.
Oakland Museum of California, Oakland Tribune Collection, gift of ANG Newspapers

The Oakland A's celebrate their World Series win over the San Francisco Giants, October 1989. Before Game 3 of the series, the 7.1 Loma Prieta earthquake shook the Bay Area forcing the series to be delayed 10 days.
Oakland Museum of California, Oakland Tribune Collection, gift of ANG Newspapers

99

World Series. The team won the next World Series, too, and in the 1974 season, managed by Alvin Dark, became the "Team of the Decade," winning their third consecutive World Series title — the last team in baseball to do so.

Oakland gained another flamboyant owner when former advertising executive Franklin Mieuli relocated his NBA Warriors from San Francisco to Oakland in 1972. In 1975, featuring Rick Barry as their only established star, the Golden State Warriors amazingly found themselves in the NBA world championship against the heavily favored Washington Bullets. Led by coach Alvin Attles, who skillfully rotated his players throughout the season and series, the Warriors swept the Bullets in four games for the world crown.

Although the Raiders made it to Super Bowl II, they were Oakland's only major league team without a world title, and they came to training camp for the 1976 season determined to end years of playoff frustration, including three straight losses in conference finals. Coached by John Madden and led by quarterback Ken Stabler, the team swept through the regular season with a 13-1 record and vanquished the Pittsburgh Steelers in the conference title game. In the Super Bowl match Oakland dominated the Minnesota Vikings, 31-14. Oakland now stood alone with New York City in winning world titles in the three major sports in such a brief time period.

Despite the fact that the team had enjoyed years of consecutive sold-out games and were adored in the city, there was trouble between Davis, the team's managing general partner, and the Coliseum administrators. Davis wanted seating expanded and luxury boxes built to generate greater revenue. In 1980 the NFL had voted down the Raiders' proposal to move to Los Angeles and the team, league, city and county became involved in extensive litigation.

Fan support never wavered, however, and Oakland began the 1980 season with a great revamped lineup, including starters who had been released by other teams, such as quarterback Jim Plunkett, defensive end John Mutuszak and running back Kenny King. Almost miraculously, they fought their way into Super Bowl XV, winning a convincing 27-10 victory over the Philadelphia Eagles. More than 100,000 fans turned out in a downpour along city streets and the city hall plaza to honor the world champs. Sadly, the Raiders would spend only one more year in Oakland. Davis finally prevailed in court and moved the team to Los Angeles.

The A's were talking about a move as well. Instead, they were sold to local ownership, the Haas family, who pledged to make the club an integral part of the community. They kept their promise and attendance blossomed. In 1989 the invigorated A's won 99 games and swept the San Francisco Giants in the first trans-Bay World Series — a game at Candlestick Park that was interrupted by the October 18th Loma Prieta earthquake. The following season the A's won 103 games. Pitcher Bob Welch won the Cy Young Award and Rickey Henderson was named League MVP. Mark McGwire hit 39 homers and José Canseco 37. They swept the Red Sox for the pennant, but lost to Cincinnati in the World Series. The franchise, however, had demonstrated that major league baseball could draw in Oakland, if properly promoted. In 1988 the team attracted more than 2 million fans, and drew more than 2.5 million in 1990 and 91.

Meanwhile, Los Angeles was not the monetary windfall Al Davis had anticipated and he started looking for yet another place to relocate his team. In 1995, lured by a $200 million guarantee from Oakland and Alameda County to renovate the Coliseum, build luxury boxes and pay him more than $50 million in expenses and "loans" that were not required to be repaid, he returned, semitriumphantly, to Oakland. Fans, perhaps still feeling the sting of the team's earlier abandonment, or perhaps just sick and tired of Davis, did not flock to Raiders home games. Sellouts were a rarity as the team failed to capture its championship magic, and ticket prices were the highest in the league. Soon, Davis and the city and county were back in court again, the owner saying he was "duped" into returning to Oakland, the two governments contending that it was taxpayers who were the real victims as they were forced to bail out the financially troubled lease arrangement. By 2000, legal rulings seemed to indicate that the Raiders would be required to play in Oakland through the 2010 season.

Being "major league" had won Oakland international renown but also had created a new order of franchise shifts, lawsuits, player work stoppages and draw-downs on the public treasury. The character of athletics in Oakland had changed forever.

100

Wide RECEIVER FRED BILETNIKOFF AND QUARTERBACK KEN STABLER, A PROLIFIC SCORING DUO, WATCH A SCRIMMAGE FROM THE SIDELINES AT THE OAKLAND RAIDERS TRAINING CAMP IN SANTA ROSA, JULY 1971. THE TWO STARS PLAYED TOGETHER FROM 1970 TO 1978 AND EARNED A SUPER BOWL WIN IN 1977.

Oakland Museum of California, Oakland Tribune Collection, gift of ANG Newspapers

CHApter 9

Oakland's SOBRIQUET AROUND THE TURN OF THE 20TH CENTURY, "ATHENS OF THE PACIFIC," REFERRED TO THE CULTURAL AND EDUCATIONAL ATTAINMENTS OF A YOUNG TOWN THAT TOOK PRIDE IN ITS QUALITY OF LIFE. IN "FREE TO ALL," WILLIAM STURM DESCRIBES THE CITY'S FIRST LIBRARIES. IN "GROWING THINGS," ERIKA MAILMAN REVELS IN OAKLAND'S HORTICULTURAL TRADITION AND PARKS.

Free to All

Oakland's early libraries were private. The first, opened in 1857 and dubbed the Oakland Philomathean was supported by annual dues and featuring lectures to which the public was invited. When it dissolved 10 years later, its 295 volumes were bequeathed to the newly formed Odd Fellows Library, supported and patronized by members of the Independent Order of Odd Fellows. The library's collection of 4,300 books was housed in a building on the northwest corner of 11th and Franklin streets.

In 1868 Dr. Samuel Merritt and other civic notables founded the Oakland Library Association to make books available to more citizens. The association raised funds for a collection and a one-story wood-framed building on the southeast corner of 12th and Washington. Six years later they moved to 14th and Washington, next to City Hall. Accessibility to the association's volumes, however, was greatly limited by an annual membership fee of six dollars. An *Oakland Tribune* writer protested in 1874, "No city the size of Oakland ought to be without a public reading room, free to all, citizen or stranger."

In 1878 the California legislature passed the Rogers Act, which enabled cities to fund and support public libraries. Oakland became the second California city (after Eureka) to establish one. The Oakland Library Association donated its collection and building, to which a second story was added, and on November 6, 1878, the Oakland Free Library was opened to the public. That same year, "Reading Rooms" — precursors of branch libraries — were opened in West and

East Oakland. An early patron remembered "the little old Public Library" with fondness and a measure of awe: "The first floor was for newspapers and the few magazines then published; the second for fiction and the reference department. It stood a little back from the street and one climbed a few steps to enter a hallway about ten feet wide; there in front of you loomed two large swinging doors, covered with a dark green material like oilcloth of slightly rough texture. At left of these, winding stairs led to the hall above and again the same kind of doors barred your entrance to Oakland's center of culture." In those days there was no public access to the stacks. A librarian at a desk just inside the doors took the patron's order, disappeared and returned with the desired tome.

The first director of the Free Library was Ina Coolbrith, who would one day become California's first Poet Laureate. Coolbrith was a friend to Bret Harte and Joaquin Miller and mentor to Mary Austin and Jack

City funding for the library was meager, however, and Coolbrith's public denunciations of municipal parsimony eventually cost her her job. Years later, her feelings somewhat softened, she remarked, "I am prouder of being the first public librarian in California than I am of being the first woman author, for I think the public libraries have been a greater help to the people."

By the turn of the century, Oakland's growing population was placing great strains upon its public library. The new director, Charles S. Greene, former editor of the *Overland Monthly* (to which Coolbrith also contributed), obtained funds for a new main building from steel magnate Andrew Carnegie, then freshly embarked upon national library endowments. Carnegie donated $50,000 for a new structure with the stipulation that the city must provide the land. A private subscription drive launched by the Ebell Society, a local women's philanthropic club founded in 1875 secured a site on the southwest corner of 14th and

London, who as a famous writer, wrote to Coolbrith: "The old Oakland library days! Do you know you were the first one who ever complimented me on my choice of reading matter?... I was an eager, thirsty, hungry little kid — and one day at the library I drew out a volume on *Pizarro in Peru* (I was 10 years old). You got the book and stamped it for me; and as you handed it to me you praised me for reading books of that nature. Proud! If you only knew how proud your words made me!"

Grove streets. The splendid new main library, designed by Bliss and Faville, with murals by Arthur Mathews and others, opened June 30, 1902. It featured a youth room and expanded services for younger patrons. Under Greene's leadership Oakland's branch library system grew, with Carnegie endowing four more buildings: Golden Gate, Alden (now Temescal), Melrose and 23rd Avenue. All but the 23rd Avenue branch are still in operation.

104

The PERIODICAL ROOM AT THE OAKLAND FREE LIBRARY, C. 1914. NOTE THE SIGN ON THE FRONT TABLE: "THIS TABLE IS RESERVED FOR LADIES."

Oakland History Room, Oakland Public Library

Oakland's three city museums, created between 1911 and 1922, were semi-autonomous, governing themselves but officially under the oversight of the library commission. The Oakland History Room retains extensive museum files. In 1961, a bond measure was passed to form a new Oakland Museum with its own overseeing body, the museum commission.

During the 1920s and 1930s the library responded to the needs of a growing immigrant and working class population by purchasing foreign language books and setting up small collections in factories. During World War II, as war defense workers streamed into the Bay Area, Oakland's population diversified still more. A local bond measure passed on May 8, 1945, provided funds for two new branches, Elmhurst and Lakeview, and a new main library. On January 8, 1951, the new main branch opened at 14th and Oak streets near the shore of Lake Merritt. Designed by the noted architects Miller and Warneke, the new edifice exemplified the streamlined look favored in postwar public buildings. It contained a "California Room" which later evolved into the Oakland History Room, the city's main center for the history of the community.

From the 1960s onward the library expanded to meet the needs of Oakland's increasingly multiethnic population. With strong community support, the Latin American (César E. Chávez) branch opened in 1966; a bookmobile providing library service direct to neighborhoods started in 1965; and construction on an Asian branch library was finished in 1976. In the 1970s services were established for disabled patrons and the Oakland Library joined cooperative library systems to enhance its reference resources and increase its inventory. The new Dimond branch opened in 1980, followed by Brookfield Village (1992), Asian (1995), Rockridge (1996) and Eastmont (1998). In 1994 the Northern California Center for Afro-American History and Life, renamed the African American Museum and Library at Oakland, joined the library system. The museum, whose research archives on African-American history and life are open to the public, will be housed in the Charles S. Greene library, following that building's current extensive renovation.

106

In 1978 library staff and the organization Volunteers for Oakland created a telephone service, Cityline, to inform citizens with information about city programs, regulations, services, special events, vital statistics and "anything having to do with Oakland and its citizens." In 1984 the library launched a Second Start adult literacy program and in 1994 created Partners Achieving School Success (PASS) homework centers as part of the system's commitment to the needs of youth. A bond measure to increase library funding passed overwhelmingly in 1998, demonstrating that Oakland continues to value its libraries. In all its endeavors strong support has come from Friends of the Oakland Public Library, the Library Commission and more recently, the Oakland Public Library Foundation.

Electronic media have become a highly visible part of today's library, auguring great changes in the future. The "little old public library" fondly recalled by a pioneer patron has been transformed through more than a century of changing visions. Yet the librarian, whether at the desk or in the community, remains as vital to library service as in the days of the city's first library — a personal, human contact with books and the world of learning. In the 1920s a patron who had moved away from Oakland returned to the library and inquired, "Where is the librarian who was here 30 years ago?" When told that he must be referring to Ina Coolbrith, he said, "Coolbrith, that was the name. She gave me a book of Homer, and she gave it with a smile. I have been away from here for 30 years but I always remembered her — her smile."

Growing Things

Plants thrive in Oakland's Mediterranean climate and rich soil, and many of the first German, Italian and Portuguese settlers there were farmers. Fruit Vale was an orchard of 700 Bing cherry trees planted in 1856 by German immigrant Henderson Luelling. Before long, the Oakland foothills were covered with cherry orchards and other fruit farms, and Fruit Vale was transformed into a major fruit-growing center. New plants from Australia, China and Africa were introduced by explorers and sold at fairs and expositions. By 1868 there were 168 different nurseries in Alameda County. The 19th-century gardens of great mansions that once ringed Lake Merritt vibrated with bright colors and exotic species.

Oakland Municipal Rose Garden, June 1, 1949, later renamed Morcom Amphitheater of Roses
Oakland Museum of California, gift of Bob Rishell

Plants from Oakland's commercial nurseries were taken by truck to the Southern Pacific trains, thence to ferry for the trip across the bay to the San Francisco. The Domoto brothers on 55th Avenue were the first to operate a truly large-scale Japanese nursery in America; in 1902 they offered 230 varieties of chrysanthemums. In 1917 Hirokichi Hayashi, whose nursery was on 73rd Avenue, patented a flexible paper sleeve and installation machine for protecting plants during transit.

The Oakland Rose Garden was the idea of dentist Charles Vernon Covell, who convinced the Business Men's Garden Club to back his idea in 1931. Landscape architect Arthur Cobbledick, the club's president, designed the garden as a composite of famous gardens of Italy. Within three years, the garden became a reality, built by laborers paid from the city's unemployment relief coffers. Set in a naturally bowl-shaped site on Jean Street, off Grand Avenue, the formal design features raised terraces and geometrically radiating walkways. A central pool and cascading fountain lend the musicality of water to the scene. The roses are trained to bloom in May, according to head rosarian Rene Batoon, and the garden has capitalized on this by holding an annual Mother's Day ceremony — in earlier years called "Rose Sunday." Attendance for the affair in 1936 was 25,000. Today only a few hundred attend.

In 1953 the garden's name became the Morcom Amphitheater of Roses to honor Mayor Fred Morcom, who planted its first bush. A children's miniature rose garden was created in 1995, with 60 bushes to represent each of Oakland's elementary schools. Batoon, who has been head rosarian since 1988, tends the garden's

107

estate boasted a 50-foot glass conservatory, which no longer exists, and a greenhouse complex with four separate hothouses for distinct flower varieties, such as orchids and poinsettias. Cinerarias, narcissus and daffodils grown at Dunsmuir won first prize and anemones won second prize at the 1915 Panama-Pacific International Exposition.

Although the Hellmans enjoyed their blossoms *in situ,* the flowers were grown to be cut. Blooms were regularly sent to friends and family, and arrangements within the mansion were color-coordinated with each room. Mrs Hellman had water lilies, culled by servants in a boat, resting on her breakfast tray every morning.

Victory Gardens were encouraged as a patriotic activity during World War II. Among a garden's virtues, stated a pamphlet at the time: "[It] makes the family income more elastic, it brings health in fresh foods and outdoor exercise, and what is more important, to my way of thinking, it teaches the whole family many wholesome lessons. And now that we have a war to win, a vegetable garden can contribute directly to national safety."

Among Oakland's local flower societies are the East Bay Rose Society, initiated by the founders of the Oakland Rose Garden; the Sydney B. Mitchell Iris Society; the Cactus and Succulent Society; and the East Bay Bonsai Society. Most of them hold annual flower shows at the Garden Center in Lakeside Park on Lake Merritt. The park was designed by John McLaren, who also landscaped the 1894, 1915 and 1939 San Francisco world fairs and the country estates of Leland Stanford and William Ralston.

In November 1999 the East Bay Bonsai Society and volunteers opened the Bonsai & Suiseki Display Garden at the park — one of only two such gardens in California. *Suiseki* are stones in which viewers see natural formations that may suggest landscapes or other images and that encourage a meditative state.

7,000 bushes. Among his favorites are the Prima Donna, "a shocking pink rose that grows tall," and the lavender Lagerfeld. Amid the garden's profusion is the Pride of Oakland. Created in 1977, this pink rose grows along both sides of the stepped cascade. Of the approximate 5,000 roses in the garden, about half are believed or known to have been historically there. The garden was almost lost in the 1970s, when the city, who owns the land, made a backroom deal to sell it for development. Neighborhood activists protested, and with the support of *The Tribune's* Peggy Stinnett, succeeded in derailing the sale.

Some of the Rose Garden's bushes were once kept fenced in against deer at the Dunsmuir estate on Peralta Oaks Court in the Sheffield Village area. An elegant 37-room mansion, Dunsmuir House was built in 1899 as a gift from coal magnate Alexander Dunsmuir to his wife. He died on their honeymoon and his wife died in 1901. The property was sold to I.W. Hellman, a San Francisco banker, in 1906. He and his wife had intended it for summer use but after the great earthquake struck, they moved there permanently. Under the Hellmans' care, Dunsmuir gardens became famous throughout the Bay Area. The

Laomia McCoy, Miss Oakland 1969, at the Dahlia Garden

Oakland Museum of California

Chapter Nine

The garden features 100 trees, with 50 on exhibit at a time. The prize specimen is a nearly 400-year-old tree given to U.S. Minister to China Anson C. Burlingame by the Japanese government in the mid-1800s. Lakeside Park is also the scene of a traditional Japanese Tsukimi festival each October, a collaboration between the Oakland Office of Parks and Recreation and the Fukuoka Sister City Society, with music, dance, displays and moon-viewing through telescopes in the garden.

Tulips have been shown every spring since the 1960s at historic Mountain View Cemetery. "Tulip Days" feature plants arranged by color in beds surrounding the central fountain at the cemetery's entrance. Mountain View opened for business in 1865. Its sweeping design was planned by Frederick Law Olmsted, the visionary landscape architect who designed the U.S. Capitol grounds and Central Park in Manhattan.

Oakland's extensive park district came about through a coalition of East Bay communities, but only after a long gestation period. In 1866 Olmsted had called on city officials to create a greenbelt of parks along the crest of the Contra Costa hills, extending into

the city of Oakland through canyons, with "scenic lanes," or natural park strips, on either side of the many creeks that flow into the bay. In 1906 city planning consultant Charles Mulford Robinson again urged creation of parkland, and some of his recommendations were enacted by Mayor Mott. Nine years later Dr. Werner Hegemann, an Oakland city planner, outlined a city plan for Berkeley and Oakland calling for shoreline, city and canyon parklands. Finally, in 1930, the time was right. Frederick Law Olmsted's sons, landscape architects, and Ansel F. Hall of the National Park Service, drafted a feasibility study of the park and recreational needs of East Bay communities. The report, including maps and pictures, was a compelling statement of the need for such parks. It emphasized preservation of land that had multiple uses and was easily accessible. Citizens of nine cities petitioned the East Bay Municipal Utility District to release watershed lands it was preparing to sell off to developers. State Assemblyman Frank Mott, the former Oakland mayor, drafted AB 1114, authorizing the establishment of a regional park district and a board to govern it. The bill passed in 1933 and Gov. James Rolph signed it into

110

East Bay regional parks provide relaxation for parents and fun for children, August 1941. *Oakland Museum of California, City Clerk's Office/ City of Oakland*

Redwood Regional Park, August 1983 *Oakland Museum of California, gift of Independent Documentary Group Photo by Bob Walker*

law. It was the first law of its kind in the United States. The project had one more hurdle — seemingly insurmountable. It was the height of the Depression, and voters in nine cities were asked to tax themselves in order to form the district. The miracle happened on November 6, 1934, when East Bay voters approved the initiative by a large margin.

A nationally revered open space advocate, landscape architect William Penn Mott Jr., provided strong advocacy leadership as Superintendent of Oakland Parks from 1946 to 1962. The only American to have headed major park agencies at the local, regional, state and national levels, he was key in expanding and protecting parkland resources.

Today the East Bay Regional Park District comprises 55 parks: recreation areas, regional parks, botanic and geologic preserves, historic farms, caves and mines, and shoreline parks and trails. Oakland alone has 12 of these parks within its borders and the remaining ones — some 100,000 acres in all, connected by 1,000 miles of trails — are less than an hour away. Among these, Huckleberry Botanic Regional Preserve on Skyline Boulevard, an amazing ecological island of California native plants, is one of the great "islands in time" in California.

Harlan Kessel contributed to this chapter.

111

THE

nEigHbORHOOds

North Oakland

Vicente Peralta hardly had received the northern portion of his father's land when European immigrants, eager to cut and sell the old-growth redwoods in the hills, settled there and began exploiting its resources. After a long legal battle, a Supreme Court ruling upheld Peralta's title, but he had to sell land to stem his losses. Settlers began growing fruit and vegetable crops, which later led to building canning and packing plants. One, the Josiah Lusk Canning Company, stood on Claremont Avenue at 51st Street. Opened in 1868, it had become the largest cannery in the world when it closed two decades later.

In 1869 Oakland constructed its first streetcar line along Telegraph Avenue to 40th Street, leading to the development of North Oakland. The line was extended to Temescal Creek in 1870; the terminus at 51st and Telegraph became the center of a business district. The introduction of electricity to the rail service enabled the area to develop further, and commercial and residential districts were built alongside the streetcar line. By the beginning of the 20th century, North Oakland was a country suburb for affluent Oaklanders.

After 1906, San Francisco refugees built new homes in the ethnically diverse communities of North Oakland. Golden Gate or Klinknerville, located near San Pablo Avenue and 56th Street, developed particularly rapidly. After World War I, as other neighborhoods in the district began to decline economically, the Golden Gate district became an entrepreneurial center for African Americans. Evidence of this legacy is hard to find today. Freeway construction, redlining and poverty hit this neighborhood during the 1970s and 80s, and it little resembles its former self.

The greater mobility of the population after World War II, and the popularity of the automobile, led to a transportation revolution. In the late 1940s streetcar lines were replaced with freeways and during the next two decades BART stations were constructed around the city. In the 1960s Interstate 580 was built along the borders of North Oakland, West Oakland and Chinatown/Central. The MacArthur BART station opened in 1972. Its construction, unfortunately, severed main arteries along Grove Street (now Martin Luther King, Jr. Way), compromising a once-healthy commercial area. The Rockridge BART station opened in 1973 with a happier result; BART provided an injection of commercial activity into the Rockridge area. The Grove-Shafter Freeway was completed in the 1980s.

In the 1970s the city invested in citywide community development programs designed to make improvements throughout North Oakland. However, assistance was not equal below and above Telegraph Avenue. Residents and businesses in the African-American communities of low and moderate means below Telegraph were denied opportunities to maintain or improve their properties. Above Telegraph, banks and lenders were active, and communities such as Rockridge began to thrive. The lack of private lender support in districtwide revitalization efforts is one of the major causes for the deterioration that currently challenges many Oakland districts.

North Oakland faces unique problems and opportunities. Some of these have to do with the encroaching influence of Berkeley and Emeryville on the district's borders. Neighborhood organizations and associations are working on major revitalization projects. The Martin Luther King, Jr. Community Plaza, once home to University High School and Merritt College, recently reopened as a center combining commercial, cultural and vocational training, community services and 23 housing units. ■

Chapter 10

NATIVE SPIRIT

The ANTIQUITY OF LOCAL HUMAN SETTLEMENT IN THE EAST BAY SURPRISES MANY WHO WERE EDUCATED TO VIEW OUR AREA'S HISTORY IN TERMS OF A MERE COUPLE OF CENTURIES. IN "VANISHING SHELLMOUNDS," **SANDRA SHER** DETAILS THE GREAT OHLONE SHELLMOUNDS, THOUSANDS OF YEARS OLD, THAT ONCE RINGED SAN FRANCISCO BAY. IN "HEART OF THE COMMUNITY," **SUSAN LOBO** DESCRIBES CONTEMPORARY NATIVE AMERICANS IN OAKLAND — AN INNOVATIVE AND ENERGETIC INTERTRIBAL POPULATION.

Vanishing Shellmounds

The East Bay shellmounds, like hundreds of others that rose along the shores of San Francisco Bay, were native village sites. Typically situated where creeks or streams emptied into the bay or estuaries, their locations provided critical freshwater and the combined resources of overlapping ecological zones. Shellfish, freshwater fish, waterfowl, eggs, sea mammals, small and large game, tules for balsas (canoes), acorns, seeds, bulbs, berries, greens and a myriad of other useful and edible items were utilized by the native population. These first settlers of the region had a sophisticated, intimate and spiritual relationship with the land they occupied.

Aboriginal life seems to have been well ordered, grounded in traditional practices and beliefs that enveloped everyday life. Hunting and health, the utilization of shamans (healers with spiritual powers) and a comprehensive view that linked native people to their land and every living creature on it — all of this was part of the spiritual life that could not be separated from the acts of daily living. Malcolm Margolin phrased it this way: "The relationship between people and animals was not one of exploitation but of reciprocity."

Over centuries of occupation, the Ohlone villages gradually rose above the surrounding plain, taking the form of mounds. These mounds contained not only the remains of shellfish and other debris, but also tools, all manner of household ceremonial items, and human burials as well. Some reached astounding heights and massive lateral spread. The Emeryville Shellmound, one of the tallest, reached a height of 32 to 40 feet.

Archaeologists believe that a sparse population first settled along the shores of San Francisco Bay at least 5,000 years ago. The era when many of the large shellmounds flourished began approximately 2,500 years ago. Remarkably, despite millennia of occupation, the native people of this area left so light an imprint on the land that the shellmounds were among the few physical traces of the "pre-contact" era to survive into "historic" times.

The shellmounds in Oakland were occupied by the Ohlone (Costanoan) people — a linguistic and partly cultural grouping that extended from the Carquinez Strait south to Point Sur (including the San Francisco peninsula). The Spanish mission system later decimated but did not totally eliminate this native population, and there are descendants of these people alive today. The descendants prefer "Ohlone" rather than the Spanish-derived term of "Costanoan."

In 1907 University of California graduate student N.C. Nelson walked the shores of San Francisco, San Pablo and Suisun bays, mapping and numbering 425 shellmounds. Many of the numbered mounds had already vanished, due to municipal and industrial expansion. Others had been partially or wholly carted away for use as fertilizer, road ballast or chicken feed. The mounds at Emeryville and West Berkeley survived long enough for scientific interest to catch up with them at the turn of the 20th century, but the shellmounds in Oakland were largely destroyed during the latter half of the 19th century. Nonetheless, we have some scraps of information about them.

One of Oakland's shellmounds stood near the foot of Broadway, No. 314 on Nelson's map. This area was the original town center when Oakland was founded in 1852. Another mound, No. 314a, had definitely disappeared by the time Nelson was making his rounds, but it had been located just below the neck of Lake Merritt, perhaps a half mile from the Oakland Museum. A little

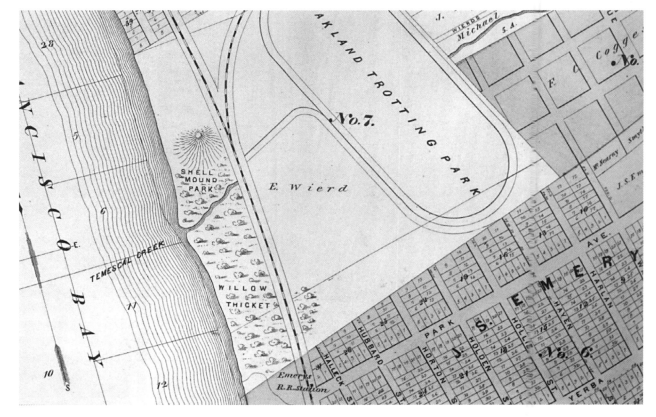

A GATHERING AT THE INTERTRIBAL FRIENDSHIP HOUSE

Intertribal Friendship House

Photo by Anthony Garcia

further south, No. 315 designated a mound in a marshy area near 14th Avenue and the Brooklyn Basin. The 14th Avenue creek would have been the source of fresh water in that vicinity.

An Oakland mound not included in Nelson's original survey was located south of No. 315 and southeast across the water from the southern tip of Government Island. In the 1850s it was part of Shell Mound Ranch, a large nursery. The mound reportedly occupied two or three acres and rose 10 to 15 feet above ground level. In 1875 this area was subdivided and sold as the "Shell Mound Tract."

Still further south, the Sather Tract was a known Indian site from which artifacts and bones had been removed for years. Located between Fruitvale Avenue and High Street and bordering on marshy land, it appears to have been cut through for the Tidal Canal project, completed in 1902.

Oakland may have had other shellmounds, unrecognized or lost so early as not to have been recorded. Additionally, there were campsites, as Trestle Glen or "Indian Gulch" possibly was, and native quarries. Altogether, these sites were Oakland's very first neighborhoods. Their loss has weakened our links to Oakland's past and deprived us of irreplaceable repositories of native culture.

Heart of the Community

For thousands of years, California Indian people lived in what is now called the San Francisco Bay Area, linked with one another and distant tribes through trading, traveling and intermarriage. In the 1770s and onward, native people were placed under tremendous stress with the incursions of Spanish and later Anglos into their homelands. Population levels declined tremendously and cultures were disrupted. As the area urbanized, the original native people found themselves marginalized or they created specialized niches for themselves. Although ancestors of the original people continue to exist into the present, they have been nearly invisible to non-Indians, who often held the misconception that native peoples had vanished.

In the 1930s and 40s a series of events took place that attracted new Indian migrants to the Bay Area, beginning an intertribal base for Oakland's present Native American community.

During World War II, many American Indians in the armed forces passed through the area or were stationed nearby. During the same period students at Indian boarding schools often participated in summer work programs in the Bay Area, or after finishing their studies were placed as domestics in local non-Indian homes. Some oral histories of this period, collected for the Community History Project at Intertribal Friendship House in Oakland, speak of isolation from other Indian people and a sense of loneliness. "Here I didn't have any friends," Ethel Rogoff (Laguna Pueblo) remembered. "I was brought up in boarding school. I was used to all kinds of friends then. I really missed it when I first came out here. I used to lie in bed and cry sometimes because I was homesick; I mean homesick."

Indian people searched out one another to assuage this loneliness. Sometimes bars were a focal point for meeting, or organizations such as the YWCA. Eventually, these first migrants of many diverse tribes formed clubs like the Four Winds, based at the Oakland YWCA, with social and recreational functions. They formed basketball, bowling and softball teams. Most of these people were young and unmarried and initially planned to stay only a short time. Some eventually returned home to rural areas and reservations, but others stayed in the city and became the founding generation of the Bay Area American Indian community.

By 1954 Indian people began arriving through the federally-sponsored Relocation Program, which ostensibly tried to encourage assimilation into the mainstream. Oakland was one of the initial designated sites on the West Coast. A large number of relocatees came from the Plains and Southwest, and for many, it was their first experience living off reservations, out of state and in an urban area. Although the programmatic aspects of the Relocation Program changed over the years, most typically a relocatee was granted transportation into an urban area, some initial assistance from the Bureau of Indian Affairs (BIA) in finding and paying for housing and, occasionally, job training.

Soon after initial assistance ceased, many relocatees found apartments or rental housing in low-rent districts throughout the city. Indian people did not have a preference for creating American Indian ethnic neighborhoods, and BIA employees encouraged this dispersal, as it was considered a step towards "melting into" the population

118

Native AMERICANS, NEWLY RELOCATED TO OAKLAND, RECEIVED JOB TRAINING THROUGH SUCH PLACES AS THE PACIFIC AUTOMOTIVE CENTER, 1971.

Intertribal Friendship House

© 2000 Ilka Hartman

Chapter Ten

at large. Thus, early in the history of the American Indian community in the Bay Area, the spatial pattern that continues today was established.

For the new migrants, the move into the city was stepping into the unknown, and arrival was often a sudden jolt of reality. Many had minimal English language or urban survival abilities, and their job skills often were not suitable for the existing job market. Subsidized training was typically limited to welding for men and cosmetology or secretarial work for women. Moreover, the assistance of a few months' duration could not meet the often-complex, diverse and immense needs of the relocatees, who found themselves in an alien environment far from their homes, extended families and tribal territories.

Even prior to relocation, Indian people in the Bay Area had established a series of agencies and organizations, sometimes with the collaboration of non-Indian groups, such as the American Friends Service Committee and the "Y." These organizations

and those that came later have served as nodes on a very fluid community network. Dispersal and regrouping is a familiar survival strategy for American Indian people. Ray Moisa, who grew up in an urban area and lives in the Bay Area, wrote in *News From Native California*, "In one of those cosmic ironies of sublime magnitude, the BIA's efforts to assimilate us have, in a word, backfired. By bringing together in the cities Indians from all tribes, relocation has contributed to Pan-Indianism, the movement to forsake individual tribal differences in favor of common goals. The great orators and chiefs of our past who counseled unity would have been proud."

One of the instrumental organizations in the Bay Area Indian community was Intertribal Friendship House (IFH), founded in 1955 in conjunction with representatives of the American Friends Service Committee and still in operation. As one of the first urban Indian community centers in the United States, IFH became a stimulus and an informal model for the establishment of similar urban Indian centers throughout the United States and Canada.

Over the years, IFH offered a variety of social service and social programs, including educational activities, summer youth programs, elders' programs, social service counseling, crisis intervention, holiday dinners and a shop. To the present the facility in downtown Oakland continues to be a community meeting hall and conference center and is rented for receptions and other family events. During these activities, people have come together to provide mutual support, exchange information and ideas and socialize. The organization has provided a neutral ground where communitywide questions could be discussed and dealt with. There also, adjustments and compromises among the growing number of tribes regarding beliefs, values, behavioral styles and long-standing intertribal histories were worked out. Ways were found to validate tribal identity while building a multitribal community. During the early years following relocation, activities that drew from the entire Indian community, such as sports clubs, pow-wows and political action groups were established.

A new pan-Indian consciousness began to emerge, fueled by a long history of loss of lands, brutality, racism and forced migration. The 1960s provided a context in which to question the social order, and the Indian community leapt into the activity. One relocatee who was trained as a welder recounted for the IFH Community History Project how he was working at U.C. Berkeley during the fall of 1965 when he heard the speeches at Sproul Plaza. Later he joined in the demonstrations. The Black Power movement, born in Oakland, flourished in some of the same neighborhoods where Indian people were living. In the mid-1960s, there was a short-lived occupation of Alcatraz Island by a group of Bay Area Indians, the precursor of the larger-scale, 18-month occupation in 1969. By that time Red Power was an idea circulating throughout the Indian community, and the American Indian Movement (AIM), with roots in Midwestern cities, had a strong Oakland contingency.

The social awareness of the 1960s affected structure, leadership and power relationships within the American Indian community. The non-Indian boards and staff members of organizations such as Intertribal Friendship House were ousted, and these organizations became Indian-controlled. A number of additional institutions were established, many of an educational nature, that recognized the expanding needs of the community and utilized the creativity and energy of a generation that had grown up in the multitribal urban setting and who brought such concepts as "empowerment" and "Indian identity" into the life of the community.

During the 1970s Native American Studies programs were created at Bay Area campuses. Additionally, the Indian and Chicano-run D.-Q. University outside of Davis was established. A group of concerned parents in Oakland started a small preschool that eventually evolved into Hintil Ku Caa, a cultural enrichment school that continues to flourish as part of the Oakland Public Schools. It has had a major impact on the local Indian community and is a model on a national level of educational alternatives that respond to specific cultural needs.

Throughout the 1980s the community continued to evolve and diversify in terms of age, tribal representation and economic well-being. By 1990 there were over 30 Indian-run organizations in Oakland and numerous special interest groups. Among these were pow-wow organizations and drum groups, a contemporary Indian art gallery, sports clubs, radio programming collectives and organizations including United Indian Nations, American Indian Child Resource Center, The International Indian Treaty Council, California Indian Legal Services, The Native American Health Board, Indigenous Nations Child and Family Agency, Unity Village and The Family Healing Center. Each of these organizations has experienced a unique history, and many embody a dynamic ability to shrink, expand or transform their character as a reflection of American Indian community needs, external pressures and available resources.

In contrast to the late 1960s and 70s, organizations today address political and social issues primarily through legal approaches, education and the wielding of influence to sway thinking. While tribal identity remains strong, American Indians are thinking about and participating in national and hemispheric indigenous concerns. And Oakland, as before, is the heart of the Bay Area Indian community.

121

THE

neigHbORHOOds

Fruitvale

During the Gold Rush, the first European settlers in Fruitvale established orchards and vegetable gardens. Newcomers in the 1870s built factories, dairies and mills. The California Cotton Mill was constructed along the Southern Pacific Railroad tracks near 23rd Avenue. German settlers opened beer gardens and Portuguese farmers established several of the early dairies.

Fruitvale enjoyed a period of affluence from the late 1800s into the early years of the new century, culminating with its annexation to the city of Oakland in 1909. Once the site of numerous grand estates, the area still boasts many bungalows of architectural interest and the Cohen-Bray House, one of the last of the stately Victorian mansions in the area.

The island of Alameda was originally a peninsula in the Kennedy Tract section of Fruitvale. In 1874 a strategic decision was made by the federal government to improve the harbor by channeling the waters of San Leandro Bay into San Antonio Creek. The land connecting Alameda to Oakland was severed and the port, estuary and harbor areas were enlarged, putting Oakland in the position to handle any type of cargo in competition with the port of San Francisco. The project was completed in 1902.

From the turn of the century until Prohibition, Fruitvale was a weekend tourist spot. San Francisco residents crossed the bay and took trolleys out to visit the orchards and beer gardens. In 1910 the Oakland Tribune published an article touting Fruitvale as an ideal area for home builders and buyers. The article described it as "the best there is in the way of residential property... with its delightful climate, deep rich soil, luxuriant growth of trees, plants and flowers, wonderful transportation facilities, splendid schools, numerous social organizations, excellent library... [and] up to date stores and shopping places that indicate an active, progressive people."

In the late 1920s commerce developed along the streetcar line on East 14th Street (now International Boulevard). Residential neighborhoods stretched a few blocks on either side. The crossroads of Fruitvale Avenue and East 14th had four commercial banks and several large businesses and was described by the *Tribune* as being "exceeded in importance only by the downtown district itself."

The Latino community in Fruitvale grew in the 1930s with new settlements of Mexican immigrants arriving to work in the fruit canning and packing industries. African Americans, Asians and Pacific Islanders also came to the area in search of opportunities. Many of their children and grandchildren continue to live in the district, participating in its community life and working for its well-being. ■

Chapter 11

PERMISSION TO DANCE

Blues, CLASSICAL AND WORLD MUSIC, BALLET, DANCE THEATER AND AFRICAN DANCE ALL HAVE VITAL OAKLAND HISTORIES. CHIORI SANTIAGO EVOKES THE VIBRANT SONGS AND URGENT RHYTHMS OF THE CITY.

It's eight o'clock on a Saturday night in the 1940s, and Oakland is jumpin'. Zooters are polishing their two-tone wingtips and giving a final tug to their wide lapels before heading downtown to McFadden's ballroom. Men in tuxedos, their hair brilliant with pomade, escort gowned ladies up the steps of the Oakland Auditorium to watch Orley See conduct the Oakland Symphony Orchestra. Elsewhere, a mariachi band crowds into a restaurant to serenade for tips; a blues singer plucks a mournful chord in a club on Seventh Street, and a dancer is poised to perform a solo so wild and unexpected that the next morning patrons will wonder what they saw.

For much of its early history, Oakland was a hard-working city with little time for formal entertainments. There were speakeasies and nightclubs, of course, and church choirs and dances for the good folk, along with chamber music, popular theater and, always, the folk traditions of music and dance that brought people together in every neighborhood. Over time the city would enjoy stints in the national spotlight — as a center for West Coast blues, as a place of classical innovation and jazz revival, and as ground zero for world music. First, though, Oakland had to get permission to dance.

Public dancing was a problem in 1913. Oakland is, after all, a port city, with all the attendant rowdiness that might be expected when muscled labor takes a night off. "The man who invented the 'turkey trot' dance ought to be hamstrung," Mayor Mott reportedly declared during debate on an ordinance that would restrict public dances. "All our troubles over dances are due to these fancy dances. They ought to be all abolished."

Mott and the city council were standing against the tide. In 1919, with no place to go on Friday nights, young men began to organize "pay dances," hiring

bands and advertising a shindig via handbills and word-of-mouth. One of these enterprising fellows was Al Marshall, who organized dinner dances at the Hotel Claremont on the Oakland-Berkeley border. By 1922 weekend dances were so popular the city considered opening a municipal dance hall.

In the dance hall realm Sweet's Ball Room is legendary. An avid ballroom dancer, William Sweet gave up a professorship in agriculture at U.C. Berkeley to open Sweet's Ball Room in 1920 first on 20th Street,

then Broadway. A second ballroom, Sweet's Persian Gardens, was opened in 1931 at Grand Avenue and Webster; later, under different management, it became the Ali Baba. Frank Sinatra and the Tommy Dorsey Orchestra performed at Sweet's fourth ballroom at 1414 Franklin. Different days of the week were devoted to different ethnic groups. On Sundays, for instance, Sweet's Ball Room was the site of regular *tardeadas,* or afternoon dances, featuring top acts from Mexico — Pedro Infante, Jorge Negrete and María Victoria — booked by promoter Guadalupe Carlos.

Other enterprises invited people to dance: ballrooms named McFadden's, Linn's and the Sands. Benny Goodman's orchestra supposedly made its West Coast debut at McFadden's in 1936. Local luminary Sid Hoff and his orchestra toured all the dance halls, opening for visiting big bands. Two years after Goodman blew into town, city fathers threw up their hands and allowed the

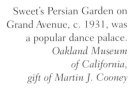

126

A SMALL MUSIC STUDIO IN WEST OAKLAND, C. 1942

Oakland Museum of California,
© Dorothea Lange Collection,
gift of Paul S. Taylor

127

Chapter Eleven

first open-air dance, sponsored by the City Recreation Department at Jefferson Playground, complete with a 12-piece orchestra.

In their heyday the ballrooms and tiny nightclubs provided steady work for musicians and launched quite a few careers. Pete Escovedo was a student at McClymonds High School just opening his ears to jazz when he and fellow student Ed Kelly decided to put together a Latin jazz quintet. "He wanted to know if I played percussion and I said, 'I'll learn,'" Escovedo recalled in an interview. "I made a set of bongos out of coffee cans — really! I used those until my buddy Al Lairos bought me a set of timbales." Later Escovedo

Bob Geddins, "father of the Oakland blues," shows off some of his awards from the height of his production career, 1983.
Oakland Museum of California, Oakland Tribune Collection, gift of ANG Newspapers

joined a band led by pianist Carlos Frederico (who played in various bands around the Bay Area until his death in 1997). "Every week I'd take this flour sack and put my timbales in it and catch the bus down San Pablo Avenue to the gig. It was a happening time. The mambo and cha-cha were big, and all the ballrooms were jumping."

About the time Escovedo's family was relocating to Oakland from the Central Valley in the late 1930s, bluesman Johnny Otis was getting his start as a drummer in the West Oakland Houserockers. The blues scene

surged as workers traveled to Oakland's shipyards from Texas and Louisiana, bringing the songs and sound that would evolve into "Oakland blues." As historian Lee Hildebrand describes it, "the music had a distinctive brand of guitar-playing and a virtual absence of the harmonicas that were so prevalent in Chicago-style music." Its purveyors included Ivory Joe Hunter, Lowell Fulson, Pee Wee Crayton and Jimmy McCracklin. They reigned in the clubs along Seventh Street, where "in those days, you could find gambling dens, whorehouses and almost anything you wanted — including trouble," Hildebrand writes.

The Oakland blues might have stayed on Seventh Street if not for Bob Geddins, a blues songwriter and producer who scouted the area for artists to record in his nearby studio. He was the first to record Fulson, selling his records from the trunk of his car. He recorded Jimmy Wilson singing Geddins' own "Tin Pan Alley," an homage to "the roughest place in town" — Seventh Street. Several of his artists had national hits in the 1960s, until the blues fell out of popular favor and Geddins lost his artists and some of his copyrights to larger labels. His death in 1991 went unnoticed in the local news, except for a funeral notice that acknowledged, "He originated the Oakland Blues."

While the adventuresome roamed Tin Pan Alley, those of more sedate tastes were applauding the rise of the classical arts from some other grassroots beginnings. The Oakland Symphony Orchestra was founded in 1934 by civic boosters and conductor Orley See, formerly a violinist with the Philadelphia and San Francisco orchestras. The symphony was a merger of two groups led by See — an instrumental ensemble in residence at the Oakland YMCA since 1925 and the Wildwood Violin Choir. The symphony's first season of four concerts was held in the lobby of the YMCA.

"See has made a definite musical entity of the orchestra, winning praise both for his interpretations and for his ability to deal with the perplexing problems connected with the maintenance of a 90-piece non-professional orchestra," wrote Fred Noland in *The Oakland Tribune* in 1936. That summary would prove prophetic. See retired in 1957 and Piero Bellugi led the orchestra through 1958. Gerhard Samuel then became music director, presiding over a period of expansion that included formation of the symphony chorus in

128

1959 and the symphony youth orchestra in 1964, and a tripling of the season's schedule, from eight concerts to 24. The orchestra was then the largest performing arts organization in the East Bay. A Ford Foundation grant of $1.35 million in stabilization and endowment funds in 1966 cemented its status as a major institution.

A new conductor, Harold Faberman, took over in 1971 and the orchestra continued to grow, introducing a pops series, free concerts, a minority orchestral fellowship program and music in the schools. It also won an ASCAP Award for Adventurous Programming in 1977. Yet the financial foundation supporting this pinnacle of accomplishment was beginning to crumble. A weak board, a management prone to infighting, indifferent fund raising and unhappy musicians chafing under Faberman's leadership contributed to a gradual diminishing both of attendance and financial contributions. Still, the orchestra continued its ambitious course. Hoping to boost attendance, trustees purchased the Paramount Theatre in 1972 and began a million-dollar renovation of the Art Deco movie palace.

The Paramount's construction in 1930 had been a symbol of hope in the middle of the Depression, providing not only an architectural landmark but entertainment and jobs. Designed by Timothy Pflueger, the combination vaudeville and film house was a marvel of metallic filigree, gilded plaster bas relief, fanciful grillwork and a towering mosaic facade above the marquee. It was so lavish that it was already obsolete when it opened. Filling the nearly 3,000 seats was daunting, and with operating expenses at $27,000 a week, the Paramount closed its doors just six months after its gala opening in December 1931 and stayed closed for a year. When it reopened, it "had settled down to being just a movie theater," recounted a city-funded history of the theater.

The renovation of the Paramount in all its glory was a triumph but an expensive one: the symphony association was able to raise less than a quarter of the final $4 million price tag. Although attendance was increased by 160 percent, the organization was deep in debt. To ease the burden, trustees transferred ownership of the Paramount to the city and moved part of its endowment into its operating budget, a move that eventually would prove fatal. Before the end, however, there were bright spots, especially in the hiring of Calvin Simmons as conductor in 1979. The brilliant and personable Simmons won over donors, the public and the musicians. "Things got better during the Simmons era," recalled trumpet player Tony Caviglia. "It was so much more pleasant, community-oriented, like a family. He truly was beloved." The entire Bay Area mourned when Simmons died in a boating accident in 1982.

Still, the symphony association continued to spend beyond its means while ticket sales dropped and management strife went unaddressed. Tensions between musicians and management culminated in a vote to strike in 1985. In 1986, as players filed a charge of unfair labor practices, the symphony, nearly a million dollars in debt and having squandered its endowment, filed for bankruptcy. Stunned citizens wondered if the symphony's death was indicative of a greater cultural disease sweeping the city.

The Oakland Symphony at the Paramount Theatre, c. 1980
Oakland Museum of California, Oakland Tribune Collection, gift of ANG Newspapers

If so, the symphony's rebirth four years later as the Oakland East Bay Symphony illustrated the city's ability to rebound. Led by an entirely new organization launched by musicians and orchestra supporters in 1989, the new orchestra boasted cross-genre collaborations, a strong music-in-the-schools program and, in conductor Michael Morgan, a director who personifies Oakland's character. Originally from Washington, D.C., Morgan is warm yet commanding, modest and extremely sure of himself. He is committed to establishing American classical music in the souls of everyday citizens and willing to devote hard work to the demands of artistic survival.

Oakland's dance history is a rich one, with innovators like the African-dance maestra Ruth Beckford and a ballet company of intriguing roots.

Raoul Pausé, a well-known teacher of ballet, was a free spirit. In 1948, after a fire destroyed his home studio, he taught in a rented space above an auto parts store in the 4600 block of Telegraph Avenue. From the beginning he guided students in an iconoclastic curriculum that reflected his personal passion for artistic expression. Rather than be constrained by the demands of classical ballet style — which he dismissed as "display dancing" — he urged students, "Light the light inside."

One of his attentive pupils was 14-year-old Ronn Guidi, whose family owned Blanche's Coffee Shop, a fixture on MacArthur Boulevard. Pausé's emphasis on joie de vivre as opposed to stringent technique impressed the youth. "I remember that once Raoul bought me a ticket to see Margot Fonteyn in *Swan Lake*," Guidi recalled in a commemorative memoir, *Oakland Ballet: The First 25 Years*. "When I came back... I said, 'You know, she hopped on a pirouette.' So he bought me another ticket and said, 'Now go back and see the ballet.' It was a lesson I never forgot."

The Korean War interrupted Guidi's ballet education, but he returned from military service with plans to teach. He ended up dancing with Pausé's ensemble, known in various evolutions as Pausé Ballet, the California Ballet Company and by 1960, the Oakland Civic Ballet. Three years earlier, the energetic Pausé had also formed the Oakland Players Guild to produce the dance dramas that were his passion. The OPG made its debut in August 1957 with *Eye of Darkness*, a retelling of the Orpheus myth.

Pausé devoted more time to theatrical pursuits, including a commission by the Oakland Raiders football

130

team to produce "a spectacular corps of 'Raiderettes'" featuring 100 baton twirlers, dancers, pompom girls and cheerleaders in pirate-theme costumes. Meanwhile, Guidi assumed more responsibility for the daily duties of running the ballet company. Eventually, artistic differences would drive apart the master and his star dancer. Guidi decided to form his own company to concentrate on ballet.

In September 1965 the Oakland Ballet offered its first performance at Berkeley's Little Theater; Guidi could only afford to pay the dancers $10 per show. For the next several years, the company was a "gypsy caravan," touring tiny stages at schools and churches. Their break came in 1973, when the Oakland Symphony moved into the restored Paramount Theatre and was casting about for additional revenue. Trustees decided they needed a holiday show to fill the theater during December and asked Guidi to stage that perennial favorite, *The Nutcracker Suite*. Guidi agreed, with the caveat that he would create new choreography emphasizing the story's mystical overtones. The show became a local tradition, and the Oakland Ballet developed a national reputation for imaginative revivals as well as original work.

Oakland became a center for African-based dance through the work of Ruth Beckford and her students. A disciple of famed dancer-choreographer Katherine Dunham, who introduced the movement of the African Diaspora to American modern dance, Beckford represented a number of "firsts," including first black student enrolled in U.C. Berkeley's modern dance department in 1944 and first black member of the Anna Halprin-Welland Lathrop dance company in San Francisco in 1945. At age 21, fresh out of college, she applied for a job with the City of Oakland Parks and Recreation Department. She hoped to teach tennis; they wanted someone to teach "rhythmics."

"They didn't know what to call modern dance," she said in an interview. "I knew I wanted the girls to move." The initial four classes grew into a citywide program. From 1953 to 1975, she operated Ruth Beckford African-Haitian Dance Studio. "It was a real novelty. No one had drummers playing for dance classes. We had artists coming in to sketch the dancers, and I allowed spectators in the advanced classes because I felt every class should be a performance instrument."

She offered her first full concert of African-Haitian dance at U.C. Berkeley in the mid-1950s. "It was standing room only, with an all-white audience," Beckford recalled. "They were curious. Most black people back then were ashamed to say the word 'Africa.'" Thanks to Beckford's influence, that attitude

African dance master and author Ruth Beckford at a booksigning, September 1979
Oakland Museum of California, Oakland Tribune Collection, gift of ANG Newspapers

131

changed. Two of her students, Deborah Brooks Vaughn and Halifu Osumare, established influential venues for African-based dance. Vaughn, with fellow dancer Elendar Barnes Harrison, founded Black Dimensions Dance Theater in 1972 to teach and perform African-derived dance in all its forms, from traditional to jazz styles. It was the first company in the Bay Area to produce an annual performance season of African-American dance, beginning in 1990.

Osumare opened Everybody's Creative Arts Studio in 1977 in a tiny space on 51st and Broadway. The casually run enterprise encouraged dancers of all stripes and offered a spectrum of modern, jazz and ethnic dance. Malonga Casquelord's Congalese classes drew crowds of passionate devotees; several other teachers founded companies or went on, as did Osumare, to head university dance departments. "Everybody's" became a flashpoint for a quickly-expanding national interest in world music. Reincorporated as Citicentre Dance, the organization today is an anchor tenant in the city-funded Alice Arts Center.

Oakland has produced great jazz artists and what many musicians call "the best jazz club in the world." Yoshi's started as an afterthought at a Japanese restaurant in Oakland owned by Yoshi Akiba and her partner, Kaz Kajimura. Akiba, an amateur dancer,

built a small stage and seating area next to the main dining room with the idea of holding occasional salons and musical events. The stage was inaugurated with a dance performance by Akiba herself and a bit of free jazz performed by friends. Local musicians heard about the venue and asked to perform there; in 1986, Kajimura found himself booking touring acts on a regular basis. The arrival of a full-time booking agent, Jason Olaine, turned the room into a full-blown "nightspot" featuring the likes of McCoy Tyner, Betty Carter, Sonny Rollins, Tito Puente and dozens of other luminaries. In 1997 the restaurant was forced to move from its leased space, which turned out to be a blessing. With city assistance, a new club and restaurant were built in Jack London Square. The venue is a gem of intimate proportions, great sightlines and acoustics that musicians love. Acoustics so good, in fact, that patrons can't hear the rumble of the trains, passing just beyond the club's walls, on their way to the C.L. Dellums Amtrak Station.

Throughout the day the whistles of those slow-moving trains are some of Oakland's best music, reminding all who listen of the city's working-class roots, the blow-out-the-stops energy that spun off into creative activity, and the fortune seekers deposited by this very train who over the past century have made the city sing.

132

Sailors DOMINATE THIS ARMISTICE DAY BALL AT THE OAKLAND AUDITORIUM, NOVEMBER 1943.

Oakland Museum of California, Oakland Tribune Collection, gift of ANG Newspapers

Chapter Eleven

THE

nEigHbORHOOds

The Hills

The Oakland hills, officially the Contra Costa Range, are extraordinary. There are creeks, groves of oak and bay and stands of redwood, hiking trails and neighborhoods with million-dollar views. The oldest redwood clear-cut in the world, and the oldest secondary growth, are found there. European settlers began harvesting redwoods in 1840, and by 1860 all of the ancient giants, once used by sailors at sea to spot the entrance to the Golden Gate, were gone. Anthony Chabot, the French Canadian engineer, created his first water reservoir in the hills, using a hydraulic mining method, and the city's first water retrieval system, the precursor of East Bay Municipal Utility District. Alameda and Contra Costa counties were linked through the hills in the 1937 by the Caldecott Tunnel.

The Lower Hills stretch from the Grand Lake area south to 35th Avenue between Interstate 580 and the Warren Freeway (Highway 13). Known for quiet streets and 150 neighborhood associations, these rolling hills once were covered with 217 acres of cherry trees planted by Friedrich Rhoda. In the 1860s his Royal Ann cherries became the first California-grown fruit to be sold on the east coast. Surrounding the orchards were beer gardens and a large settlement of German Americans. The area attracted visitors looking for weekend getaways at hillside resorts and summer cabins.

Indian Gulch was a long-standing attraction in the Lower Hills. It was renamed Trestle Glen in 1893 after a streetcar trestle was built to carry passengers across the gulch. Around 1915 citizens urged the city to acquire the site as a public park, and several unsuccessful attempts were made. Developers outbid the city and development started in 1918. Most of the native oaks, laurel and buckeye were cleared from the glen, including the last virgin stand of Oakland's original oaks. Four years later Trestle Glen was divided and prepared for development. Today its spacious homes on modest lots remain some of the most attractive in the city.

The Laurel and Glenview hill neighborhoods developed early, between 1910 and the 20s. Lakeshore and Grand avenues, surrounding the affluent town of Piedmont, became central locations for growth in the 1920s and 30s. Commerce expanded rapidly through the next few decades and housing spread eastward. The Montclair District in the Upper Hills named in a 1920 contest after Montclair, New Jersey, was a site for summer cottages. The neighborhood boasts its own multiuse public park, shopping center and wooded, winding streets.

The South Hills include the Oakland Zoo, with its modern open-space habitats. Nearby are beautiful residential areas such as Grass Valley. The North Hills, at the borders of Berkeley, North Oakland and Piedmont, were devastated by fire in 1991. On October 20, 1991, fire broke out just north of the Caldecott Tunnel in an area of densely built homes surrounded by an abundance of eucalpytus trees and Monterey pines. Fanned by high winds, the fire roared through the hills of Oakland and Berkeley for three days, killing 25, injuring 125, burning more than 1,600 acres and destroying more than 3,800 residences. The beauty of the hills masks such dangers. The Hayward Fault lies just underneath Highway 13, and there is concern about a serious rupture on the fault, quiescent for many decades. The area continues to be vulnerable to fires. Nevertheless, by 1999 nearly all the destroyed structures had been rebuilt. ■

Chapter 12

TRANSFORMATIONS

Earthquakes ARE A FACT OF LIFE IN CALIFORNIA. BIG ONES ARE DEVASTATING, BUT THEY CAN LEAD TO POSITIVE CHANGES IN THE WAY A CITY SEES ITSELF. **ANNALEE ALLEN** WRITES ABOUT TWO EARTHQUAKES' AFTER-EFFECTS ON DOWNTOWN OAKLAND.

Whenever a major earthquake strikes, the effects are often felt for some time. Depending on the extent of damage, communities begin to look very different once broken structures are cleared away and new buildings take their place. Two earthquakes stand out as distinct turning points in Oakland's history as well as in its physical development. The 1906 and 1989 tremors on the San Andreas Fault both precipitated notable changes — especially to the city's center, the district surrounding City Hall.

Compared to San Francisco, Oakland experienced comparatively little loss of life in the 1906 earthquake. Structural damage was relatively light and no devastating fires broke out. Of the thousands of refugees who made their way to Oakland, many remained permanently. Oakland's population grew from 67,000 in 1900 to 150,000 in 1910, an increase of over 100 percent.

To coordinate the disaster relief in Oakland, Mayor Frank Mott was joined by California Gov. George Pardee, a lifelong Oaklander, who traveled by train from Sacramento and was on the scene within hours. Response headquarters were housed at 14th and Washington streets in City Hall — a quaint four-story, wood-frame Victorian structure with a bell tower. According to Pardee family archives, the governor did not return to the capitol for several weeks following the earthquake. His family home on 11th Street and Castro had been leased to others for the duration of his term, so he slept on a cot in the mayor's office while directing recovery efforts.

As the city gradually returned to normal, Mott, a proponent of the era's popular "City Beautiful" movement, began advocating for funds to pay for a new "20th Century" city hall. A planning concept of the Progressive era, the City Beautiful movement called for grand civic structures and public amenities such as parks, libraries, scenic plazas and boulevards. Other cities and towns across the country

were erecting stately civic centers and sweeping away "old fashioned" 19th-century structures, considered to be "white elephants."

In 1909, through municipal annexation, much of East Oakland and portions of North Oakland were claimed within city limits, increasing Oakland's radius to 53.4 square miles. The same year, Oakland voters approved a $1,150,000 revenue bond to construct a new city hall. A nationwide design competition involving 28 applicants was held to select the architectural team. New York-based Palmer and Hornbostel's winning entry called for a new sort of civic headquarters. A traditional granite-faced base of three stories, which would contain the council chambers and executive offices, supported a high-rise, nine-story office tower. A gleaming terra cotta-clad cupola, Renaissance-Baroque inspired, topped off the 343-foot-tall building. Mayor Mott heartily approved the jurors' choice, saying the

new City Hall, "being out of the original and conventional style, will attract notice everywhere and will put Oakland in the front ranks of modern cities in the magnificence and attractiveness of its chief public building."

The Spirit of Oakland

A VIEW OF THE NEW, MODERN CITY HALL AND THE OLDER VICTORIAN CITY HALL IN FRONT OF IT, 1914. H.C. CAPWELL AND TAFT & PENNOYER DEPARTMENT STORES ARE SEEN NEARBY ON 14TH STREET.

Oakland Museum of California, gift of Herrington and Olson

Chapter Twelve

BUSY SCENE ON BROADWAY, C. 1915
Oakland Museum of California, gift of Jo Ryan

The Spirit of Oakland

In a much-publicized trip to the West Coast, President William Howard Taft attended the building's groundbreaking in the fall of 1911. A rousing parade down Broadway afforded Oakland citizens the rare opportunity to cheer for their national leader. Following the parade, Taft ferried across the bay for a ceremonial groundbreaking for the Panama-Pacific International Exposition. To accommodate the anticipated fair-going throngs, new hotels on both sides of the bay had been proliferating. One of the grandest of these was the Hotel Oakland, designed by Walter Bliss and William Faville and built in 1912.

In 1914, Oakland City Hall was ready for occupancy. Its opening coincided with Mott's decision to take a bride, and reporters dubbed the new high-rise "Mayor Mott's Wedding Cake." It was, in fact, the first "skyscraper" city hall in the country and stood taller than any other building in the region. For a brief time, according to Oakland History Room files, it was the tallest structure west of the Mississippi. Its Victorian predecessor was pulled down and the plaza was enlarged. A live oak tree was planted in 1917 in honor of Jack London. New buildings soon replaced earlier structures in the immediate vicinity, including a number of department stores: Capwell Sullivan and Furth and Kahn Brothers, with its elliptical dome gilded in gold leaf (both designed by Charles W. Dickey), and the Taft

and Pennoyer dry goods emporium. At the triangular gore of San Pablo, 14th Street and Broadway rose a distinctive eight-story flatiron building, modeled after the famous New York City flatiron, which became the banking headquarters for the First National Bank. It was called the Broadway Building.

A rush of other downtown construction took place in the decade after the quake. The new landmarks, prominently sited on corner lots, featured projecting cornices, classical ornamental details in the Beaux-Arts mode and steel-frame "earthquake proof" construction. Banking halls, theaters and restaurants lined Broadway, while shoppers crowded into stores on Washington, Clay and San Pablo. This building boom continued through the 1920s, with more construction occurring further "uptown" near 19th Street. Many façades featured the newly popular Moderne and Art Deco treatments. Throughout this heady period, streetcar lines on the main thoroughfares carried passengers from outlying districts. Downtown was everyone's destination.

The Depression and World War II years slowed development. The once-elegant Hotel Oakland was converted into a military hospital in 1943 and a residence for senior citizens. As the 1950s and 60s came and went, the city's central district seemed to be frozen in time. Years of construction on BART clogged downtown. Freeways hastened migration to the suburbs where, after the war, people found affordable housing. Businesses and stores soon followed. The Broadway Building lost its last banking tenant, Wells Fargo, in

141

1967. Kahn Brothers (later Rhodes, then Liberty House) closed for good in the mid-1980s. The city administration, in need of more room, acquired the old Taft and Pennoyer store on Clay and converted it to office use, dubbing it "City Hall West." Capwell's was demolished to make way for a parking garage, and City Hall Plaza took on a somewhat scruffy, unkempt appearance. Although built to high standards for its day and listed as a landmark on the National Register, by the late 1980s "Mayor Mott's Wedding Cake" was increasingly seen as seismically inadequate and hopelessly outdated. A commissioned study pointed out structural deficiencies in the seven decades-old building, with needed repairs in the tens of millions of dollars. Mayor Lionel Wilson, along with city council members and their staffs, moved out and rented space in a new city center complex across the street.

The Loma Prieta earthquake struck at 5:04 p.m. on October 17, 1989. It measured 7.1 on the Richter scale and lasted 15 seconds. All city workers were safely evacuated from City Hall and the annex. Others were

less fortunate. Just a mile away, the two-tiered Cypress structure collapsed, killing 42 motorists. Damage was especially heavy in West Oakland. City Hall, too, was heavily damaged, with visible surface cracks throughout. If the tremor had lasted several seconds more, experts believed, the building's clock tower would have come crashing down. A portion of the brick veneer of the Hotel Oakland did fall onto the sidewalk, leaving a gaping hole. City Hall West was a total loss, and the city manager was forced to lease nearby vacant office space to house hundreds of employees. Fortunately, the Federal Emergency Management Agency (FEMA) agreed to reimburse Oakland the millions of dollars in extra rent for up to five years. For months, city leaders waited to hear FEMA's decision about City Hall — whether to replace it with a new building or to restore the National Register landmark no matter the cost.

Finally, in 1991, a favorable ruling came. FEMA agreed to fund full restoration, including the latest seismic technology — a base isolation reinforcement system engineered to safely absorb shocks generated by a 7.1 quake. The $80 million work was carried out by VBN Architects. In the course of demolition, a "time capsule" from 1911 was discovered behind the interior brick walls. It contained photographs, books, maps, city documents, flags, a bible and a list of contents. Missing were 1911 gold and silver coins that apparently had been "liberated" before the last brick was laid.

Although City Hall would reopen, the problem of the excess leased office space still had to be solved. Proceeds from the Redevelopment District, insurance reimbursements and a $103 million dollar bond cleared the way for a new city administrative complex. Among the

142

(Far left)
Frank Ogawa Plaza in front
of the newly refurbished
City Hall, 2000
Photo by Robert A. Eplett

The Federal Buildings at
City Center, 2000
Photo by Robert A. Eplett

alternatives studied was a scheme to incorporate the damaged Broadway Building into a new structure, combining the historic portion with an attached wing at the rear. Three older buildings in the block across 15th Street from City Hall would be demolished and a new six-story, 332,000-square-foot structure built in their place. The empty Kahn's/Liberty House store — rechristened the Rotunda Building — would eventually be rehabilitated for commercial mixed use. City Hall Plaza would be increased half again in size, and surrounding streets would be transformed into pedestrian promenades.

As plans unfolded, Craig Kocian, the city manager, directed staff to meet with those concerned about the loss of still more historic buildings. Since the earthquake several organizations, including the National Trust for Historic Preservation, the local chapter of the American Institute of Architects and the Oakland Heritage Alliance, had been monitoring the status of damaged landmarks. Recognizing that demolition of existing older structures would further erode the historic

fabric of downtown, city staff committed to nominating the district for listing on the National Register of Historic Places. Other agreed-upon mitigations included a façade-improvement program, with grants and loans for property owners in the district, and a marketing campaign promoting the downtown to new businesses. These became legally binding when they were incorporated into a final environment impact report.

In 1994, with city council approval and broad-based community support, staff sought responses from architectural and construction teams, inviting entries for a new administration complex project. Design guidelines stressed the importance of respecting the context of the surrounding historic buildings. The winning team was Hensel Phelps, architect, and Fentress Bradburn, construction. A new time capsule was placed within the walls, containing publications, a signed photo of Mayor Elihu Harris, five tickets to a Raiders' game, pins, a flag and more — but no coins.

In the fall of 1998, nine years after the Loma Prieta earthquake, the campus-like city hall complex was dedicated to the memory of longtime city councilman Frank H. Ogawa. As part of the administration's commitment to protect the legacy of downtown Oakland's rebirth, the city initiated regularly scheduled walking tours, offering visitors the opportunity to learn how significant seismic events eight decades apart set in motion the civic center's two amazing transformations.

Chapter 13

A WRITER'S PLACE

EXPLORING THE CITY'S LONG LITERARY TRADITIONS, **JOAN BOER** WRITES THAT OAKLAND IS A PLACE TO TRY SOMETHING NEW, RAIL AGAINST INJUSTICE AND FEEL AT HOME.

... This place of enormous wealth

And abject poverty

This Oakland

Where the red man

once danced freely

Where Califia was said to rule

Where living was a golden dream

And all things were possible

... This united nation

On the brink of discovery

This East Bay city

Of refugees and dream seekers

I now call home

— Opal Palmer Adisa

Poets and writers were in a buoyant mood on January 4, 2000. The world hadn't ended, computers hadn't crashed, and Oakland had a new mayor and a new spirit. The inauguration of Jerry Brown, admired for his support of the arts when he was California's governor in the 1970s, was cause for hope and celebration. Some of the city's best poets gathered at the Oakland Museum of California for an evening of short readings. Opal Palmer Adisa, originally from the Caribbean, read her love song to Oakland, "This City I Now Call Home."

Poet Jack Foley, who organized the readings, said the key word for the event was diversity. "Oakland is an exciting, enormously diverse place to live, and we want to celebrate that," he wrote in the program. "We also hope and believe that the election of Jerry Brown will mean an increase in Oakland's pride and self-consciousness."

Haiku

THE BIG
YELLOW
LEAF
S
P
I
N
S
through
the
silver
down
pour
— Smacks
my

wind
shield

FOUR DEER
and
a great
blue
heron
in a
field.
brake
lights
up
a
head
!

— MICHAEL MCCLURE

Today's Oakland writers take pride in their literary ancestors, whose dreams of a true democracy, justice for all and the dignity of the working man have inspired their descendants through the decades.

As the third millennium dawned on a prosperous America, Oakland had more than its share of problems. Poverty left many of its residents too exhausted to struggle for a better life. The public schools were in disastrous shape. The city had been battered badly in the flatlands by a 1989 earthquake and in the hills by a 1991 wildfire. Still, poetry and literature continued to flourish. In his Oakland hills home, renowned poet and playwright Michael McClure wrote haiku. In the flatlands, young people performed their hip hop at MamboJambo. Poets shared their work at Walden Pond Books, Grand Avenue Coffee Mill and Java House.

Lucha Corpi, a Chicana mystery writer, finds strength in Oakland's integrated neighborhoods and the opportunity they present to explore all cultures. "It's not so much that we're sharing the same space, but we're learning to live the American dream. We get tested every day in terms of tolerance," she said.

After the 1991 Oakland fire, author and activist Ishmael Reed wrote in *Money Can't Buy You Love:*

[W]hen it appeared certain that Oakland was experiencing another catastrophe, we started to think of moving elsewhere ... But we'll probably stay in Oakland. Why?... Oakland is like a journeyman fighter, bloodied and battered, one eye nearly shut, jaw swollen, behind on points, but still capable of a comeback during the last ten seconds of the twelfth round. I have a hunch Oakland will not only come back, but thrive. We live in Oakland because of its fighting spirit.

That spirit, born of Oakland's multicultural character and the search for social justice, encourages an openness to new ideas and values, says Jack Foley. "It's a situation that allows for contradiction. There are different things going on here simultaneously. There is not one fiber running through the whole, but an overlapping of many fibers. We don't suffer here from what Jennifer Stone calls 'hardening of the categories.'"

The rich, diverse urban life in Oakland forms the backdrop for some of the best local fiction. In such a diverse culture, one's own identity is an issue to explore, and Oakland's authors often create heroes who struggle to find their place in the world. So it is with the Chinese-American protagonists in Maxine Hong Kingston's *The Woman Warrior* and *Tripmaster Monkey: His Fake Book,* the ambitious black academic Benjamin Puttbutt in Ishmael Reed's *Japanese By Spring* and the author himself in Floyd Salas' wrenching memoir about the destruction of a Spanish-American family, *Buffalo Nickel.*

In the early days of California, when newcomers left their pasts behind to come west, it was easier to reinvent oneself. Samuel Clemens became Mark Twain, Francis Harte became Bret Harte, Cincinnatus Miller became Joaquin Miller to honor Joaquin Murrieta, the bandit hero of his poem, and Josephine Smith became Ina Donna Coolbrith (1841-1928), the first Poet Laureate of California.

Joaquin Miller (1837-1913) went further than most in transforming himself. He also changed or romanticized the facts of his early life and played to the hilt the character of the rugged frontiersman, affecting, as his contemporary Twain (1835-1910) recalled, "the picturesque and untamed costume of the wild Sierras." Miller was particularly successful with this pose in

Joaquin MILLER, C. 1890
Oakland Museum of California, gift of Miss Jean Bradford Fay

Chapter Thirteen

England, where he (and Twain as well) resided for some time. Miller did well enough with his writing to buy 75 acres in the Oakland hills with a full view of

the Golden Gate. The land is now Joaquin Miller Park, and one tiny cottage still stands. The literati of Oakland and San Francisco often gathered at "The Hights," as he insisted on spelling it, to get away from the stresses of the cities below. Among attendees were the acerbic journalist and short story writer Ambrose Bierce (1842-1914?), Jack London (1876-1916) and poet George Sterling (1869-1926), who became London's best friend much to the chagrin of Bierce, who considered London far too radical in his politics.

Issues of social justice are often at the forefront when races, cultures and classes mix. Like many early writers, Miller saw in the open-hearted Western frontier the best hope for the young American democracy. In Swinburnian cadences, he poured out his populist feelings in his poem "In San Francisco:"

> The brown brave hand of the harvester,
> The delicate hand of the prince untried
> The rough hard hand of the carpenter,
> They are all upheld with an equal pride;
> And the prize it is his to be crown'd or blest,
> Prince or peon, who bears him best....

148

Jack London, Oakland's most famous literary son and America's first significant working-class writer, admired Joaquin Miller, but his was a different kind of frontier. As biographer Richard O'Connor put it, "Instead of buckskins he would flaunt the red sweater of the revolutionary." London had an impoverished childhood that helped make socialism attractive. He credited Oakland for making a literary career seem possible. In a 1914 letter he told an admirer that two "wonderful things" had happened to him as a small boy, without which he would never have become a writer. The first was finding a tattered copy of the novel *Signa* by Ouida (Louise de la Ramee, 1839-1908), which "opened up to me the possibilities of the world of art." The second was coming to Oakland to live, where "I found access to the great world by means of the free public library of the City of Oakland.... It was this world of books, now accessible, that practically gave me the basis for my education." The title character of his novel *Martin Eden* (1909) is similarly immersed in books and exhilarated with learning:

A rarely seen portrait of author Jack London taken by prominent San Francisco photographer Laura Adams Armer, 1901
Oakland Museum of California, gift of Mr. and Mrs. Austin Armer

Poets Edwin Markham and Ina Coolbrith chat together, c. 1920.
Oakland History Room, Oakland Public Library

Martin had ascended from pitch to pitch of intellectual living, and here he was at a higher pitch than ever. All the hidden things were laying their secrets bare. He was drunken with comprehension. At night, asleep, he lived with the gods in colossal nightmare; and awake, in the day, he went around like a somnambulist, with absent stare, gazing upon the world he had just discovered. At table he failed to hear the conversation about petty and ignoble things, his eager mind seeking out and following cause and effect in everything before him.

In his adventure stories London grappled with the great questions of life and death and the struggle to survive with dignity and integrity. He was a dashing, hard-living, heavy drinker, fast with his fists — a romantic and an adventurer to the end. That came in 1916, when he died at 40 apparently of uremic poisoning at his Beauty Ranch in Sonoma (now Jack London State Park). He is buried there near the ghostly stone ruins of Wolf House, his dream home whose destruction by a mysterious fire just before completion nearly broke his heart.

London's socialism may also have been spurred by the work of two other Oakland residents — Henry George (1839-1897), whose political essays he admired, and the passionate poetry of Edwin Markham (1852-1940). Markham was a 47-year-old Oakland grammar school principal when the *San Francisco Examiner* published "The Man With the Hoe" in 1899. It was reprinted all over the world and made Markham a great deal of money. The poem, inspired by the Jean-François Millet painting that had been recently exhibited in San Francisco, is an indictment of a system that brutalizes the common laborer. It ends with a challenge and a warning:

How will it be with kingdoms and with kings —
With those who shaped him to the thing he is —
When this dumb Terror shall rise to judge the
world,
After the silence of the centuries?

In his essay "Fallen Western Star: San Francisco as a Literary Region," poet and critic Dana Gioia holds up "The Man with the Hoe" as the quintessential Bay Area poem — a representative work for the best that would follow over the next century. "It offers a populist and progressive but unillusioned view of existence. It dramatizes the lone individual against the system without idealizing the protagonist into an unrealistically noble figure," writes Gioia.

Delilah Beasley (1867-1934) is another Oakland writer who used her pen for social justice. Born in Cincinnati and orphaned at an early age, she supported herself by giving therapeutic massages and wrote on the side. In 1910, when she was 44, a wealthy female client paid her way to come to Berkeley. She worked as a feature writer for the *Oakland Sunshine,* a newspaper for Oakland's black community, and in 1923 the Oakland Tribune hired her to write a weekly column, "Activities Among Negroes." She was the first African-American woman on the staff of a major metropolitan daily. The column was not merely a chronicle of events but a vehicle for enlightening readers about the black experience and promoting interracial cooperation. She was instrumental in halting the use of racial epithets in the local press. Her most lasting contribution was her 1919 history of black pioneers, *The Negro Trail Blazers of California.* The first person to write such a history, she was a trail blazer herself. She is rightly credited with preserving and correcting the record of black participation in building the state.

Perhaps the wittiest Oakland writer whose work exposed chicanery and championed the disenfranchised was Jessica Mitford (1917-1996), who once said, "You may not be able to change the world, but at least you can embarrass the guilty." Her 1963 exposé of the excesses of the funeral industry, *The American Way of Death,* was an eye-opener that led to reforms. She also railed against the defects in the prison system in *Kind and Usual Punishment,* the prosecution of anti-war activists in *The Trial of Dr. Spock,* and the questionable practices of obstetricians in *The American Way of Birth.*

Mitford ran away from her aristocratic English family at age 19 with her cousin, Esmond Romilly, to fight the Fascists in the Spanish Civil War. The couple married and later found their way to America. Romilly lost his life as a fighter pilot in World War II and the young widow, with an infant daughter, came to California, where she married Robert Treuhaft, an Oakland attorney. Both were members of the Communist party but left the party in 1958. A rebel to

Delilah Beasley, c. 1910
*Oakland History Room,
Oakland Public Library*

demonstrating literary excellence and a multicultural viewpoint, often those likely to be overlooked by mainstream publishers.

Oakland was the childhood home of two of the most experimental writers of the last century: Gertrude Stein (1874-1946) and Robert Duncan (1919-1988) — neither of whose art became identified with the city. Duncan, a poet known for his syntactical jumps and eccentric spellings, lived during his adult productive years in Berkeley and San Francisco, and Stein, who grew up on a 10-acre property in East Oakland, moved to Paris, where she found fame as an art critic, writer and host to some of the greatest artists and writers of the 20th century. She wrote in the third person about her youth in *The Making of Americans* (1908): "It was a very good kind of living... the... children had in their beginning, and their freedom in the ten acres where all kinds of things were growing, where they could have all anybody could want of joyous sweating, of rain and wind, of hunting, of cows and dogs and horses, of chopping wood, of making hay, of dreaming, of lying in a hollow all warm with the sun shining while the wind was howling..."

When Stein returned to Oakland in the mid-1930s, the family estate was a run-down housing development. "What was the use of my having come from Oakland," she lamented in *Everybody's Autobiography* (1937), "it was not natural to have come from there yes write about it if I like or anything if I like but not there, there is no there there."

"We thought otherwise," Jessica Mitford responded in *A Fine Old Conflict* (1977). "Oakland was still at the frontier, where the issues were sharper, the corruption cruder, the enemy more easily identifiable.... There was nothing abstract about the class struggle in Oakland."

Anyone who has returned to a scene of childhood to find it drastically altered might feel as Stein did, but most writers who have settled here as adults wouldn't trade the energy and excitement of modern Oakland for her comfortable recollections.

For Opal Palmer Adisa, Oakland is a mecca for writers, "a fertile place that calls to artists," and Lucha Corpi, who sets her mystery novels there, agrees: "Every writer needs a village. This is my village."

the end, at the time of her death Mitford was involved in a crusade to "Send a Piana to Havana," with her son, Benjamin Treuhaft.

Equality and justice were also the goals of writers Ishmael Reed, Reginald Lockett and Floyd Salas when they met in 1989 to form PEN Oakland, the only affiliate of PEN Center USA West and International PEN specifically chartered to benefit local, and particularly minority, writers. Reed (b. 1938) is a highly honored author and academic who taught at Harvard, Yale and Dartmouth and is now on the faculty of the University of California, Berkeley. Salas (b. 1931) is a prizewinning novelist, poet, teacher and former boxer who is proud to say he has based his life on Jack London's. Lockett (b. 1947) is a poet and owner of Jukebox Press, a publishing cooperative in Oakland. PEN Oakland gives yearly awards to works

151

Conclusion

OAKLAND AND THE REGIONAL REALITY

CHARLES M. WOLLENBERG PUTS OAKLAND'S PRESENT AND FUTURE INTO A REGIONAL HISTORICAL PERSPECTIVE.

Oakland's HISTORY HAS ALWAYS BEEN AFFECTED BY THE BAY AREA'S REGIONAL DEVELOPMENT. THE GOLD RUSH NOT ONLY CREATED AN "INSTANT CITY," SAN FRANCISCO, BUT PRODUCED AN INSTANT METROPOLITAN REGION, WITH INTERDEPENDENT SMALL BAYSIDE COMMUNITIES LIKE OAKLAND PROVIDING GOODS AND SERVICES TO THE NEW URBAN MARKET. THE BAY ITSELF WAS THE REGIONAL TRANSPORTATION AND COMMUNICATION LINK. DURING THE 1850S AND 60S, HORACE CARPENTIER, OAKLAND'S ILLEGITIMATE FATHER, MADE SURE HE CONTROLLED THE CITY'S WATERFRONT AND THUS ACCESS TO THE REGIONAL ECONOMY.

The arrival of the transcontinental railroad in 1869 transformed Oakland into a city, making it an integral part of the Bay Area's urban core. But the railroad's corporate policies also made sure that Oakland was a junior partner: the corporation located its rail yards, round houses and shops in Oakland, but company head-quarters were in San Francisco. Blue-collar workers moved into modest new homes in West Oakland, but the men who ran the railroad built their ostentatious mansions on San Francisco's Nob Hill. Oakland may have done the work, but San Francisco still gave the orders.

The 1906 earthquake quite literally shook up the regional balance of power, sending thousands of refugees and hundreds of businesses from San Francisco to Oakland. At the same time, new electric rail systems encouraged rapid urban expansion in the East Bay. During these years Oakland won back control of its port and promoted construction of a regional water system. By the 1920s the city was an industrial center, "The Detroit of the West," and downtown Oakland was a prosperous commercial district, though still second in importance to downtown San Francisco in the Bay Area economy.

152

The 1920s also marked the beginning of the automobile age, but it took Depression-era public works projects, the Bay Bridge and the first bore of what was to become the Caldecott Tunnel, to establish the supremacy of the car in the regional transportation network. Also during the Depression years, Oakland's political economy was affected by the recovery of organized labor in the Bay Area, particularly following the 1934 San Francisco General Strike. In the 1940s the flow of billions of federal defense dollars into the region produced a dramatic economic recovery. Oakland shipbuilding boomed as never before or since, and new military projects promoted the development of the waterfront and airport. Most important, the wartime labor shortages produced huge new migrations of African Americans and Latinos into the city.

But postwar developments turned the regional tide against Oakland. An explosion of suburban growth produced middle-class "white flight" and resulted in a pattern of increasing residential segregation. Industrial jobs joined the flight to the suburbs, the most dramatic case being the move of General Motors from East Oakland to Fremont. Beginning in the 1960s downtown Oakland was disrupted by seemingly endless BART construction and a series of ill-conceived redevelopment projects. During the next two decades, Oakland's economic base was further eroded by the decline and fall of old "smoke stack" industries. New white-collar jobs either stayed in San Francisco or skipped over downtown Oakland to suburban locations, such as the Interstate 680 corridor.

Oakland certainly had some solid accomplishments during the postwar years, including the emergence of the city as the Bay Area's premier port and the evolution of some of the region's most pleasant and lively neighborhoods. But residents increasingly identified with their separate communities and districts rather than the city as a whole. Voters often opposed efforts by the political and business establishment to promote downtown recovery through massive public subsidies. Indeed, the most dramatic economic development in the central part of the city during these years occurred in Chinatown, and it was produced by the arrival of a new generation of Asian immigrants rather than as the result of any city policy or program.

In the late 1990s the regional tide again shifted, this time at long last in Oakland's favor. Silicon Valley was now the Bay Area's economic engine, and its remarkable prosperity influenced the entire region. The dot-com revolution particularly affected San Francisco, promoting astronomical increases in real estate prices. Regional traffic problems and environmental concerns promoted new interest in "smart growth" proposals to reduce suburban sprawl and encourage urban infill. In these circumstances, downtown Oakland and its adjoining neighborhoods, with their relatively affordable property values, BART connections and established urban infrastructure, became attractive locations for both commercial and residential development. After years of being concerned about urban deterioration, central Oakland residents suddenly found themselves faced with problems of economic and social gentrification.

If Oakland can address these problems and promote the recovery of its central district in a manner that serves rather than displaces current residents, the benefits will be enormous. Balanced downtown recovery would not only promote new business and employment growth, but also create a civic focus for the renewal of the entire city. A viable downtown could become a common ground of economic opportunity and cultural expression for Oakland's diverse population. This, in turn, could contribute to an increased sense of civic identity and community. There is indeed a brave new regional reality out there — and Oakland's prospects are looking good.

A portion of Oakland's waterfront and skyline, spring 2000
Photo by Robert A. Eplett

153

Conclusion

COntributors

Photos by Joe Samberg

EDITOR: ABBY WASSERMAN is a free-lance writer, editor and researcher who has published extensively in newspapers and magazines. Her research projects include *One of Us: Richard M. Nixon and the American Dream* by Tom Wicker and *J. Edgar Hoover: The Man and The Secrets* by Curt Gentry. She is author of *Portfolio: Eleven Native American Artists* and editor of *Praise, Vilification & Sexual Innuendo, or How to Be a Critic: The Selected Writings of John L. Wasserman, 1964-1979* (Chronicle Books). Since 1989 she has been editor-in-chief of *The Museum of California* magazine, the quarterly magazine of the Oakland Museum of California. A native Bay Arean, she lived in Oakland from 1990 to 1999. She holds a bachelor's degree in education from San Francisco State University and a master's degree in educational theater from New York University.

PHOTO EDITOR: DIANE CURRY is a photography researcher in the Oakland Museum of California History Department and an award-winning Irish step dancer. She completed her master's degree in history with an emphasis on public history at California State University, Hayward, in 1999. Recent research projects include the exhibition, *Gold Fever: The Lure and Legacy of the California Gold Rush*, and the accompanying book by J.S. Holliday. She was born and raised in the Bay Area.

MICHAEL DOBRIN ("Claims, Characters and Commerce"), an avid sailor who for many years berthed his sailing craft on Oakland's Estuary, has written extensively on Western maritime history. He is a former editor of *Bay & Delta Yachtsman* and has contributed articles and photographs to *Sea, Cruising World, Up Here* and *Wooden Boat*, among other journals. A former public information officer at the Oakland Museum of California, he was guest curator of the museum's exhibition *Yachting's Golden Years: 1910-1940* and co-curator of *Hot Rods and Customs: The Men and Machines of California's Car Culture.*

CHIORI SANTIAGO ("Traces of the Peraltas" and "Permission to Dance") has appreciated Oakland's spirit for many years in her role as an art and dance critic and feature writer for *The Oakland Tribune, San Francisco Examiner* and other Bay Area and national publications. She is associate editor of *The Museum of California* magazine. An East Bay resident since 1959, she earned her bachelor's degree in history from the University of California, Berkeley.

BRENDA PAYTON ("The Politics of Invention") writes a column three times a week for *The Oakland Tribune*, where she has been a columnist for 18 years. Formerly on the staff of the Center for Investigative Reporting, she has taught reporting, news and feature writing at San Francisco State University. Her many awards include citations from the National Association of Black Journalists, the California Newspaper Publishers' Association and Meiklejohn Civil Liberties Institute. She lives in Oakland.

KAREN TSUJIMOTO ("Artistic Harvest") is senior curator of art at the Oakland Museum of California. Her special area of interest is the modern and contemporary art of California. She has organized exhibitions and written books on the art of Joan Brown, Dorothea Lange, Wayne Thiebaud and Peter Voulkos, among others.

WILLIAM WONG ("Chinatown Roots"), in his 32 years in journalism, has worked on national and local newspapers, appeared regularly on television as a commentator and been a pioneer among Asian-American journalists. A book of his essays on race relations, affirmative action, multiculturalism and Asian-American politics and identity, *Yellow Journalist*, will be published by Temple University Press. He is a native of Oakland Chinatown.

CATHERINE B. DOBRIN (The Automobile Age in "Wheels & Wings"), a fourth-generation Californian and East Bay native, has a degree in history from Oakland's Holy Names College and maintains an avid interest in regional history. For

154

more than 20 years she has been affiliated with the automotive industry as a public relations executive in partnership with her husband, Michael.

BOB MIDDLETON (Ceiling Unlimited in "Wheels & Wings"), a fourth-generation San Franciscan, is manager and chaplain of the International Maritime Center, an ecumenical ministry to the Bay Area's working waterfronts. He holds bachelor's and master's degrees from UC Berkeley. From 1977 to 1997 he worked for the Port of Oakland, serving four years as public relations director. He resides in "the Oakland suburb of Piedmont" and is a candidate for ordination as a deacon in the Episcopal Church.

MARY ELLEN BUTLER ("Grace Under Pressure"), an award-winning journalist, worked for a variety of public and private sector organizations from the mid-1960s through the mid-90s, including daily newspapers in Oakland, Berkeley and Washington, D.C. She is author of two books: *Oakland Welcomes the World* and *Prophet of the Parks: The Story of William Penn Mott, Jr.*, and editor of *Black Women Stirring the Waters*. A graduate of UC Berkeley, Butler's professional memberships have included the National Association of Black Journalists and the National Conference of Editorial Writers.

PHIL MUMMA ("Safe at Home"), former associate director for public programs at the Oakland Museum of California, received his bachelor's and master's degrees in journalism from the University of Missouri. He founded *The Museum of California* magazine and has written widely on a variety of California issues. For more than four decades, he played baseball and softball at nearly every level. He currently coaches softball at the high school and Olympic Development level and owns a softball training facility in San Ramon, California.

WILLIAM STURM (Free to All in "For the People"), an Oakland native, is a librarian in charge of the Oakland History Room and the consulting historian of this book. He received his undergraduate degrees in history and philosophy at San Francisco State and his master's degree in library science from UC Berkeley. He joined the staff of the Oakland Public Library in 1965 and in 1978 assumed his History Room post.

ERIKA MAILMAN (Growing Things in "For the People") is the editor of the *Montclarion* newspaper and writes a weekly column on Oakland history for the paper. She is on the board of directors of Oakland Heritage Alliance and is one of the early members of Friends of the Oakland Fox Theater. Her free-lance work has appeared in *Art & Antiques* and several local publications, including *Oakland* magazine, *Urban View* and the *Nob Hill Gazette.*

SANDRA SHER (Vanishing Shellmounds in "Native Spirit") is a graduate of UC Berkeley and a free-lance historian. She "stumbled on" the subject of the East Bay shellmounds while doing other historical research. Over the next 10 years she worked to chronicle the history of these local mounds, which she considers richly and critically significant for both native descendants and the larger community.

SUSAN LOBO (Heart of the Community in "Native Spirit") is author of many articles and books and editor of *The American Indian Urban Experience* (AltaMira Press, 2001). She is administrator of Intertribal Friendship House in Oakland.

ANNALEE ALLEN ("Transformations") is a weekly columnist with *The Oakland Tribune,* writing on topics relating to landmarks and local history. Since 1992 she has been a member of the city's Landmarks Preservation Advisory Board. A past president of the Oakland Heritage Alliance, she is coordinator of the city-sponsored Oakland Tours Program. Born in San Francisco, she grew up in Berkeley and graduated from UCLA with a degree in art history. She has lived in Oakland's Rockridge neighborhood since 1978.

JOAN BOER ("A Writer's Place"), a former reporter and editor for ANG Newspapers, is a history buff with a special interest in literature and the theater. An art docent at the Oakland Museum of California, she also edits the bimonthly docent newsletter and is the coordinator of the museum's Speakers Gallery. Her weekly "Lively Arts" column appears in the *Valley Times/San Ramon Valley Times.*

CHARLES M. WOLLENBERG, PH.D. ("Oakland and the Regional Reality") received his bachelor's, master's and doctorate degrees in history from UC Berkeley. His many books include *Photographing the Second Gold Rush: Dorothea Lange and the Bay Area at War 1941-45, Ethnic Conflict in California History* (co-author), *Golden Gate Metropolis: Perspectives in Bay Area History,* and the forthcoming *Berkeley: A City in History.* He is a history instructor and chairman of the social science department at Vista College in Berkeley.

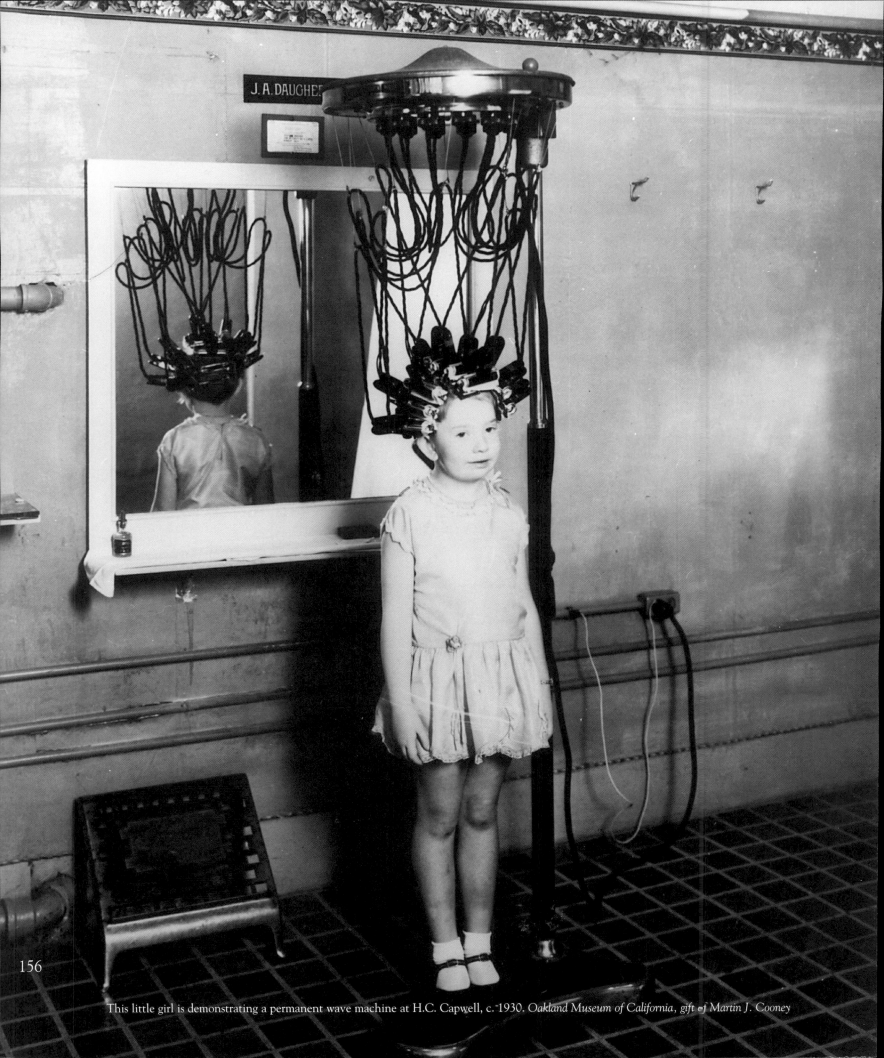

This little girl is demonstrating a permanent wave machine at H.C. Capwell, c. 1930. *Oakland Museum of California, gift of Martin J. Cooney*

PartNers iN OAklanD
Table of Contents

157

BuilDing a GreaTeR OaKland

Oakland real estate development, management and construction companies shape tomorrow's skyline, providing and improving working and living space for area residents.

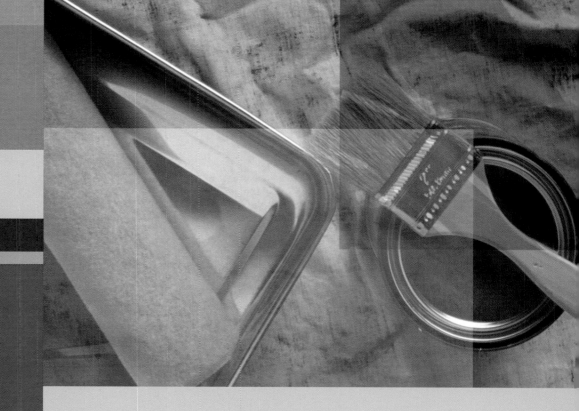

Bigge Crane and Rigging Co.

Bigge has always thought big. In the early years of the 20th century, when Bigge was established, the company moved trunks and cargo from the docks in the East Bay to the Oakland Hills for 25 cents each. But Henry W. Bigge had a bigger picture in mind for his business. During the 1920s, Bigge saw great opportunity in the heavy hauling business in the rapidly growing West. Nearly 100 years later Bigge Crane and Rigging Co. is still family owned and managed, and the scale of its operations is more enormous than its founder could possibly have envisioned.

Bigge is the No. 1 heavy engineering, transport and rigging contractor in California, the biggest in the business of hoisting and hauling the heaviest and most enormous of construction components. The company's expansion is due to its history of innovative solutions to any problem involving transport and hoisting. Bigge holds more than 30 patents for its equipment designs. Over the years, it has performed with such consistent excellence that it has been awarded the Specialized Carriers and Rigging Association's "Outstanding Rigging/Transportation Job of the Year" 18 times in the 36-year history of the international competition, more than any other crane company in the United States.

Early Bigge crane installing a 72-inch storm drain, Grand Avenue, Oakland, 1929

Henry W. Bigge in drayman's leather apron, 7th Street, Oakland, 1919

The history of Bigge parallels the history of the 20th century. Through the decades, Bigge has kept ahead of the newest engineering and technological innovations. Bigge's General Engineering Contractor's

license was obtained in 1931, one of the oldest licenses still active in California. Over the years it has played a key role during some of the century's finest moments and its greatest calamities. When buildings went up or freeways collapsed, Bigge was there. As construction sites got larger and more complicated, Bigge's equipment

and engineering solutions were a match for any lifting or transportation challenge.

The company was founded in 1916 and today Bigge is still family owned and operated. The founder, Henry W. Bigge, stayed on until 1980 when Brock and Marlene Bigge Settlemier purchased the company. Brock Settlemier started with Bigge in 1958, has been its president and CEO since 1980 and has moved the company into national and international prominence. Marlene serves as vice president of finance. The Settlemiers' two sons, Reid and Weston, are key players on the Bigge management team. Reid is president of Bigge Equipment Co., and Weston is executive vice president and COO of the Bigge Group of companies.

During Settlemier's tenure, Bigge Power Constructors was activated and the company has expanded into heavy crawler crane rental, nuclear power construction, refinery maintenance, crane dealerships and professional engineering consulting. In the 1990s Bigge acquired Shaughnessy and Co., a Seattle-based heavy hauling and transportation company. Bigge also purchased Concord Crane and Rigging Co., which supplies crane rentals, performs heavy refinery maintenance and services industrial customers in the North Bay, Solano, Marin and Modesto counties. Bigge Equipment Co., the crane dealership, was also incorporated as was BEAR High Reach to rent and service access equipment. Bigge Development Co. manages the Bigge Groups's real estate.

During the 1930s, Bigge participated in the construction of two of the Bay Area's greatest landmarks — the Golden Gate Bridge, completed in 1937, and the Oakland Bay Bridge, finished in 1936. Bigge transported the structural steel and massive floor girders and beams for both bridges.

World War II demanded the utmost from the country's defense contractors, and Bigge played a vital part in the production of warships at Kaiser's Oakland Shipyard No. 3. Bigge provided cranes, labor, supervision and specialized trucking equipment to transport, install, rig and set the enormous ship substructures. When a Japanese submarine was captured off the California coast in 1942, on a pro bono basis Bigge transported the enemy ship on its 48-state fund-raising tour to raise money for War Bonds.

The peaceful 1950s allowed Bigge to move into maritime construction where the company provided

Multiaxle trailers hauling bridge girders to the Golden Gate Bridge, San Francisco, 1936

specialized barge services, erected and relocated dock-mounted container cranes and engineered heavy lift rigging systems for the refinery and petrochemical industries. Bigge's Crane Certification Co. was founded in 1958. ■

Bridge cranes and crew stabilizing the Cypress Freeway overpass after its collapse in the Loma Prieta earthquake, October 1989

161

Recovery of Japan Airlines
jet *Shiga* from
San Francisco Bay, 1968

Rebuilding Cypress Freeway
eight years after the
Loma Prieta earthquake
destroyed it, 1997

Hauling and erecting BART
girders, 120 feet long and
150 tons, Oakland, 1966-1969

A dramatic event occurred in November 1968 when a Japan Airlines DC-8 missed its landing at the San Francisco airport and ended up in the San Francisco Bay. Bigge's team of divers and engineers arrived with heavy equipment, cranes and barges to recover the aircraft, successfully lifting, loading and transporting the jet to the United Airlines maintenance facility in south San Francisco. Amazingly, the plane was repaired and flew again.

Over the years the size and magnitude of Bigge's projects has increased. Bigge has had a hand in most of the large construction projects throughout California, including establishing a satellite branch to assist in the

development of the San Luis Dam, the California Aqueduct and the Oroville Dam, which in 1968 was the largest earth-filled dam in the country. Locally, Bigge has been a major player in many important construction sites. When BART was built, Bigge's cranes, rigging equipment and personnel transported and erected more than 3,500 girders for the rapid transit line. Bigge erected the precast concrete for the Oakland International Airport. Facilities for the Golden State Warriors, the Oakland A's and the Raiders were built with Bigge's cranes, as was the erection of the Oakland Sports Arena.

A recent Bigge challenge was its key role in the decommissioning of the Navy's top-secret spy ship, the Glomar Explorer, whose mission was to recover a Soviet nuclear submarine. After the recovery, the Glomar Explorer was mothballed until 1997 when it was towed to Hunter's Point Naval Shipyard to be converted to a deep-water drilling vessel. Bigge's biggest job was to remove the ship's heavy lift equipment. Bigge's engineers designed an ingenious system of hydraulic jacks and support platforms to remove the 1,600-ton hoisting gimbal. Their efforts earned Bigge its 10th "Outstanding Rigging Job of the Year" award.

When disaster strikes, Bigge responds. During the 1980s the company developed emergency response teams to deal with natural and manmade disasters and signed long-term contracts with local refineries, railroads and Caltrain. When the magnitude 7.3 Loma Prieta earthquake struck on October 17, 1989, part of Oakland's two-tiered Cypress Freeway collapsed. Victims were trapped under tons of rubble and debris, and the search for survivors went on for eight days. Within two hours Bigge was on the job with cranes, forklifts and emergency response personnel who installed beams and heavy jacks to prevent further collapse. Nine years later when the freeway was reconstructed, Bigge transported and erected the massive 500-ton replacement girders.

Whatever the challenge, Bigge is committed to and maintains the highest standards of quality. The company deals honestly and fairly with its customers, employees and business partners. In business for the long haul, the Settlemiers invest heavily in quality

Second- and third-generation Bigge management team, (left to right) Reid Settlemier, Weston Settlemier, Brock Settlemier, Marlene Settlemier, November 1999

assurance, safety standards, long-range planning, growth and employee training. As Bigge moves ahead, the company's management is aware that hoisting and rigging projects in the future will become ever more complex, competitive and risky. To prepare, Bigge has dedicated itself to mastering new techniques and implementing practices that will meet and exceed every challenge. ■

Changing bleachers from baseball to football in Oakland Coliseum — 9,000 seats in 22 hours

163

Madison Park REIT

Since 1985 real estate developer John Protopappas has been providing Bay Area residents with an attractive alternative to apartment dwelling — the upscale "live-work" space. Those familiar with New York's trendy SoHo district will recognize live-work spaces as large lofts typically found in converted warehouses or factories in urban areas. These spaces tend to have high ceilings, an abundance of natural light and large expanses of floor space and walls, appealing to people who want to exercise individuality in decorating or who need ample room to both live and work in their homes. Historically favored by artists, live-work spaces now appeal to a wide range of businesspeople and telecommuters.

As president and chief executive officer of the Madison Park REIT (Real Estate Investment Trust), Protopappas is head of the first real estate investment trust in the country to specialize in live-work spaces. According to Protopappas, the original live-work inhabitants were willing to put up with a lack of amenities to live in the abandoned warehouses and obsolete factory buildings that met their needs.

In most areas of the country, particularly San Francisco and New York, live-work spaces are condominium developments. The REIT is a natural outgrowth of the fact that live-work spaces have become state of the art and that new telecommunications options like high bandwidth Internet and World Wide Web services give live-work residents many more lifestyle choices than suburbia can offer. Some lofts in San Francisco's South of Market district (SOMA) are approaching the $1 million sales price. In fact, the area is so popular that in 1996 the City Planning Department found that of 532 residential units built in the city, 157 were in SOMA, giving it more construction activity by far than any other neighborhood in the city.

Protopappas, who has developed and managed several live-work space buildings in the Bay Area, believes that the growing interest in live-work makes it an even better investment than traditional apartments for the rental market. One of its many benefits is that live-work spaces are a means of revitalizing older neighborhoods. Suitable buildings for conversions are

predominantly found in larger urban areas, and city officials are cooperative because they want to preserve historic structures, as well as find a use for buildings that are now standing empty.

From the real estate investor's viewpoint, older buildings often are considered unwanted sites, resulting in lower purchase prices. The costs of rehabilitating live-work spaces are less than the cost of new construction, in part because one of the chief appeals of live-work space is the rough, unfinished, industrial look. Many tenants install their own improvements to highly personalize their spaces. This pride of ownership

The Oakland Tribune Tower, a historic landmark on the city's skyline, reopened in fall 1999.

The courtyard at the Exchange Studios building provides a welcome garden in an urban setting.

164

results in long-term tenants who tend to take better care of the property. The result for the investor is lower management costs and higher occupancy rates.

Protopappas became involved with live-work spaces almost by chance. He had purchased a 45,000-square-foot furniture outlet, which he intended to convert into self-storage spaces. But further analysis showed that the self-storage market was overbuilt, and he decided to go into the live-work space industry because of the growing demand for this type of space.

Today Protopappas is considered one of Oakland's live-work space pioneers and has spent much time working with the city to draft zoning regulations that recognize that the properties should come under neither residential nor industrial building codes, but deserve special regulations that reflect their eclectic mix of uses. The most successful developments, he has found, are those with 30 or more units. They give the developer economies of scale and are large enough to make common-area amenities, ranging from courtyards and fountains to laundry rooms, financially viable.

Tenants who rent properties in the Madison Park REIT receive an average of 1,200 square feet, and pay about $900 to $1000 per month. In Oakland, the average rent is $700 a month for conventional apartments. Protopappas is in the process of developing family-friendly live-work spaces. These larger units will measure about 1,600 square feet and offer separate bedrooms. Almost all of Protopappas' tenants are professionals, a third of whom work from home.

The cost of renovating an existing building comes to an average of $60 per square foot, compared to $105 per square foot to build a new complex from the ground up. Because the cost of purchasing and renovating a live-work space building is also lower than that of a comparable apartment building, Protopappas sees live-work spaces as a good vehicle for investors in a REIT. A Real Estate Investment Trust is similar to a mutual fund in that it allows investors to pool funds for participation in real estate ownership or financing. It is required by law to distribute 95 percent of its annual income to shareholders.

Some REITs invest in a variety of properties such as shopping centers, apartments, warehouses, office buildings and hotels. Others specialize in just one type of property. Currently, Madison Park REIT has 10 properties in its portfolio: seven in Oakland, and one

The Exchange Studios Building provides an ideal live-work setting for an architect.

each in Emeryville, Novato and Napa. Protopappas has his eye on several other properties in nearby areas including San Francisco, San Jose, Berkeley, Sacramento, Santa Rosa and San Leandro.

One of the most famous properties in the Madison Park REIT includes the historic Oakland Tribune Tower building, which was damaged in the 1989 Loma Prieta earthquake. With its prestigious landmark status from the Oakland City Landmark Advisory Board, the Tribune Tower and its clock have long been perhaps the best-known feature of Oakland's skyline.

Protopappas predicts a permanent change in the real estate apartment market and that the desire for such live-work rentals will continue to grow in the Bay Area and other markets such as New York, Chicago, Portland and Los Angeles. ■

A penthouse occupies the top floor of the American Bag Building in Oakland's Waterfront Warehouse District.

165

Elliott and Elliott Roofing Co.

A roof overhead is one of life's basic necessities, but who spends much time thinking about it? Out of sight and mostly out of mind, a roof generally doesn't become a priority until it wears out, the rains come and it starts leaking. That's when a good roofing contractor becomes a building's best friend. One of the Bay Area's best-known and most reliable roofing contractors is Elliott and Elliott Roofing Co., which has been on the job in the Bay Area since 1918. Thousands upon thousands of roofs later, it's clear that this family-owned firm is indeed a roof's friend in need.

The founder of Elliott and Elliott was Charles D. Elliott who was born in Boston in 1875. As a young man he worked as a ships carpenter at a time when vessels were still crafted from wood. At the end of the 19th century, Charles moved to San Francisco. There he met Nellie Crowton, a native of England. They were married in May 1899. A year later their son, Aaron Leslie Elliott, was born and three years after that, they had a daughter they named Grace. The family stayed in San Francisco until the 1906 earthquake when they migrated east to Oakland. Since Charles was an experienced carpenter, he found work as a roofer, installing wood shake roofs. He worked as an installer for 12 years and then joined forces with his young son and founded the company that still bears their two surnames.

> ## "Experience and hard work have earned Elliott and Elliott a sterling reputation through eight decades of the 20th century… "

Elliott and Elliott, which opened for business in 1918, has been handed down from father to son and is now in the capable hands of the sixth generation of Elliotts. The company's success has been built on the founders' strong commitment to the very highest standards: taking pride in their workmanship, dealing honestly with every client and providing service that is personal and trustworthy. Since roofers often come by their business through referrals, the Elliotts understood that their reputation was their most important asset. Their business grew in response to their integrity and the quality of the service they provided. This commitment to being the best became the cornerstone of what is a proud family tradition. Founder Charles Elliott believed passionately that customer satisfaction was the greatest satisfaction, and it is a point of pride for Elliott and Elliott that many of its current customers are children, grandchildren and even great-grandchildren of early clients.

Aaron Leslie Elliott was a young man when he went into business with his father and fell in love with an English girl named Maude Longman. Aaron and Maude were married in 1920 and stayed in Oakland for two years. In 1922 they moved to Santa Barbara to open their own roofing company. Six years later, when Charles was having financial difficulties in the Bay Area, the couple sold their business and returned to Oakland. Together they took on the task of restructuring Elliott and Elliott, and both worked very hard to ensure the business became a success. Aaron installed the roofs while Maude loaded up the trucks and kept the books. Over the years they became the parents of three boys, Charles, Leslie and Russ. Their son Leslie joined the family firm in 1940 and assumed leadership of the business after his parents died.

True to the Elliott family tradition, Leslie encouraged his son Robert to join the firm, and together they headed Elliott and Elliott until 1995. Then it was the turn of the fifth generation to run the company, and Robert's two sons, Robert and Mark, are at the helm of the venerable contracting firm. As a pair, Robert and Mark divide up the duties and take on those they most enjoy. Robert goes out on the job, supervising all aspects of roof construction. He's an old pro, having been at it since he was 13, and knows virtually everything about the roofing business. Mark runs the office, managing the company's marketing strategy and developing the software that handles the costing, invoicing and collection. He's also taken the firm into cyberspace and maintains Elliott and Elliott's Web site.

Back when Elliott and Elliott was founded, roofs were fairly simple. Today, technology has developed a wide array of roofing materials that are both safe and beautiful. Today's roofing materials are fire-safe, long-lasting and high-tech. Old materials have new treatments, and styles, textures and colors can be selected to complement the design of every building, both old and new. Elliott and Elliott is skilled in all areas. Carpenter Charles would be amazed by the wide range of choices that the company has available for roofing, including tar and gravel, wood singles, fire-treated shake, cedar shake shingles, composition shingles and tile. Elliott and Elliott also installs skylights, gutters, downspouts and plywood decking. The core of the company's business, some 70 percent, is in residential, but Elliott and Elliott has worked on substantial commercial projects as well. Many prominent Oakland residences and Bay Area businesses and institutions, including the University of California at Berkeley, are crowned by Elliott and Elliott roofs.

The company will tackle any roofing project, large or small, new or repair. In fact, it advertises itself as the one-stop source for all roofing needs. The first step is an inspection and evaluation, with a look at the total roofing system, not just the roof itself. That includes carefully analyzing the roof deck, the flashing, chimney caps, downspouts and gutters, vents and flues. Included in the potential scope of work is a full range of services that includes installation, maintenance and repair. The firm's in-house sheet metal shop custom fabricates flashings, leaders, gutters and accessories to meet every specification.

Careful files are kept so that all customers receive timely reminders about periodic roof inspections. No one understands better than Elliott and Elliott how the years and the elements can take their toll on a roof. Wind, rain, sun and pollution wear away at even the most advanced roofing materials. Left neglected, roofs will fail, usually in small, subtle ways that go unnoticed until severe damage forces a complete replacement. Elliott and Elliott offers timely inspections, which can correct problems early on and avoid expensive re-roofing. This attention to all aspects of a customer's roofing needs that has earned the firm the trust and repeat business of its many satisfied clients.

Experience and hard work have earned Elliott and Elliott a sterling reputation through eight decades of the 20th century, and both Robert and Mark are confident that the company's growth will continue well into the future. Robert is the father of sons Corey and Kevin, and Mark is the father of daughters Paige and Taylor. When the sixth generation of Elliotts grows up, the four will inherit a business that is deeply rooted in the history of Oakland and respected for its commitment to the highest standards of quality, service and innovation. ▧

The fleet of Elliott and Elliott trucks ready to roll in the 1940s

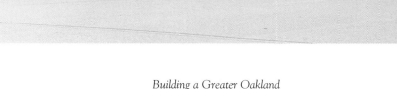

167

M.A. Lindquist Co., Inc.
Lindquist-Van Hook Co.

Construction. This one word sums up M.A. Lindquist and Lindquist-Van Hook Company. The combined companies give each construction project the priority treatment that it and the client deserve. The entire team is involved in every step of the process from feasibility studies and concept design, to the actual building and construction through occupancy and completion. Whether acting as general contractor or construction manager, creating a new structure or renovating an existing one, their approach is to ensure jobs are on time, on budget and of unsurpassed quality.

The firms of M.A. Lindquist Co., Inc. and Lindquist-Van Hook Co. are deeply committed to the Oakland community. Through their combined presence of investments and construction, the firms have made Oakland their home for doing business and investing in the community's future.

Projects are both privately and publicly financed and include such notable historic renovations as the Overland House, the seismic retrofit of the Paramount Theatre, the renovation of the Golden Gate Library and the Charles Greene African American Library & Museum.

Projects have included the Jack London Square Cinema, Pizzeria Uno restaurants, the Maintenance and Repair Center for East Bay Municipal Utility District and numerous class A office renovations and new construction.

Outside of the Oakland area, the firms have constructed facilities in Berkeley, Contra Costa County

Golden Gate Library

(Far right)
Clarence Van Hook and
Mark Lindquist

The Charles Greene
African American
Library & Museum

(Far right)
The Presidio Club
House Restaurant

The Presidio Club House

and San Francisco, including the recently completed Club House at the Presidio Golf Course with Arnold Palmer, the new Rental Car and Freight Facilities at the San Francisco International Airport, and numerous renovations and new construction for the Catholic Diocese of Oakland.

Mark Lindquist (a third-generation Oaklander) and Clarence Van Hook are both committed to the business community and its future. Outside of their business roles, the firms are involved with the Salvation Army of Oakland, the Oakland Black Business Development Corporation, the Oakland Chamber of Commerce and the Oakland Horseback Program for Disadvantaged Youth (Wildcat Canyon Ranch). Lindquist and Van Hook believe the city of Oakland is poised for greatness in the 21st century.

The goal and commitment of the two companies are to be a driving force for the betterment of the Oakland community, to be committed and inclusive with all subcontractors and vendors with whom they work and to make Oakland the best city that it can be. M.A. Lindquist Co., Inc. and Lindquist-Van Hook Co. welcome the opportunity to discuss their abilities and strengthening the vision for Oakland in the 21st century. ∎

Bostrom-Bergen Metal Products

For years after the 1989 Loma Prieta earthquake, Oakland's City Hall stood empty. An architectural showpiece, and the country's first high-rise government office building when it was completed in 1914, City Hall was rendered a ghost town. Once a monument to civic achievement, it was now a monument to nature's wrath.

The earthquake left the building structurally compromised. A huge crack ran the width of the signature clock tower. The building was red-tagged and evacuated the day after the disaster. Pragmatism suggested the building be razed and a new one erected in its place. The Federal Emergency Management Agency (FEMA) favored this course of action. Oakland's citizens, however, favored sentiment over pragmatism. They wanted to preserve the history and restore the grandeur of City Hall, even though restoration would cost 50 percent more than reconstruction. After months of discussion with FEMA, sentiment prevailed. The citizens of Oakland got their way.

Bostrom-Bergen Metal Products helped restore Oakland City Hall to its 1914 splendor.

One of the companies they turned to for help in rebuilding City Hall was Bostrom-Bergen Metal Products, which was only fitting since Bostrom-Bergen helped build modern-day Oakland in the first place.

Founded in 1960 by Oakland residents Milton Bostrom, a longtime ironworker, and Donald Bergen, a young businessman, Bostrom-Bergen provided the fabricated steel that fueled much of Oakland's growth in the 1960s, 70s and 80s. In fact, Bostrom built the company's original fabrication plant himself.

The technology of steel fabrication has changed in the four decades since. Bostrom's original fabrication plant was replaced by one with automated processes, and newer welding and forming equipment. The company has since added another fabrication plant in Fresno and has sister companies Meddco Metals in Hayward and Bergen Southwest in El Paso, Texas. What has remained unchanged is Bostrom-Bergen's ability to produce customized materials upon demand — in sizes ranging from a one-square-foot anchorage, to a five-ton weldment, to a 10-ton, 60-foot beam. If it needs to be formed, bent, drilled, cut or welded to exacting specifications, Bostrom-Bergen is able to comply.

This was the expertise Oakland sought when Bostrom-Bergen Metal Products got involved in helping the city recover from the latest great earthquake, while helping it prepare for the next. The company took on several seismic retrofitting projects in the wake of the quake, but City Hall provided one its bigger challenges. Bit by bit, the historic building was raised off its foundation by enormous jacks. That's when Bostrom-Bergen went to work — with 15,000 man-hours at the fabrication shop and 60,000 man-hours in the field. The company packed thousands of tons of structural steel beneath City Hall. Then it installed "isolators," a bed of shock absorbers upon which the building rests. The isolators will allow the building to shimmy and sway during subsequent earthquakes, releasing stress instead of absorbing it.

The City Hall project totaled $85 million. When it was finished in 1997, the building stood, as it had 83

Oakland residents can see Bostrom-Bergen's work all around them — even at Children's Fairyland, where the company refurbished the theme park's trolleys with donated material and labor. The work of Bostrom-Bergen's 100 employees is all over Northern California as well, from the Diablo Canyon and Rancho Seco nuclear power plants, to Folsom Prison, to various schools, hospitals and office buildings.

Bostrom-Bergen is a regional company with a local conscience. After 40 years it remains committed to building Oakland's future as well as rebuilding the city's past. ◼

Once Oakland City Hall was raised off its foundation, Bostrom-Bergen installed thousands of tons of custom-manufactured materials and a bed of shock-absorbing isolators.

years earlier, as a shining example of Beaux-Arts-style architecture and as a symbol of the city's spirit. While it may have been Bostrom-Bergen's best work in helping Oakland rise from the rubble, it wasn't the company's only effort toward that end.

Among Bostrom-Bergen's contributions to the East Bay are: helping to retrofit the venerable Capwell's building; the Woodrow and San Pablo hotels; the area between the two terminals at Oakland's International Airport; and several buildings on the University of California's Berkeley campus.

Bostrom-Bergen also helped San Francisco renovate its quake-damaged City Hall. The San Francisco landmark, built to replace a building destroyed in the 1906 earthquake, remained open after the Loma Prieta temblor. But it was clear it wouldn't withstand another significant jolt. San Francisco City Hall was renovated at a cost of $181 million. Bostrom-Bergen contributed 2,500 tons of material and 170,000 man-hours to the project.

Bostrom-Bergen is still in the business of constructing buildings from scratch. Under current owners Douglas Johnson, who joined the company in 1962, and David Olson, who came aboard in 1970, the company furnished structural steel and miscellaneous iron for the Golden State Warriors' new practice facility. It also helped build a heliport at Children's Hospital, the largest pediatric facility between Los Angeles and Seattle.

The Golden State Warriors' new practice facility was built with the aid of structural steel and miscellaneous iron supplied by Bostrom-Bergen.

Thanks to seismic retrofitting by Bostrom-Bergen, Oakland's Woodrow Hotel is braced for future earthquakes.

171

McGuire and Hester

Californians who drink the clean water that comes from the great reservoirs of the Sierra would be surprised to learn how two partners from Ireland contributed to the construction of their state's great aqueducts.

Michael J. McGuire emigrated from Ireland in the 1890s. After having been a successful U.S. Treasury Bonds fund-raiser and union member with the boiler-makers, McGuire decided to start his own construction business in 1926. He began installing sewers for new and existing residences in Oakland, Berkeley and Piedmont.

In 1931 he took on a partner, another immigrant from Ireland by the name of Mike Hester, and extended the scope of the company's operations until they covered all the Bay Area counties. At first, they worked for other contractors, gaining a good reputation for drainage work on such major Depression-era projects as the Alameda County Courthouse in Oakland. By 1935 they quit using their 1921 Buick touring car as a mobile tool shed when they bought their first pickup truck.

McGuire and Hester grading equipment finishes off a recent railroad track replacement project for Caltrain in Fremont.

In the early 60s, when suburban Mountain View was mostly farms, McGuire and Hester laid huge drain pipes as the city braced for growth.

Their first headquarters was in Michael J. McGuire's Oakland house at 14th Street and Hopkins. The company moved in 1938 to a 16-acre parcel at the foot of 66th Avenue in East Oakland. The waterfront property, surrounded by dairy farms, ran down to San Leandro Bay. It was common to see cattle barges floating down nearby Damon Slough, their unsuspecting passengers bobbing to Butcher Town in San Francisco. Today, much of the acreage is covered by the Alameda County Coliseum.

During World War II, the two partners quickly became major Bay Area players, laying all the underground utilities at the massive Oakland Army Base and nearby Naval Supply Depot, as well as large military projects at Mare Island, Hamilton Field and Merced. The company also installed a section of the massive Hetch Hetchy water system for the city of San Francisco.

The partnership continued to grow, and in 1947, McGuire and Hester was incorporated. In 1948 Michael J. McGuire passed away and Mike Hester subsequently purchased his remaining interest in the firm.

In the 1950s the property was split as the Nimitz Freeway (Interstate 880) pushed south to the suburbs, and the Port of Oakland condemned a portion for development. McGuire and Hester clung to its remnant until 1988, when it moved to its current location on Railroad Avenue, a 4.5-acre plot just south of the Oakland Coliseum.

In the 1950s and 1960s as the Bay Area spread, so, too, did McGuire and Hester expand its operations in Northern California. This growth was assisted by the addition of the second generation, Joseph M. Hester and Robert E. Hester, sons of Mike Hester.

In 1962 McGuire and Hester constructed the prototype of the California Aqueduct Canal — 10 miles of canal and appurtenances around the city of Livermore supplying water to the Santa Clara Valley. It was on this project that McGuire and Hester developed methods and techniques for trimming and lining canals that would later show up in major water projects in California and worldwide.

In the early 1970s, under the leadership of Joseph M. Hester, the company's capabilities gradually expanded into all types of underground construction, as well as grading and paving, reinforced concrete structures and mechanical work. The company undertook major landmark urban projects in the 1970s and 1980s, including the Market Street beautification in San Francisco, from the Embarcadero to 7th Street; the Powell Street Cable Car Mall and turntable; Napa Downtown Mall and Clock Tower; and the City of Concord Plaza.

In 1988 McGuire and Hester received the prestigious "Meeting the Challenge of the Difficult Job" award from the Associated General Contractors of California. The recognition honored the company's work for the Nevada Irrigation District, which consisted of installing 1,700 feet of 66-inch reinforced concrete pipe on a 45-degree steep mountain side.

Until his death in 1991, Mike Hester came to work every day and had a lifelong avocation as a philanthropist. He helped found Oakland's Saint Vincent de Paul Society soup kitchen. Today his son, Joseph, carries on the family tradition of philanthropy. He heads the Michael and Maureen Hester Foundation, which sponsors education-oriented projects, aimed primarily at Oakland's inner-city children. From its inception in the 1960s, the foundation has contributed almost $3 million to various projects. In 1998 Joseph Hester received the "Scout of the Year" Award for his and his wife's dedication to emergency foster care to which they have taken in more than 300 children on an emergency basis.

Joseph Hester has also been very involved with the construction industry. He has served as district manager and chairman for the Association of General Contractors, and on the board of the Teamsters' Health and Welfare Trust for 15 years, where he also served as chairman. He also helped found an organization to provide representation to the underground contractors in the Bay Area. Today that organization is known as Engineering & Utility Contractors Association (EUCA).

In 1990 the third generation took on the daily operations of the company. Michael R. Hester, son of Joseph M. Hester, succeeded as president.

Under Michael R. Hester's leadership, McGuire and Hester developed a reputation for emergency work. This reputation involved the company in the repair of such major catastrophes as the collapse of the Cypress Freeway in the 1989 Loma Prieta earthquake, the Oakland Hills firestorm of 1991 and various floods and landslides within the Bay Area during the "El Niño" winter of 1998. The company's emergency

Work proceeds on a state-sponsored outfall storm drain to carry runoff into the ocean near Half Moon Bay.

response capabilities resulted in several of its personnel being asked to join an elite national search and rescue team that went to Northridge in Southern California following the earthquake there in 1994.

The company expanded its underground division through its involvement with numerous microtunneling projects throughout the Bay Area. This included one of the first microtunneling projects to be performed in Northern California, the Everglades Sewer Rehabilitation Project for Union Sanitary District completed in 1993.

Newly laid asphalt marks the path of a multiuse recreational trail for the East Bay Regional Parks District in Pittsburg.

The legacy of McGuire and Hester is considerable and embedded in Oakland's history. Today's management continues to play a strong role in the industry. Michael R. Hester has been active in EUCA, serving as its president in 1996. Robert Doud, chief financial officer, currently serves as a board member of EUCA and as a trustee of the Operating Engineers Trust Funds. McGuire and Hester, with more than 150 dedicated employees, looks forward to future involvement with the fortunes of Oakland and the Bay Area. ■

173

Meyer Plumbing Supply

For some, the measure of a great civilization like that of ancient Rome is its ability to have indoor plumbing. A mere 150 years after California's birth in crude mining camps, the state has become the seventh-largest economy of the world, and plumbing is taken for granted. While most people never think about it, plumbing is an essential comfort and marks not only civilization, but the milestones of history throughout the ages. Similarly, the origin and expansion of Meyer Plumbing Supply mirror the growth and development of Oakland.

In 1904, on the porch of a small farmhouse in the Napa Valley, a man put his arm around the shoulders of his then 17-year-old son. As they gazed over the green rolling hills, his father shook his head and handed his son a $10 gold piece. "There is no future for you here, boy. Best get off to San Francisco and make your fortune there."

W.J. (Jack) Meyer hitchhiked and walked all the way to San Francisco, the likes of which he had never seen before. It bustled with carts and wagons, dirt roads, three-story buildings, loose women, and ships bringing goods to the stores lining Market Street. Stunned by the sights surrounding him, Jack stopped to pet some dray horses hitched to the side of a warehouse. A man burst out of the building and asked Jack if he knew anything about horses. Jack responded boldly that he did, and R.W. Kinney hired him on the spot to work in the warehouse of R.W. Kinney Company, a plumbing supply store.

Jack had begun to build a new life when the great San Francisco Earthquake of 1906 demolished the building. Undaunted, R.W. Kinney moved to Oakland across the bay and took the young man from Napa Valley with him. Jack stayed with Kinney for 21 years and learned the business inside and out until he started a series of partnerships first with Cyrus W. Abbott in 1925, then Frank Wirthinger in 1932 — with a $5,000 loan, a large safe and 5,000 square feet of

W.J. Meyer (left) and Frank Wirthinger, 1944

George Meyer, founder of Meyer Plumbing Supply, 1970s

warehouse space provided by R.W. Kinney himself. Meyer and Wirthinger Wholesale Plumbing Supply was located in the center of town on the corner of Ninth and Franklin streets in Oakland. At the time, wooden sidewalks bordered the streets, and despite the Depression, the area boomed in new construction.

Meyer Plumbing Supply emerged in 1953, when Jack's son, George R. Meyer, and his wife Geraldine (Jerry), bought Wirthinger's share and the Franklin Street building.

In 1978 George sold the Franklin Street building to the Bay Area Rapid Transit District (BART), which planned to tunnel under the building. George moved his store and warehouse to Second Street near Jack London Square to a building previously occupied by a roofing company.

One afternoon George, who always took Fridays off to play golf, left the moving of the store to his son, John, and a few of his friends, all home from college. The scruffy lads, working over summer vacation to earn school money, had decided to move the old R.W. Kinney safe to the new store. They inched the safe, a four-foot-high cube of thick iron onto the prongs of a forklift and while one boy drove, the others accompanied it on foot, all the while trading raucous laughter and jokes. No one, not even the police questioned the boys-who-could-have-been-thieves, although the caper was reported in the *Berkeley Gazette*. The safe is still in use at Meyer Plumbing Supply.

In 1983 Jed and Helen Myall and partners Bud and Barbara Weymouth purchased the business and building. Jed's father, an Oakland-born native, had worked in the plumbing supply business. Jed himself joined the industry after graduating from Arizona State University. Jed's knowledge and Bud's accounting experience combined to give Meyer Plumbing Supply a solid business foundation.

A year before purchasing Meyer Plumbing Supply, Jed had started American Plumbing Supply International (APSI) in San Jose. After acquiring the building, Jed relocated APSI to Oakland where it occupied separate offices in the Meyer warehouse. Together the businesses served both the domestic and international markets from one large facility. Location of the business and warehouse near the Port of Oakland was key to building the international component. Today the international company has offices in Singapore, Guam, Hong Kong and Shanghai, China, and in Manila, Philippines. The international operations enable foreign contractors access to American plumbing products.

Over the years Meyer Plumbing Supply has changed its mode of operation to accommodate shifting competition. With the advent of home center markets where large warehouse-like stores carry plumbing and other home building and repair items, Meyer has become more selective with its product. An authorized American Standard dealer, it has gradually shifted to upscale products and imported European products. Its warehouse is approximately 35,000 square feet with a

6,000-square-foot yard meaning convenient and quick loading for contractors.

Meyer Plumbing Supply will keep abreast of changing technologies and adapt its business accordingly. In the future there will be greater emphasis on water conservation, cleanliness, handicap accessibility and design. More people will want low-flush toilets, infrared, sensor-operated faucets, heated toilet seats, and sleek, durable designs incorporating the features of French, Italian and German state-of-the-art products. To accommodate these demands, Meyer Plumbing Supply is building a Web site linking customers with manufacturers and eventually e-commerce.

Since 1906 Meyer Plumbing Supply has always been a family-operated business. Meyer Plumbing Supply is a member of the Western Suppliers Association (WSA) and the Oakland Metropolitan Chamber of Commerce. It donates annually to the Leukemia fund raiser sponsored by the local KGO radio and television station, and to Oakland charities. Involvement in the community includes helping disaster survivors. In 1991 after the East Bay Hills Fire, Meyer Plumbing Supply joined with a number of other businesses to provide a one-stop exhibit to assist fire survivors identify resources for rebuilding in the charred zones.

Meyer Plumbing Supply is proud to have employees who have been with the company for 25-30 years, collectively bringing more than 150 years of plumbing experience and knowledge to assist contractors in making the right decisions for their projects.

Contractors and individuals alike shop at Meyer not only for the quality products, but for the quality service. At Meyer, a contractor can rely on good advice, because he is dealing with good friends who take pride in offering good service in a friendly, fun environment. ■

Warehouse employees, c. 1979, (top row, left to right): Bob Mesa, Brian McCole. (bottom row, left to right): Bob Floyd, Fred Everingham, Steve Mitchell, Charlie Oaks, Don Volker; (foreground) Don Reynolds

(Left to right) Peter Krainock, Jed Myall, Bud Weymouth and Julie Apana, 1998

175

Broadmoor Electric Company

Broadmoor Electric Company, located in San Leandro's industrial district, is a woman-owned, second-generation electrical contracting firm that specializes in commercial, retail, residential, government, institutional and industrial projects. Broadmoor, the second electrical company — and now the oldest electrical contracting firm — in San Leandro, serves Northern California with a focus on the East Bay, San Francisco and San Jose. Broadmoor handles any size project, from a job under $100 for a residential customer to a $3 million contract for a large commercial or industrial concern.

Broadmoor is handling the electrical remodel of the landmark Oakland Tribune Tower Complex.

Broadmoor Electric Company began operation on July 13, 1945, in the Broadmoor area of San Leandro, with a focus on repair of major appliances, refrigerators and washing machines. In August 1945, Art Souza bought the interests of John Davis, one of the original owners. He started a new partnership for major appliance repair and began electrical contracting. In December 1945 the business was moved to another East 14th Street location, and a franchise was acquired for Hotpoint appliances, Bendix radios, Youngstown steel cabinets and Prestoline electric ranges.

The company was incorporated on March 10, 1948.

Patricia L. Raposo (far right) and the staff of Broadmoor Electric Company

In May 1948, Broadmoor engineered the moves of two local companies — and it was these projects that shaped the company's new direction, with a focus more on electrical contracting than the sale of appliances. The company continued to expand its operation, and in 1959, signed its first $1 million contract with Continental Can Co. for projects in San Jose, Oakland, Pittsburg and San Leandro. In February 1965, Broadmoor purchased the property on Republic Avenue where it has since been located.

Broadmoor's vice president, Merced Souza, who had served the company for 41 years, died in May 1986, and on January 1, 1987, Art Souza, president and founder, retired from the company. (He died in January 1999 at the age of 93.) Souza's daughter, Patricia L. Raposo, who came into the company in 1960, became president and CEO on January 1, 1987.

Broadmoor operates two divisions — the maintenance/repair division, which performs small service calls on a scheduled and emergency basis, and the construction division, which accommodates new building construction, including retrofits and remodels. Broadmoor's expertise is wide-ranging. In addition to design/build capabilities from a highly skilled and experienced staff, Broadmoor personnel has the expertise needed for technical installations of Point of Sale (POS), Uninterruptable Power Supply (UPS), programmable controllers, fiber optics, and Local Area Network (LAN) systems for offices and plants. Broadmoor can also handle the needs of many local manufacturers in industries such as food processing, plastic extrusion, plastic and metal injection molders, and general and specialty machine shop work.

One memorable Broadmoor project involved installing temporary power in the Oakland City Hall tower, damaged by the 1989 Loma Prieta earthquake. Broadmoor handles numerous projects for Albertson's, Inc., for both new construction and remodels. For Sysco Foods, Broadmoor designed and built a complete refrigeration project, including electric pallet jack battery chargers and 36-volt chargers.

Broadmoor handled all the electrical needs for the new San Jose Repertory Theatre (1998); recently completed a $1.9 million remodel and renovation project for the California College of Arts & Crafts' San Francisco campus (formerly a Greyhound maintenance repair building); and is completing a $1.3 million remodel project for the landmark Oakland Tribune Tower Complex. ■

176

Eandi Metal Works

More than 70 years after Jack Eandi, a renowned ornamental ironworker, founded Eandi Metal Works in 1928, the business is still known for its quality ironwork, whether ornamental or structural.

Jack Eandi was born in 1900 in Turin, Italy, and came with his parents to Oakland in 1905. After finishing the eighth grade, he served an apprenticeship at Romak & Stubbe to become a journeyman ironworker. When the United States entered World War I, Eandi went to work for a local shipyard. Despite being only 17, his skill led him to be named a foreman, responsible for engine-room floors. After the war, he returned to work at Romak & Stubbe. In 1923 he married Hazel, whose parents were Welsh immigrants.

Eandi Metal Works was first located in a shop behind the Eandi home. Neighbors complained about the noise, so Jack Eandi sank his savings into an old foundry building on the corner of 23rd Avenue and East 11th Street, and there he produced the stylized ornamental ironwork for which he became nationally renowned.

During World War II, he shut down his business and engaged in furthering the war effort by building stairs for ships. When he resumed his business, he enlarged the building. In 1956 his son Roger, who had earned a civil engineering degree from San Jose State University, came into the business. The first two structural bays in the shop were erected, and the business began producing both structural and ornamental ironwork.

Jack Eandi retired in 1965, and Roger Eandi took over the business. The last two structural bays were built, and the building now covered the entire block and surrounding warehouses. Roger Eandi operated the expanding business

with the aid of his vice president, Ed Bolio. During the 1980s, third-generation Eandis began joining the family business. Joseph Eandi joined as field crane operator; his twin brother, Jonathan Eandi, also joined. After serving an apprenticeship with an outside firm, Jeff Eandi, a licensed civil engineer, joined the company on a full-time basis in 1991. John Clark (Lisa Eandi's husband) joined the structural shop in 1981. Lewis Eandi, Lisa's twin brother, joined the business in the early 1990s as a field ironworker. Today Roger Eandi is president and CEO; Jeff and Joe Eandi are executive vice presidents; Lewis Eandi is project manager; and John Clark, structural shop superintendent.

Jack Eandi's renown as an artisan of quality, creative ornamental ironwork and as a nationwide consultant has given the company a firm reputation for quality work that continues to the present day. His stylized ornamental ironwork is still found on many Oakland businesses and residences, and his legacy has attracted outstanding mechanics and artisans from Italy.

Eandi Metal Works has carried out many jobs in Oakland and beyond. In the remodel of the Monterey Bay Aquarium, Eandi created the elliptical-shaped anchovy exhibit. In the first Oakland Airport building stage, Eandi Metal Works created the first five gates that had jetways. Eandi has also handled several ancillary projects for the Oakland Coliseum, including handrails and bleachers' support structures. Present Eandi projects in downtown Oakland include historical remodels of Swan's Market and The Rotunda. Eandi also has the contract to create fire escape stairs and conduct some seismic retrofitting for the Oakland Tribune Tower Complex renovation project. ■

Roger Eandi participated in the design of the landmark bell tower for St. Paschal's Baylon Church in Oakland.

ManuFacturinG & DisTRibutioN

In addition to producing exceptional goods for individuals and industry, Oakland manufacturing and distribution companies provide employment for area residents.

Wood Tech, Inc.

Wood Tech, Inc. is a minority-owned company that provides wood furniture solutions for high-end commercial businesses in the Bay Area and nationwide. Wood Tech has developed a line of flexible wood case-goods and seating, pre-engineered so that the size, configuration and edge detail of the standard case-good furniture can be customized through simple adjustments to suit a customer's particular needs. With five levels of pricing, Wood Tech has the solution to fit almost any company's budget.

Wood Tech, Inc. was founded by Hector R. Castaneda and Juan Diego Figueroa in December 1993, when the business was incorporated. Castaneda and Figueroa, as principals, completely self-funded the company at the time of its origin. Wood Tech, Inc. began serving the public in August 1994.

Bringing Expertise and Experience to the Table

Both owners were born in Mexico. Castaneda was born January 2, 1948, in Ciudad Guzman, Jalisco, where he grew to adulthood. He received a degree in accounting in 1962 from the Instituto Comercial in Ciudad Guzman and came to the United States in 1971. He began work for Modern Mode, became a supervisor and gained considerable experience during

Juan Diego Figueroa, principal of Wood Tech, Inc.

Hector Castaneda, principal of Wood Tech, Inc.

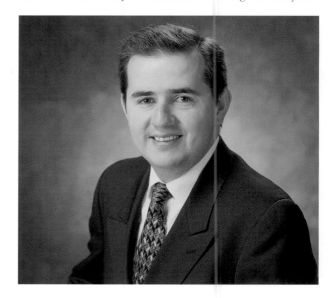

the 17 years he was with that company. Castaneda then became affiliated with another local manufacturer, where he was a major stockholder. During the five years he was with that company, he gained many management skills, and that, added to his prior experience, made him adroit in handling quality control and finishes.

Juan Diego Figueroa was born February 3, 1964, in Guadalajara, Mexico, and spent his first 13 years in the town of Atoyac, Jalisco. He received a bachelor's degree in general education from the Universidad Autonoma de Guadalajara in 1981. Figueroa came to the United States in 1982. During his first year in the United States, he worked at a variety of jobs before landing what he terms his first "real" job in 1983 with Modern Mode, where he started as an operator assistant. Both there and at another company by which he was later employed, Figueroa quickly gained new skills until he became an expert in making facilities capable of handling custom wood furniture projects. In his last position before starting Wood Tech, Inc. with Hector Castaneda, he was the person in charge of all custom work, responsible for engineering, purchasing materials and construction.

When Castaneda and Figueroa decided to begin their own business, they brought to the table the expertise needed to succeed. Their skills and experience complemented each other, for both had become

180

proficient in handling the two most difficult parts of the contract wood furniture business — Figueroa as a master of custom capabilities and Castaneda as an expert in the area of quality control and finished product. The two men became equal partners in their business.

Castaneda and Figueroa began their business in Oakland, as they knew the good labor force they wanted to attract was available locally. Wood Tech created many opportunities for skilled workers, and all of its present supervisors and key employees had previously gained experience working for Modern Mode. (This company has since gone out of business.) As the saying goes, "experience matters," and in the case of Wood Tech, Inc., this maxim proved true. The company's reputation was gained not by happenstance but by its proven abilities — in creating beautiful, functional office furniture, in working well with noted architects, and in its ability to comply with stringent industry codes and regulations.

A Debt-Free Operation

The business was completely self-financed at the onset and is completely debt-free today. Beginning with only a small staff, the company has experienced phenomenal growth in less than five years in operation. In each of its second through fourth years, Wood Tech doubled its sales. The company achieved a long-desired goal of topping the million-dollar mark in one month's sales in 1999.

In January 1998, the owners purchased the facility on Malat Street it had leased since 1994. In 1999 they completed a substantial addition to the existing building. As the business is debt-free, the owners/stockholders are able to refinance their working capital and other company needs.

Top-Quality Products

Wood Tech produces only high-quality products at competitive prices. It has accomplished a competitive edge, pricewise, by manufacturing efficiently with the least amount of waste and employee overtime.

Wood Tech uses only top-quality architectural veneers in which all the patterns are alike. This use of matching patterns produces a pleasing effect for the viewer. While the company deals primarily with five standard wood species in the contract furniture designs — cherry, maple, white oak, mahogany and

Wood Tech, Inc.

walnut — it has the capability of buying any exotic veneer that's available on the market from local or other West Coast suppliers. Designers who might desire furniture finished in Brazilian burls, bird's-eye maple, macore, beech, eucalyptus or zebrawood, for example, would find that Wood Tech, Inc. can satisfy their needs. The company uses the best-quality lacquers and finishes on all its products.

Cherry, maple and white oak are the three woods presently most popular with architects, designers and businesspeople, but tastes change. In the 1970s — just three decades ago — architects and designers adhered to the current trend by using mostly white oak and walnut; in the 1980s mahogany became the "in" wood. Yet within the five standard woods that Wood Tech uses are many choices for customers. Those choosing cherry wood, by way of example, may select from among these different shades of the wood: warm, deep, bourbon, merlot, harvest, natural and caffe.

Wood Tech works with professional, established architectural and design firms to create the lines it offers.

Inside the shop at Wood Tech, Inc.

181

Current lines are known by the names of Rival, Arcos, Monterey, Woodside and Piedmont. One award-winning designer Wood Tech has collaborated with is Wayne Morgan, who has established many designs for well-known companies in this industry. David Ebert of Fee Munson Ebert has created the Interval series conference table, square chair designs and 800 U Series chair. Wood Tech is also proud to work with other designers and prominent architectural firms such as Gensler in other major projects.

Wood Tech made all the furniture for San Francisco City Hall's private executive offices.

Wood Tech is well known for its talent and skills to produce one-of-a-kind custom furniture pieces.

Customer Service

A true commitment to deliver the furniture on time and free of defects has been the driving force to Wood Tech's success. Wood Tech has maintained a high level of quality and on-time deliveries for several reasons. First, to remain competitive, Wood Tech must be as good as its word — it must deliver what it sells. By accomplishing this goal, Wood Tech has won the confidence and trust of its clients. A teamwork relationship between Wood Tech and a client allows supplier and customer to work together

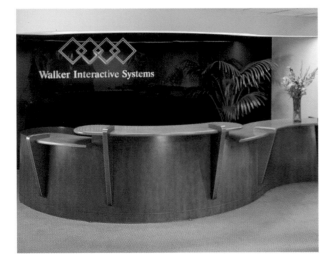

to ensure that the client's goals are met satisfactorily. By maintaining its commitment, Wood Tech has secured long-standing relationships with clients. In addition, because both Castaneda and Figueroa actively participate in the manufacturing process, working side by side with the other employees, they have created a high level of respect among the employees. Product quality has remained consistently high due to the ongoing scrutiny of owners and staff.

Notable San Francisco Projects

For Duty Free Shopping (DFS) in San Francisco, working with David Ebert and utilizing its renowned capabilities of providing custom furniture, Wood Tech combined metal, glass and wood in creating DFS' reception station. The design called for an exotic veneer. Wood Tech used quarter-figure beech. Workers used sandblasted custom-shaped glass for the transaction top, which is supported by T-brackets attached to vertical panels. Moreover, Wood Tech created furniture for DFS' boardroom, including a conference table, credenza, a special video equipment cabinet, and a counter shelf to hold decorative items such as cut flowers. Wood Tech also created chairs for the lobby.

Wood Tech secured a job for Towers Perrin in San Francisco through one of the top five architects in the country because of its successful history with this architectural firm. The client was looking for a simple-yet-unique solution for its private offices, which the architect created, and Wood Tech was able to produce the furniture at a competitive price. Wood Tech was also asked to create a tower to fit in with another manufacturer's system, a challenging request requiring Wood Tech to match the other manufacturer's veneer colors on 135 units and give the appearance that they came from the same manufacturing facility.

One recent notable Wood Tech project was for San Francisco City Hall, which Wood Tech secured due to its ability to manipulate its existing product while also creating a cost-effective solution. Wood Tech worked this project side by side with city architects well over a year before the furniture order was placed. As part of the massive retrofitting and refurbishing of this noted landmark, completed in 1998, Wood Tech created all the desks, bookcases and credenzas for 100 private offices and workstations, and conference tables for 15 conference rooms. This project called for reproduction

182

desks and, because the rooms contained a great deal of refurbished natural wood moldings, the furniture Wood Tech created had to match the existing color. Wood Tech employed the Arcos series of furniture, designed by Wayne Morgan. This was one of the first projects in which the Arcos Series was introduced.

The Monterey Series, with contrast stain finish, is Wood Tech's standard product.

Projects on the Peninsula

For Gunderson Dettmer Stough Law Firm, in Menlo Park, Wood Tech provided furnishings for 200 private offices and workstations. On this project, Wood Tech again worked with Gensler as architect. In addition, Wood Tech has handled a number of projects for other Peninsula-based companies. One project was for Applied Materials, in Santa Clara, for which Wood Tech furnished the private offices. Another project was creating conference room and private offices furniture for Spieker Properties, based in Palo Alto. Wood Tech also landed the contract to create the reception area and conference room furniture for Synopsys, in Mountain View — and in its Austin, Texas, office.

For Silicon Graphics, which operates from a campus-like setting in Sunnyvale, Wood Tech recently created conference room furniture in maple. Silicon Graphics is a long-time customer. 3Com, a major computer company located in Santa Clara, has also been a long-time continuing client of Wood Tech. Wood Tech has made about 100 conference tables and credenzas for 3Com, of maple and oak. As both Silicon Graphics and 3Com are continually expanding their facilities, Wood Tech is repeatedly called upon to provide additional furniture. It secured the $500,000 contract to furnish a new Palo Alto medical center and was awarded this project because of its competitive price and ability to meet the required tight lead times.

Arcos Series Nets Wood Tech a Major Award

In June 1999, at Neocon, the largest contract furniture show in the United States, Wood Tech entered its Arcos Series. Out of 980 entrants, Wood Tech received the Silver Award for "The Best of Neocon" for exceptional design and quality. This prestigious award, given by the design segment of the furniture industry, IFMA and the IIDA, will help Wood Tech gain more national recognition.

The Arcos Series, the 1999 Neocon Show Silver Award winner

Doing Business on a National Level

Wood Tech has been primarily a Bay Area manufacturer since its beginning, five years ago. In 1998 Wood Tech began making plans to expand its market nationally. This national presence started with a limited distribution to test the waters and to find the company's niche. In 1999 Wood Tech hired several representatives around the country. While realizing that its first five successful years have come from Bay Area business, Wood Tech is forecasting that approximately 20 percent of its volume will soon be coming from outside the Bay Area. ■

183

Hansen *good* Coffee

Since its inception more than 100 years ago, John Hansen & Sons Coffee Company has been a family-owned-and-operated business — probably the oldest such coffee roasting company in the Western United States.

Johan "John" Cilius Hansen emigrated from Denmark in 1888 and eventually settled in Pleasanton, California. He operated a tavern called Big John's, catering mostly to the local farmers and dairy workers in the area, on what is now Hopyard Road. In 1894 "Big John" sold his tavern and moved his family to Oakland. With several partners, John purchased Monarch Coffee and Spice Mills, which became the forerunner of what has become known as Hansen *good* Coffee. Originally a small, wholesale grocery-type operation located on the shores of the Oakland estuary (which is now part of Lake Merritt), it catered to the needs of the wooden sailing ships of that era.

Hansen, noted for his high-quality fresh-roasted coffee, struck out on his own in 1902. He purchased Monarch Coffee and Spice Mills from his partners and remained sole owner until 1917. At that point, he brought his sons Carl and Rudolph (Rudy) into the business, renaming it John Hansen & Sons, the name it retains to this day. At that time, Carl had been gaining experience as a "tea taster" for MJB Coffee Company, and Rudy was working at Hills Bros. Coffee Company. Both companies were then located in San Francisco. Carl's skills as a tea taster were so highly regarded that, upon learning of his intention to leave MJB and join his father's business, the owner of MJB offered to double his salary to retain his services. Nevertheless, both Carl and Rudy opted to join the family business. Several years later, John built the roasting facility at 4th and Clay streets, where the company still operates to the present day. The Hansen family believes that this establishes Hansen *good* Coffee as the oldest continuously family-owned-and-operated coffee roasting company in the Western United States.

After John's death in 1937, Carl, the elder son, headed-up the operations at Hansen *good* Coffee. Carl demonstrated a proclivity toward innovation and inventiveness. He was awarded several patents for original tea and coffee packaging processes. But perhaps his best-known invention was in 1933, when he created a new vacuum-packing process that produced a positive pressure inside the coffee can that allowed the consumer to test for freshness by pressing a "button-like" feature on the container's lid. He named this innovation "Dome Top... Press To Test," and it was exclusive to Hansen *good* Coffee. The patent rights were later purchased by Standard Brands Company and used on Chase and Sanborn coffee products after that company settled a patent infringement lawsuit in Hansen's favor.

Carl's interests extended beyond the coffee business. He was a fine athlete and specialized in the sport of handball, which he continued to play well into his 70s. Through his promotion of sporting events as a member of Oakland's highly regarded Athens Athletic Club, he was elected to the presidency of the AAU. This was the premier regulatory

Founder John Hansen with two unidentified employees behind sales counter, c. 1933

Earliest reference to vacuum-packed coffee — in 1922 Monarch Coffee and Spice Company was located just up the street from its present location.

184

organization for Amateur Sports in the United States at that time. He went on to become a member of the U.S. Olympic Committee where in this capacity he officiated at track and field events for the Melbourne (1956), Rome (1960), Tokyo (1964) and 1968 Mexico City summer Olympic games.

Early in its history, the company was well known for its daily deliveries to restaurants, cafes and the mom-and-pop grocery stores of that era. In those days, deliveries were made by a horse-drawn wagon, a convenient method since the coffee plant was located right across the street from the horse stable. According to legend, Bill, the delivery horse, so thoroughly memorized his route that he would stop at each customer's establishment whether they expected a delivery or not. Bill then refused to move until the driver entered the establishment and either made a delivery or spent the time wishing his customers a good morning. Hence, the Hansen name became known locally not only for great coffee, but consistent and friendly service.

In the 1950s Carl bought out his brother's share of the business and, soon thereafter, brought in his two sons, Jack and Ken, thus continuing the father-and sons-tradition established by John.

In 1964 John Hansen & Sons, after acquiring the Oakland division of Day Coffee Company, took in Jack Mooney, the owner of Lusco Coffee Company, as a shareholder and merged that company's operations into the newly named John Hansen & Sons, Incorporated. The corporation eventually acquired Mooney's shares and the brothers continued to operate it after Carl's retirement in 1970. Ken bought out his brother Jack's share in 1977 and subsequently Ken's son, Rick, became his partner. The family business evolved to also include Ken's wife, Sylvia, and daughters Reneé, Susan, Ryan and Carole, bringing the business into the fourth generation of Hansens. The family tradition of passing the torch continues into the fifth generation. Ken and Sylvia's eldest grandchildren, Shaun, Courtney and Chris, all have worked at Hansen *good* Coffee as teen-agers during their summer vacations. Rick's children, Eric, Justin and Katie, although much younger, enjoy accompanying their dad to work on an occasional weekend, thus ensuring yet another generation's involvement in John Hansen & Sons.

Hansen roasting plant, c. 1930

The Hansen family has seen the transition from mom-and-pop grocery stores to large chain supermarkets. It has seen the change from small, local deliveries by horse and wagon, to bulk shipping for national and international markets. As a result, Hansen *good* Coffee now focuses on creating custom-roasted blends and private label packaging for the trade. It has also expanded into gourmet and flavored coffees. Despite all the changes, Hansen *good* Coffee still maintains its direct delivery service.

Technological advances have helped. New packaging methods are now less expensive and more effective than the old lithographed cans that have been replaced with vacuum-sealed, valve-equipped bags that maintain freshness.

Hansen *good* Coffee is recognized by many area residents on their daily BART commute to San Francisco as they pass by the familiar sign, which depicts a coffee pot with a halo, on the side of the company's Fourth & Clay streets building. Hansen *good* Coffee gives true meaning to its motto, "A Blend of Old Traditions and New Ideas." ■

Hansen family tradition continues — (top row) Sylvia, Rick and Ken, president (bottom row) Ryan, Sue and Reneé

185

Pacific Pipe Company

Brokenhearted survivors of the 1906 San Francisco earthquake and fire looked upon their beloved city and wondered what could be salvaged from the destruction. Amidst the rubble of collapsed buildings and shattered dreams, young Mayhelt Jacobs began a journey that would help rebuild the City by the Bay and provide vital components for generations of growth in Oakland.

The strength and endurance of steel gave new life to the salvaged pipes Mayhelt recovered from the charred, twisted ruins of ordinary buildings and majestic landmarks. Operating from a small shop at Main and Howard streets, Jacobs founded the Pacific Pipe Company. The reconstruction of San Francisco provided the fledgling business with a huge demand for its used and reconditioned pipes. Expanding to larger facilities, Pacific Pipe's good fortune accelerated when awarded the contract to salvage pipe from the 1915 World's Fair.

The volume of activity brought by World War I compelled the opening of the Oakland facility in 1922, where Pacific Pipe eventually consolidated all its operations. The first two bays of the Oakland plant were originally shipyard bays left over from World War I in Seattle. Jacobs had them disassembled and brought to Oakland.

Jacobs was not without competition, and in order to remain successful he added fittings and couplings to his product line and provided value-added services such as bending, machining and fabricating to facilitate the sale of pipe. By the late 1930s, the company began to distribute new pipe to complement its offering of used and reconditioned pipe.

Pacific Pipe had been concentrating on supplying the agricultural market with material for sprinkler systems when the advent of World War II forced the company to shift to industrial fabrication, providing steel pipe fabrication for the Kaiser shipyards. After the war, the company continued marketing steel as its exclusive material, taking on work requiring adherence to strict government specifications for pipe welding, pressure tubing and

prefabrication work. Pacific Pipe continued its ship repair work and was favored because of the company's famed reliability and service under demanding deadlines. The company's specialized fabrication capabilities brought new business from pumping stations, refineries, utilities and chemical processing plants. Pacific Pipe also provided the bent sections of the vacuum chamber for the Positron Electron Project.

Mayhelt Jacobs passed away in 1952, leaving the leadership of Pacific Pipe in the hands of his son Ellis H. Jacobs through the balance of the 20th century. In the ensuing decades, his management team, which included Philip and Warren Sussman, and his son Ellis B. Jacobs, added dozens of prestigious product lines such as Youngstown Sheet and Tube, U.S. Steel, Victaulic, and Kaiser Pipe and Steel (now known as California Steel Industries) to the company's offerings as the business grew to unprecedented levels. Pacific Pipe also manufactured its own line of couplings called Pacific Grip Couplings.

Bending pipes of all proportions is one of Pacific Pipe's defining abilities. Company engineers developed machines and techniques to accomplish this task

Pacific Pipe's Oakland pipe yard in the 1940s

Precision arc welding is one of Pacific Pipe's fabrication specialties.

through trial and error, driven by the philosophy, "If it can be done, we can do it." Pacific Pipe discovered ways to bend cold pipes. The homemade machines were given colorful names like "The Slingshot," "The Alligator" and "The Manhattan Project," and were true engineering marvels of their time.

On April 8, 1999, Mayhelt Jacobs' great-grandson Larry Jacobs, the company's vice president at the time, called a rare meeting of Pacific Pipe's senior level employees to gather the precious commodity of memories. In attendance were Orven Fischbach, who joined the company in 1943, Lynn H. Joseph, hired in 1952, and Pat Fitzgerald, who started in 1960. The resulting history was rich with accomplishments, which may otherwise have been forgotten with the passing of time.

Orven Fischbach recalled a contract to build the moveable bleachers for the New Orleans Stadium. The entire job was fabricated like an erector set at the plant in Oakland so that it could be easily assembled. The engineers did not have to make a single trip to New Orleans because everything fit perfectly. He also reminisced about the trials and tribulations of supplying sections of the Alaska Pipeline.

By its very nature, the business of supplying industrial pipe does not have a high profile, because once the project is finished, the last thing anyone ever wants to see again is the pipes — but nearly all of Oakland's byways, buildings and bridges have been touched by Pacific Pipe. Lynn H. Joseph noted that beneath the surface of the Bay Area's most ambitious projects and recognized landmarks is Pacific Pipe's most noteworthy work. When underground tunneling and excavation is done in water-fronted areas, Pacific Pipe supplies the underpinning supports to prevent buildings from shifting or collapsing during construction. Each vertical concrete post in the entire BART system has an internal pipe fabricated by Pacific Pipe. The company fabricated drainage systems for the Oakland Hills and Bay Area canals.

Pat Fitzgerald pointed out that some of Pacific Pipe's most prolific and unrecognized work is right out in plain sight — miles and miles of light poles for the Port of Oakland, the Oakland airport, city athletic fields and the ornate lampposts for the stunning Path of Gold on San Francisco's Market Street. Pacific Pipe fabricated handrails for the Jack London Square Amtrak Station, the Emeryville Station and the San Mateo Bridge as well as highway sign structures viewed by millions of motorists each day.

Pacific Pipe has worked closely with architects and artists in recent years in the aesthetic use of square tubing and angled pipe in building design, as seen in the huge circular forms on the San Jose Civic Center, which provide structural support while making a strong visual impact. The arches at the Oakland Coliseum were fashioned by Pacific Pipe as were the bent piping and tubing in the San Francisco Museum of Modern Art's skylight and catwalk. The company has even built special armatures used by sculptors to provide internal support for their massive castings.

Pacific Pipe is highly regarded for its apprenticeship program for pipe bending, a very specialized skill that can take several years to master. The company invests heavily in its personnel and is rewarded with talented, long-term career employees, some of whom have been with Pacific Pipe for generations and even recruit their siblings.

As science continues to develop new "wonder materials," the principals of Pacific Pipe remain very confident about the future of steel — the metal that will always evoke a sense of confidence, permanence and strength. Pacific Pipe is constantly finding ways to reinvent itself with more sophisticated products, strong partnerships with its manufacturers and progressive management techniques to compete in a changing marketplace.

It could be said that Pacific Pipe was founded with the true spirit of a Northern Californian — in the apocalyptic setting of the Great San Francisco Earthquake, Mayhelt Jacobs was the quintessential recycler. His presence of mind in the face of adversity created a vital business that has stood the test of time. ■

Pacific Pipe's Norbert LaRiza displays an example of a 16-inch induction pipe bend, fabricated for use by the oil industry.

Ellis H. Jacobs, president of Pacific Pipe, with his grandson and company COO, Larry Jacobs

Cable Moore Inc.

Cable Moore Inc. was founded in 1986 by Sandra Moore and her husband, Greg Moore, in the old Todd Shipyard in Alameda. The company began as a small wire rope and cable supplier for the marine industry. However, business quickly grew and client demand caused Cable Moore to increase its inventory. As the business grew, the company made plans to relocate to Oakland, near the double-deck Cypress Freeway. The move was made in October 1989, following the Loma Prieta earthquake, which destroyed the Cypress Freeway. However, this tragic incident did not deter Cable Moore from taking root in this part of Oakland. Later, the Moores' home did not survive the Oakland hills fire in October 1991.

(Right and below) Cable Moore fabricated and field-installed vehicle and pedestrian cable barring systems for Park Place's parking structure in Irvine, California

Cable Moore started with four workers doing small rigging, then larger rigging, for Port of Oakland clientele. The company's capabilities became larger as the business evolved and expanded to include two satellite locations. An office in San Jose caters to the construction industry, supplying off-the-shelf items for construction operations. A second shop, in Benicia, not open to the public, provides a site where all Cable Moore's machine fabrications are made. There, machinists and welders work in an uninterrupted manner. The Oakland's wire rope shop specializes in wire rope for the industrial and port industries. The rigging shop and testing facility features six 500-ton swage presses, 350-ton and 1-1,200-ton Esco presses, rotary swage machines, test bed to 150-ton capacity, and hand splicing of wire rope.

What makes Cable Moore different from other companies is that it offers one-stop shopping. Instead of having to go one place to buy wire rope and another to get fittings made, customers can do both at Cable Moore. With its machine shop business, Cable Moore makes its own fittings. Offering complete package deals has proved to be a pleasing policy for many customers, especially large construction company owners who don't want to go from shop to shop to get everything they need. But wire rope and fittings are far from the only things Cable Moore has to offer the construction industry. It also carries a full line of safety protection equipment that includes full-body harnesses, life vests and construction vests, hard hats, safety glasses and tool belts. The company also provides construction support equipment, including contractor generators, chop saws, pumps, chain saws, pressure washers, hoses and other accessories.

Ironworkers can also find virtually everything to fill their needs, including hand tools, 7-inch side cutter pliers, bolt bags, tool pouches, spikes, wire reels, wooden rulers, rebar hooks and lanyards, keels and spud wrenches.

188

Cable Moore now operates a full-service shop, employs more than 40 people and has an extensive list of suppliers. It provides earthquake restrainers and metal fabrication structural services for most of the State of California's retrofit projects. It also provides cable railings and wire rope netting for use on freeway hillsides to contain falling rocks. Furthermore, Cable Moore provides wire rope for parking structure cable railings.

Cable Moore's claim that it can provide products and services other rigging and machine companies can't is not a collection of idle words. For example, it provides wire rope, aircraft cable, guy wire, bridge strand wire and wire rope slings. Wire rope is available in sizes from one-fourth inch to two-and-one-half inches in galvanized or stainless steel and steel formats. Cable Moore also provides a full line of chains, shackles (fittings that go onto a piece of rope or chain), turnbuckles, sockets, hooks, eye nuts, padeyes, snatch blocks, crane blocks, sheaves, swivels, alloy chain slings and chain hoists. There is also a variety of cordage and splicing services available.

For the marine industry, which was Cable Moore's first clientele, the company has provided ship anchors and lashing gear to secure containers that leave San Francisco Bay headed for the Orient and other places, as well as a variety of yacht rigging and hardware. Cable Moore's ship services include complete on-board rigging services: weight testing; wire slushing and replacement; block rebuilding and replacement; mooring lines; cargo quadrennials; and below-deck rigging services.

Cable Moore has architectural cable railing systems for commercial, industrial and residential applications. These include galvanized, stainless steel, or coated

cables; stainless steel turnbuckles; threaded studs, swage terminals and hydraulic swaging tools. There is even equipment that can be rented and mobile services available.

Cable Moore is justly proud of having fabricated, supplied and installed materials for many outstanding projects. For a modernistic Weber Point project in Stockton, Cable Moore provided the tent steel fabrication and cable fittings. Sullivan & Brampton was the general contractor. Cable Moore's construction division fabricated and field-installed state-of-the-art stainless steel cable railing systems for Cisco Systems Buildings' stairway projects in Sunnyvale, and the Technology Station parking structure in Santa Clara. General contractors were, respectively, Devcon, Inc. and South Bay Construction, Inc. Cable Moore's construction division also fabricated and installed stainless steel cable terrace guardrail systems for Emerystation #1 in Emeryville. Webcor Builders was the general contractor for this project. And, tying in with Cable Moore's first clientele, the company supplied lashing gear for a Hawaii-bound barge. Nova Group was the general contractor.

Sandra Moore believes her company's success is due to being a diversified business that serves a wide range of industries; its extensive line of supplies and stock; fabrication and machine shop capabilities; and its construction division. Many of her customers are repeat customers — and to Sandra Moore, that fact alone spells success. ∎

Cable Moore designed and erected this 10-ton double bridge for Valley Forge Iron Works in Oakland.

The San Jose Sharks used safety netting designed and built by Cable Moore for The San Jose Arena press boxes.

189

The Clorox Company

In the more than 85 years since its inception in Oakland, The Clorox Company has grown into an international organization that markets and manufactures a variety of well-known products to make consumers' lives simpler and better.

The company started in 1913 when a bank president, a purveyor of wood, coal, grain and hay, a bookkeeper, a lawyer and a miner, the only one of the five who had any practical knowledge of chemistry, all invested $100 apiece in a bold new entrepreneurial venture — the nation's first commercial production of liquid bleach.

A 3 1/2-ton 1921 Moreland was the first truck purchased by the Electro-Alkaline Co., The Clorox Company's predecessor.

Plant and office employees of The Clorox Company in 1925 (then known as The Clorox Chemical Corporation) — the company's president, William C.R. Murray, is in the front row, center.

The method used to make the nation's first bleach was to convert brine, extracted from the nearby salt ponds of San Francisco Bay, into sodium hypochlorite bleach using a sophisticated, technologically demanding process of electrolysis. They called their enterprise the Electro-Alkaline Company.

In August of that year, the partners acquired a plant in Oakland, where the company is still headquartered. An engineer for an equipment supplier suggested that the partners combine the words "chlorine" and "sodium hydroxide," the main ingredients of sodium hypochlorite bleach, to call their brand "Clorox." He sketched a diamond-shaped design with the word "Clorox" in bold letters in the center and the words "liquid bleach cleanser germicide" inset in the diamond's four facets.

The company had sold 750 shares of stock by the end of 1914, resulting in $75,000 in start-up capital. Soon, five-gallon crockery jugs filled with the product were being delivered by horse-drawn carriages to Clorox's first customers: laundries, breweries, walnut-processing sheds and municipal water companies that used the bleach for industrial-strength cleaning and purifying purposes.

In 1916, an early investor, William C.R. Murray, was named general manager of the company. In those difficult early years, the directors repeatedly had to extend personal loans to pay employees and prevent foreclosure on the plant. Murray's wife, Annie, ran the couple's grocery store and was as enthusiastic about Clorox bleach as her husband. She began to carry a diluted version of the bleach available in small amber glass bottles for household use.

She gave free samples to her customers and sales exploded. The bleach was popular throughout the San Francisco Bay Area. Soon, Annie received requests for the product from as far away as the East Coast and Canada.

By 1918, inspired by her example, William Murray ordered retailers to hand out three of every four bottles for free, assuring that the company would reimburse them. The strategy worked. By 1921 the first cargo of Clorox bleach destined for the East Coast was loaded onto a ship at the Port of Oakland. Extensive national advertising campaigns followed, and by 1928, the bleach had become a commonplace sight in American homes. That year, the company went public and its stock began to trade on the San Francisco Exchange.

On the eve of World War II, William J. Roth, hired initially as a bookkeeper, took over as company president. Although those were difficult years, he established policies that ensured the loyalty of both customers and suppliers and that remain in the bedrock of the company's beliefs today.

190

Due to a short supply of chlorine during the war years, the U.S. government permitted bleach manufacturers to dilute their products. But unlike its competitors, Clorox, under Roth's leadership, chose to curtail production rather than distribute an inferior product. This decision impressed customers and cemented consumer loyalty to the brand.

Roth also chose to tear up prewar contracts that would have enabled Clorox to purchase scarce chlorine at prices unfair to suppliers. His action created a good-faith relationship with suppliers and gained Clorox a solid reputation as a company concerned with fair and equitable business practices. Roth's concerns have carried over to the present day — integrity and quality are very much ingrained in the company's culture.

In 1953, the first television commercials aired. The company continued to grow with the construction of a dozen new plants between 1938 and 1956.

Four years later, the Proctor and Gamble Company purchased Clorox, but in that same year, the Federal Trade Commission challenged the acquisition, charging that a monopoly in household liquid bleach might result. In 1969, the U.S. Supreme Court ruled that P&G must shed Clorox. That year, Clorox gained formal autonomy and celebrated by purchasing Liquid-Plumr drain opener. That fall, the ambitious company introduced its first internally developed new product: Clorox 2 color-safe bleach.

Since then, The Clorox Company has developed many products and made many acquisitions. It markets and manufactures Glad bags and wraps, STP automobile additives, S.O.S steel wool soap pads, Pine-Sol, Formula 409 and Tilex cleaners, Armor All protectant, Combat insecticides, Kingsford charcoal, Fresh Step, Scoop Away and Jonny Cat cat litter, Brita water filtration systems and Hidden Valley salad dressings, among many other well-known brands. And, Clorox products are marketed in more than 80 countries. The company is most active in North and South America, Asia and Australia.

The Clorox Company continues to innovate. Research into consumer preferences revealed that some people did not like the smell of bleach, so with the introduction of a new floral-scented bleach, Clorox increased its share of the American market to 60 percent. When Clorox introduced Lemon-Fresh Pine-Sol cleaner for those consumers who like the cleaning power of Pine-Sol but do not prefer the pine scent, annual shipment growth shot up. In addition, simple, but effective, packaging innovations to bleach bottles,

Tilex Fresh Shower daily shower cleaner, Brita water systems and more helped the company to thrive.

The Clorox Company's environmental track record is excellent. In 1993 *Fortune* magazine voted the company one of the Top 10 environmentally sound companies in the United States. Clorox's plants have state-of-the-art safety systems and training processes in place to prevent any release of chlorine into the environment. In addition, more than 27 percent of the company's packaging consists of post-consumer recycled materials. And, extensive research shows that the bleach's active ingredient, sodium hypochlorite, is environmentally benign.

The Clorox Company and its people have always made strong commitments to community involvement. Its employees volunteer countless hours and contribute financially to myriad causes. The company fulfills its commitment through the activities of The Clorox Company Foundation.

The foundation's mission is to improve the quality of life in communities where Clorox employees live and work. In Oakland, foundation grants and employee volunteers have supported reading, business-awareness and teacher-training programs in the schools. The Clorox Company Foundation also supports Red Cross readiness programs, the Oakland East Bay Symphony, Habitat for Humanity and many more community organizations.

The Clorox Company of today remains committed to the traditional values that guided its forefathers — the highest standards of quality, marketing products that provide value to consumers, and a reputation for fairness when managing a broad portfolio of world-famous brands. ■

The Clorox Company's family of brands is evidence that through the years, Clorox has become much more than just a bleach company.

191

Horizon Beverage Co.

In 1919, with the investment of a horse, a wagon and six cases of beer, Albert Markstein founded Markstein Beverage Company to distribute Golden West Beer. With the enactment of Prohibition a short time later, Albert continued to serve his customers by selling "near beer," soft drinks and soda water. After the repeal of Prohibition in 1933, the company resumed the distribution of full-strength beer. By 1934 the entire Markstein family (husband, wife and three sons) was working full time in the business.

Denny Suzuki, vice president of Horizon Beverage Co.

Cestra "Ces" Butner, president of Horizon Beverage Co.

Implementing then-innovative techniques such as pallet loading and pre-sell ordering, combined with establishing a good reputation and gaining the respect of the customer, brewer and community, the company was able to successfully negotiate exclusive distribution rights in Alameda and Contra Costa counties. The business continued to grow and by the 1960s consisted of eight distributorships in Hayward, Union City, Pittsburgh, Concord, Long Beach, Sacramento and two in Oakland. Due to the size and location of the distributorships, the Markstein brothers decided to split the business among them with Adolph Markstein and his sons maintaining ownership of the Oakland and Sacramento operations. Adolph's brothers, Albert Jr. and Walter, maintained ownership and operational control of the rest.

In October 1987 Anheuser-Busch Investment Capital Corporation purchased the Oakland distributorship from the Markstein family and renamed it Horizon Beverage Company. The day-to-day control of the business became the responsibility of Cestra "Ces" Butner, president, and Denny Suzuki, vice president. In October 1988 Butner and Suzuki purchased a portion of the business and became managing general partners, with Anheuser-Busch Investment Capital Corporation remaining a limited partner.

Butner, a Missouri native, is one of 12 children, all college graduates. After attaining a degree from the University of Missouri in 1975, he worked for Fortune 500 companies in Minneapolis and Chicago before coming to Oakland in 1980 as a brewery representative for beer wholesalers in the East Bay. In 1981 Butner accepted the position of sales manager for Markstein Beverage company. He also held positions as vice president and general manager prior to purchasing a portion of the business.

Believing it is "good business" to be actively involved in the community one serves, Butner has dedicated a significant amount of time to community service. He is currently chairman of the board of the East Bay YMCA, a past chair of the Oakland Metropolitan Chamber of Commerce and a board member of the Oakland Commerce Corporation. He

192

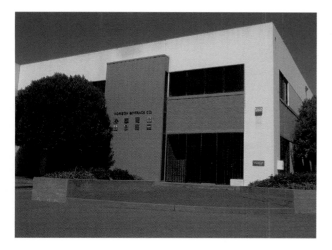

has also served on the boards of the Bay Area Black United Fund, Lake Merritt Breakfast Club, Oakland Convention and Visitors Bureau and Oakland Festival of the Arts.

As co-chair of the Economic Base Task Force of Oakland's "Sharing the Vision," Butner was instrumental in the development and adoption of Oakland's Strategic Plan. As chairman of the chamber of commerce, he led the charge for the adoption of the City Center revitalization plan and the creation of the Business Budget Advisory Committee to build the necessary link between city government and an underutilized major asset — the business community.

Denny Suzuki is an Arkansas native who was raised in Southern California. He is a graduate of Woodberry College and a Vietnam veteran. He began his career with Wisdom Imports as a brewery representative responsible for the sale and distribution of Asahi Beer in the western region, consisting of 13 states. In 1977 Denny accepted the sales supervisor position with Ace Beverage Company, the Anheuser-Busch wholesaler in Los Angeles. He also served as vice president of sales and marketing, beer division, vice president and general manager for Mission Snack Foods and Anheuser-Busch Eagle Snacks prior to purchasing a portion of Horizon Beverage Company.

Like Butner, Suzuki is also active in the community. He serves on the advisory board of the Oakland-Chinatown Chamber of Commerce, the West Oakland Commerce Association and the Asian Cultural Center.

Giving back to the community is something that is not just important to the two partners individually and personally, but collectively as well. Contributing half of the volunteers and half of the school's sponsorship,

Horizon Beverage Company's management team is a generous contributor to the Junior Achievement Program at Oakland's Hoover Elementary. Over the years, the firm has donated hundreds of hours and tens of thousands of dollars to other important causes such as national minority scholarships, product donations/promotions, and a long list of alcohol-awareness programs tailored to address everyone from grade school students to bartenders.

In January 1996 Butner and Suzuki purchased the remaining portion of the business from Anheuser-Busch Investment Capital Corporation and now have total ownership of a company consisting of 75 employees. Utilizing a fleet of 19 delivery trucks, 10 vans and two utility vehicles, the company sells and delivers more than 2,000,000 cases of product annually from a 56,000-square-foot office on 20th Street in West Oakland. The company distributes the brands of Anheuser-Busch, Redhook, Widmer, Kirin, Boston Beer, Golden Pacific and Calistoga. Under the leadership of Ces and Denny, Horizon Beverage Company is recognized by Anheuser-Busch as one of its outstanding distributors, having won the coveted Ambassador Award (for top distributors in the country) six years in a row. Horizon was also the recipient of the 1990 Oakland Chamber of Commerce's "Small Business of the Year" award.

As owners, Ces Butner and Denny Suzuki continue to carry on the established traditions of professionalism, teamwork, community involvement and customer service that have made Horizon Beverage Company a recognized leader in the beverage distribution industry. ■

Since 1987 Horizon Beverage has been a leading distributor of prominent beers and waters.

One of Horizon Beverage's 16-bay trucks

193

Tien-Hu Knitting Co. (US) Inc.

The story of Tien-Hu Knitting Company begins halfway around the world in Hong Kong's busy garment district. Tim Shing Chan, founder of Tien-Hu Group, began his career at age 16 as a factory laborer, working hand-operated knitting machines around the clock. After eight years of hard work and savings, Chan took the initiative to buy 20 hand-operated knitting machines and opened his own factory in 1968, doing mainly subcontracting jobs. Having gained more experience in dealing with buyers through selling agents, Chan founded Tien-Hu Group, a manufacturing business, in 1980. The knitting company derives its name from the Tien Hu district of Canton, China.

In the beginning, Chan did much of the essential work himself, providing made-to-order service for each customer. On the hand-operated machines of the time, a day's worth of painstaking effort was required in order to make a single sweater. Because of Tim Chan's dedication to discovering ideal uses for different fibers, as well as perfecting new stitching methods, the company slowly struggled upwards in Hong Kong's highly competitive export market. By 1987 Tien-Hu Group had become such a success that it had several branches in China and considered international expansion. As Tien-Hu Group had been making sweaters for the U.S. market for more than 18 years, Chan decided that a move to the United States would help facilitate sales.

The next year, attracted by the area's thriving Chinatown district and mild weather, Chan opened the factory in Oakland.

Today Chan is a major shareholder in a group of companies. The company employs more than 7,000 workers in six factories from the United States to China to Cambodia, and knits garments for famous names such as Ann Taylor, Cousin Johnny, Eddie Bauer, Jones New York, Liz Claiborne, Polo, Ralph Lauren and The Gap.

Jane Chan, the general manager of Tien-Hu (US), had been working with Tim Shing since 1970, first as a factory trainee, then as office manager. She was assigned to open the Oakland branch due to her outstanding performance in Hong Kong.

Tien-Hu of Oakland has distinguished itself among knitting factories by its thoroughness in developing the right knitting technique for each yarn, as technology makes more natural and synthetic fibers available for designers. These improved yarns add new softness, drape and durability to designer's repertoires and are essential to innovation in knitted garments. Tien-Hu (US) has been a force in seeking out the newest yarns available from around the world and pretesting them. This assists designers in choosing appropriate fibers and stitches for their latest designs. Each year, Jane Chan and Shirley Juster, Tien-Hu's sales representative, attend

Tien-Hu Knitting Co. (US) is located in the heart of Oakland's Chinatown.

the exclusive Pitti Filati yarn shows in Italy, where the hottest new yarns are viewed and tested by garment industry buyers from around the world. In this way, Jane is able to keep Tien-Hu (US) on the cutting edge of knitwear designs, retaining extensive knowledge as to appropriate stitches, dyes, yarns and garment finishing techniques — a unique trait among knitting factories.

Tien-Hu (US) is known for its indefatigable efforts to develop fragile or hard-to-knit yarns. Since 1994 Tien-Hu Knitting Company of Oakland has maintained a national reputation as "The Queen of Chenille" for its unsurpassed ability to knit this extremely fragile yarn into some of today's softest, most luxurious garments. Tien-Hu is also known as a leader in the testing of new microfibers, high-tech fibers and acrylics. It is currently known for its innovative use of Dupont's popular new Tactel fiber, which creates a super soft pile fabric from an unusual nylon yarn.

Currently, the Oakland factory produces 500,000 made-to-order pieces each year, primarily of the new specialty yarns. The factory has 30,000 square feet, including an extensive 10,000-square-foot storage facility for experimental and commodity yarns and 10,000 square feet for its 30 knitting machines. The machines operate 24 hours a day, seven days a week, and shuts down completely only once a year, for the much-celebrated Chinese New Year. Tien-Hu also operates a 10,000-square-foot finishing department where detailed work such as cutting, garment assembly and inspection is performed largely by hand.

As Oakland has undergone dynamic change and refurbishing over recent years, Tien-Hu Knitting Company has grown and improved as well. In the mid 1990s, the company upgraded all of its knitting equipment. This $4 million investment signified a move toward improved efficiency, capability and quality in Tien-Hu's working environs and products.

Chinatown's ever-growing population has consistently provided workers for Tien-Hu (US), and in return, Tien-Hu (US) has become a vital force in Oakland, giving back to the community by donating 2,000 sweaters per year to local churches and charities. The factory has also offered free English lessons to its 170 workers, most of whom came to the factory knowing only Chinese.

Tien-Hu (US) has a tradition of helping Chinatown's citizenry become involved in greater Oakland's cultural events. In 1998 Tien-Hu (US) sponsored all workers for the Making Strides Against Breast Cancer Walkathon in Golden Gate Park. That year, the factory also helped its workers and their families better understand California's history by providing special translated tours of the Oakland Art Museum's sesquicentennial celebration and "Gold Rush" exhibit.

In 1998, and for Tien-Hu (US)'s 10th anniversary, the company sponsored a trip to Las Vegas for all workers. As many workers speak little English and have had few opportunities to explore America beyond the boundaries

(left) Tim Shing Chan, founder of Tien-Hu Group, (right) Jane Chan, general manager of Tien-Hu (US)

of Chinatown, this was a unique opportunity to experience American-style gambling, luxury hotels and sightseeing in Las Vegas. The event proved such a success that workers requested another trip the following year. Tien-Hu also sponsored a three-day and two-night bus tour of Northern California and Oregon. The tour included Crater Lake, Clear Lake and the Napa wine country. The highlight of the trip for most workers — many of whom had never seen snow — was driving through a blizzard.

Tien-Hu of Oakland maintains a modern facility and plans to update its machinery as more efficient knitting technology is developed, possibly acquiring a number of "Knit and Wear" machines that eliminate the need for a finishing process, an improvement that could save the company thousands of dollars each year. Tien-Hu (US) looks forward to working with currently emerging fibers rumored to be made of such experimental materials as stainless steel microfibers, new rayons and even milk.

Tien-Hu (US) has had a lengthy history of caring for Oakland's Chinatown community while providing unsurpassed attention to perfecting knitting techniques for the new yarns that become available with advances in technology. ■

195

California Glass Company

California Glass Company is a major distributor of glass and plastic containers, stemware and other glasses, metal foil, polylaminate, and plastic capsules, corks, cartons, and label and case-seal adhesives for wine, beer, food, pharmaceuticals and cosmetics. Antonio Silvani founded the company, predicated upon the principles of excellent customer service, honesty and integrity, in 1934. Sixty-five years later, operating under the guiding philosophy of providing the highest-quality service to all customers, regardless of size, California Glass Company is owned and operated by the second and third generations of the Silvani family.

The company founder, Antonio Silvani, arrived in the Bay Area from Genova, Italy, in April 1906, one week prior to the earthquake that devastated much of San Francisco. Only 17 years old, he possessed a strong work ethic. During World War I, Antonio Silvani, by then a proud naturalized citizen, served in the U.S. Navy. Upon his return, he founded Bay City Bottle Supply to continue marketing sterilized glass containers, a line of work he had previously followed.

In 1933, having sold Bay City Bottle Supply, he founded California Glass Company in San Francisco to wash and resell used glass packaging. In 1936 Illinois-Pacific Glass Company (now Owens-Illinois Inc.), the largest manufacturer of glass and plastic containers, and metal and plastic closures, approached him about distributing its product lines. In addition to selling new glass containers and closures to the wine, food and pharmaceutical industries, he continued to sterilize and recycle glass containers, well in advance of today's large recycling industry.

Antonio Silvani took his children, Barbara Peri and Leonard Silvani into the business, where they remain active. Third-generation owners/operators are Cindy Silvani, L. Marc Silvani, Rick Silvani, and Cindy's husband, Doug Lacey, who is controller of the company.

For many years, California Glass Company occupied a 35,000-square-foot building, but as the company's focus gradually shifted from selling recycled glass to marketing new glass and other packaging components to wineries, food packers, microbreweries and other customers, business increased, and the company

outgrew the facility. That, combined with increasing Bay Bridge gridlock as well as the Silvanis' desire to return to Oakland, where Antonio Silvani first located, brought the company to its present site on 98th Avenue.

California Glass Company has its own warehouses, fleet of trucks, extensive inventory, and a sales staff that specializes in wine packaging components, tasting room supplies, custom-decorated containers and glassware, and food, beer and pharmaceutical packaging. Today California Glass Company services accounts throughout the Western United States, Alaska, Hawaii and abroad.

California Glass Company attributes its ongoing success in a highly competitive industry to its reputation for honesty, integrity, reliability and excellent service. The Silvanis credit their hard-working staff and loyal customers for their tradition of introducing innovations in packaging, all characteristics that distinguish California Glass Company from its competitors. ■

Antonio Silvani, company founder, whose weekly luncheons were open to employees, customers and suppliers

The present owners and operators — Leonard Silvani and Barbara Peri (second generation, seated), and Rick Silvani, Cindy Silvani, L. Marc Silvani and Doug Lacey

196

Allied Crane

Allied Crane has been building and repairing cranes designed to lift heavy materials for major manufacturing companies for nearly 25 years. Based in Oakland since 1981, the company manufactures many different types of cranes. From the mundane to specialty materials, its cranes have been used to hoist everything from nuclear materials and U.S. Navy missiles to printing presses and

airplane engines. The company designs, builds and repairs specialty cranes to handle heavy nuclear materials for fusion experiments for Lawrence Livermore Lab in Livermore, cranes for Pacific Gas and Electric, and cranes to lift turbine airplane engines for assembly and disassembly, repair and installation, for United Airlines.

When it began in San Leandro in 1976, Allied Crane specialized in crane service and repair. By 1980, however, the majority of its business focused on the manufacture of cranes. In 1984 the company modified a customized barge crane for Westinghouse Corporation that allowed the U.S. Navy to lower and submerge Trident missiles into the depths of the ocean. In 1996 the company spent four months building a 40-foot-tall, $300,000 Gantry crane capable of lifting 40 tons for Jon Federico of MAN Roland. The one-of-a-kind crane was built to assemble and install a printing press for Gannett Incorporated. This unique and sophisticated crane, equipped with a special telescoping feature that extends the crane's lift up to 60 feet, can be assembled and disassembled for easy transport anywhere in the country.

Allied Crane has also played a role in Bay Area transportation history. The company revamped cranes for a plant retrofit in Pittsburg to help convert an old U.S. Steel plant to meet the needs of Caltrans and the Bay Area Rapid Transit (BART) District. The cranes proved instrumental in helping BART and Caltrans to produce more railway cars as transportation routes were expanded in 1994. Allied Crane is also licensed by the state of California to load test, inspect and certify cranes.

Today its president, Dave Costa, manages Allied Crane. Growing up as a third-generation San Franciscan, Dave grew up fixing anything he could get his hands on. He began his career in the industry working on cranes as a crane service technician when he was 22 years old. A second partner in the firm, Vice President Paul Gershater, has more than 25 years of experience in the crane manufacturing business and joined the organization in 1990. Chief engineer Ed Block has in excess of 50 years experience. Block develops innovative ideas from the drawing board to functional systems. Dave's two sons, Tim and Chris Costa, spent much of their childhoods in and out of their father's plant. Both developed the same interest as their father in the industry and now work for Allied Crane. Tim is part of the company's structural installation division, while Chris works in its manufacturing department. They both feel fortunate to be exposed to the group of seasoned professionals that compose the industrywide respected work force of Allied Crane.

Originally located on 66th Avenue across from the Oakland Coliseum, where the company operated from for seven years, Allied Crane has been headquartered on Railroad Avenue near the Oakland Airport since 1990. The company employs 22 people at its 12,000-square-foot Oakland facility and offers a complete range of engineering capabilities. As the Bay Area and Oakland continue to grow, Allied Crane will continue to provide a lift when needed. ■

The staff of Allied Crane, 1999

Specialty Gantry crane, built to assemble and install a printing press for Gannett Incorporated

197

MarKEtplace

Oakland retail establishments and service industries offer an impressive variety of choices for Oakland residents and visitors.

Lake Merritt Hotel

Every great city holds reverence for its oldest landmarks. The contrast of baroque cornices against the backdrop of shining skyscrapers serves as a reminder that a city is a dynamic, evolving work in progress. The Lake Merritt Hotel was a stunning new addition to Oakland's Gold Coast district in 1927. Six decades later it was a pitiful candidate for the wrecking ball. The public's outcry and the courage of an esteemed developer gave the Lake Merritt Hotel the precious gift of rebirth.

Originally named the Madison-Lake Apartments, the Lake Merritt Hotel was built by a wealthy physician during Oakland's real estate boom of the Roaring 20s. Its

The Lake Merritt Hotel shortly after its debut as the Madison-Lake Apartments in 1927

breathtaking blend of Art Deco and 17th-century Mediterranean styling was a signature of famed California architect William H. Weeks. Situated on the southwest bank of Lake Merritt, the monumentally sculpted building joined the numerous lakeside residential hotels of the prestigious Gold Coast neighborhood. Exclusive home to celebrities and wealthy Oakland residents, the Lake Merritt Hotel's rooms were elegantly appointed suites with unobstructed views of the lake and city.

Historical documents suggest that the stock market crash of 1929 forced the hotel into foreclosure as Oakland's real estate market endured more than its share of suffering. Under new ownership, a glass-enclosed Terrace Room was added in 1934. The ballroom's panoramic view of the lake and elegant decor

transformed the Lake Merritt Hotel into the Oakland hot spot. The venue of lavish celebrations and performances by such music legends as Count Basie, the hotel became a vital part of Oakland's cultural scene.

The Lake Merritt Hotel thrived for many years, but began to show signs of neglect in the 1960s. The 1970s were especially hard on the hotel, operating as transient housing with few permanent residents during the city's most trying times. Abuse and apathy had taken such a toll on the property that it was slated for demolition in 1986 to make room for a condominium project. Horrified Oakland residents convinced city officials to block the demolition, forcing the owner to put the hotel up for sale, but the actual rescue was delivered by respected real estate investor Randall Berger in 1987.

An Oakland native with fond childhood memories of the Lake Merritt Hotel, Berger seized the opportunity to acquire a true East Bay landmark. Not only was he determined to restore the beleaguered hotel's dignity, he even played the role of general contractor. In total, an impressive $1.25 million would be spent on the restoration project by its completion on New Year's Day 1991.

First on the agenda was to show Oakland that something good was about to happen. The imposing cast concrete exterior and flamboyant terra cotta and stucco panels were newly bathed in a pale shade of gray. Below the building's gold-detailed crown, windows sparkled once again. Much to his delight, Berger found the structure of the old hotel to be in amazingly sound condition. The interiors, however, were a different matter.

Berger enlisted the talents of Linda Lamb, principal of Monterey-based L.S. Lamb Design Group, to create the interior design. "Create" was the operative term — not "re-create." Lamb studied photos from the hotel's heyday to gain a sense of its original style and elegance, but she used her own interpretations and instincts to rehabilitate the magnificent architectural details hidden beneath layers of unkind treatment. The treasure of existing hand-crafted flourishes provided the foundation for Lamb's artistic exercise.

200

The highest order of priority was assigned to renovating the lobby and lounge — where important first impressions must be made. Already blessed with magnificent 16-foot cathedral ceilings, the lobby became an enchanting display of elegant, but inviting comfort. Overstuffed mohair loveseats sit on plush carpeting whose pattern of taupe, cobalt blue, pale rose beige and charcoal gray provides the color palette for the entire hotel. Remembrances of the past including old theatre posters and nostalgic photos of the hotel hang on the pearlized pewter wall-covering.

A turn to the left reveals the north-facing Terrace Room. Famous for its sweeping view of the lake and park, the ballroom's rear wall is adorned with a mural series of scenes of Lake Merritt and its surrounds, painted in 1956 by Bay Area artist Andre Boratko. The Art Deco details and furnishings faithfully recapture the room's historic glory days.

Originally built as an exclusive residential hotel catering to those of wealth and fame, the Lake Merritt Hotel boasts 51 exceptionally spacious guest rooms, all but nine of which are suites. Lamb's design prowess gives the visitor a sense of the glamour of a 20s-era luxury apartment, enhanced by the conveniences expected of a modern boutique hotel. Ornately framed nine-foot ceilings, a cedar-lined walk-in closet and tapestry-style draperies blend seamlessly with the microwave oven in the kitchenette, the 20-inch cable television and the modem outlet. The Art Deco color scheme of the lobby and public areas decorates the walls and covers the floors of each guest room with warm, vibrant tones.

A half-dozen of the suites are dedicated as an "ode to the arts" to show support for Oakland's cultural associations. Themes include the Oakland Ballet Suite, the Oakland Opera Suite and the Mandelo Institute Suite. More than an enduring landmark, the Lake Merritt Hotel is well known for its good works in the Oakland community. The hotel hosts fund-raisers, awards dinners and special events to boost such charitable causes as the Black Adoption Placement and Research Center, the California Autism Society and several AIDS-awareness and prevention groups.

Two or three times a year, the social group known as Rick's Martini Club parts the curtains of time, returning the Lake Merritt Hotel to the hustle and bustle of the 20s, 30s and 40s. Members create quite a stir as they arrive in classic automobiles, decked out in vintage clothes to swing to the rhythms of the great jazz era — and drink martinis, of course. The Lake Merritt Hotel has long been a haven for jazz lovers and is a favorite hangout for musicians when they are in town. Thursday's Jazz Night in the Terrace Room has become an Oakland tradition.

Saturday nights on the terrace are usually reserved for private parties. The Lake Merritt Hotel is one of Oakland's most sought after venues for weddings, anniversaries, birthday bashes and business events, boasting the reputation for serving the best banquet dining in the East Bay.

Randall Berger has done much more than prove that all things old can be made new again. The renaissance of the Lake Merritt Hotel has become a model for Oakland's renewal — a standard by which all other community efforts can be measured. ■

Guests enjoy an unobstructed view of Oakland's Lakeside Park.

Spacious guest rooms blend modern convenience with the elegance of a 20s-era luxury apartment.

Jack London Square

With its rich history, lovely, water-oriented setting and family-friendly atmosphere, Oakland's Jack London Square (the larger neighborhood is sometimes referred to as "Jack London District") offers a unique blend of restaurants, world-class jazz clubs, shops and hotels. Bordering the Oakland Estuary, the Square also features a wide range of activities for the outdoor enthusiast such as yachting, rowing, canoeing and kayaking. Water taxis and leisurely promenades make the waterfront district a lively visitor magnet that draws more than 6 million people each year.

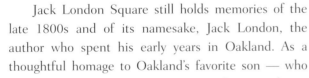

Ships line the Oakland waterfront near the end of Broadway in the late 1880s.
Oakland Library

Jack London Square still holds memories of the late 1800s and of its namesake, Jack London, the author who spent his early years in Oakland. As a thoughtful homage to Oakland's favorite son — who was actually born in San Francisco — the original log cabin in which London spent a freezing winter during the Yukon Gold Rush in 1897 was transported to the Square in 1970. Heinold's First and Last Chance Saloon, one of London's favorite watering holes, still operates in the Square today. The floor of Heinold's is slanting because of subsidence after the 1906 earthquake. In January 1998, the Friends of the Library named Heinold's a National Literary Landmark. This prestigious honor has been bestowed upon just 28 other American landmarks including San Francisco's City Lights Bookstore and the Algonquin Hotel in

New York. London built and berthed his boat, the *Snark,* in the nearby estuary. Jack London Square has other noteworthy historic aspects to it as well, but it is the tale of Jack London that lures most of the Square's visitors, who come from around the world each year. The Overland House was built in 1887 at the terminus of the transcontinental railroad. The waterfront is where Captain Thomas Gray, grandfather of the famous dancer Isadora Duncan, began the first ferry service to San Francisco in 1850. The Pony Express used the ferry to complete their delivery to San Francisco on occasion.

It is at the Square, too, that the usually more sedate Port Commissioner George Pardee, then mayor of Oakland, personally kicked down a fence that the Southern Pacific, which once claimed exclusive ownership of Oakland's waterfront, had erected across Broadway in 1893. Finally, in 1906, the California Supreme Court ended the lengthy disputes by ruling in the city's favor. Today the Port of Oakland still owns and operates Jack London Square.

Another unique aspect of the Square is the colorful tiled wall in front of Barnes&Noble, The World Wall for Peace, whose first section was dedicated at Jack London Square in a 1996 ceremony. The inspiration for the project, conceived in 1983 during the height of the Cold War, was a response to the political priority of a possible nuclear threat. Founder and artist Carolyna Marks chose ceramic

Bar owner Johnny Heinold befriended the young Jack London who frequented Heinold's Saloon, still found on its original site at the Square.
Heinold's First and Last Chance Saloon

tile, which lasts for centuries, to act as a peace development format. The international Wall now includes 30 sections in various countries, with a total of 36,000 painstaking and individually hand-painted tiles. The Square's portion totals 2,000 tiles in three distinct sections.

Today Jack London Square offers plenty of great things to do. Hungry sightseers will find something for everyone, whether their preferences are for tantalizing tortellini at Il Pescatore, succulent seafood at Scott's Seafood Restaurant, spicy salsa at El Torito, Maryland crab cakes at Kincaid's, Korean-style BBQ at Hahn's Hibachi, or prime rib at Jack's Bistro. Family-style Italian cuisine at The Old Spaghetti Factory and fabulous pizza at Pizzeria Uno's Chicago Bar & Grill are also favorites. Music lovers can take in a concert and delicious Japanese cuisine at Yoshi's. A new taste has arrived at the Square, Tony Roma's, featuring tender, juicy, world-famous ribs, seafood, chicken, steaks, prime rib and salads.

Shoppers will discover unique retail values as well — from Barnes&Noble, with more than 150,000 titles to browse, to Timeout for Fun & Games, with games for young and old. Equipment for the adventurous is available at California Canoe & Kayak. The Hat Generation has hats for every occasion and Murasaki offers fine Japanese gifts & futons. Add to that, marvelous one-of-a-kind finds from around the world at Cost Plus. Beverages & more! features a huge selection of wine, beverages, gourmet food and cigars.

After shopping or a fine meal, visitors can take a ferry ride to San Francisco, stroll along the scenic boardwalk, or stay the night in the Waterfront Plaza Hotel, all against a backdrop of beautiful Pacific waterfront vistas. A Web site and 24-hour hotline keeps callers apprised of the many special events, concerts and activities available year-round at Jack London Square.

Jack London Square was voted the No. 1 local attraction in the East Bay by *Oakland Tribune* readers in the 1999 "Best of..." listings. Recently, live-work loft spaces have flourished in the district. High-tech start-up companies and artists are drawn to the area by its massive variety of cafes, bookstores, bike paths and shopping opportunities. Entrepreneurs are encouraged by the city's policy favoring the development of non-traditional, higher-density, mixed-use lofts with ground-floor retail and restaurants. Construction of some 700 units began in 1999. Future plans include more open space for recreation, office, hotel and retail space with shopping malls and grassy meadow areas set aside for outdoor entertainment and performances. A series of public plazas and boardwalks is also planned to help create a safe "neighborhood" atmosphere that encourages visitors to explore the waterfront and its shops and restaurants. Many changes are taking place, but a sense of history and the memories of a great American writer remain, making Jack London Square a wonderful blending of the old and new, and a place that everyone can enjoy. ■

After dinner or before a show at Yoshi's, visitors can take a relaxing stroll along the wide pedestrian pathways at Jack London Square.

Brand new marinas line the water's edge at Jack London Square for recreational yachts and daytime boaters to call home.

203

Summit Bank

During the recession of 1982, when the finance industry quivered in anxiety, Shirley Nelson decided to start Summit Bank. Most industry analysts would have considered the decision bold, perhaps foolish. But Nelson — a single parent who knew little about starting a bank — had an astute, observant mind and unfailing confidence.

Born in Celina, Tennessee, nestled in the Appalachians, Nelson graduated from high school at 16 and left home for the big city of Nashville. There she worked as a cashier, met her naval officer husband and moved to Alaska. When her son was three months old, she found a job in a fish packing plant, and after one night of smelly fish, she became a bank teller, a prestigious job by Tennessee standards. Three years later, Nelson became a junior teller at Central Bank in Oakland when her husband was transferred to the Alameda Naval Station. Nelson had always assumed she would rise to become CEO, and she did.

A gracious, comfortable lobby filled with Persian rugs, fine paintings and antique furniture allows customers to relax while being served.

By the early 1980s, Nelson was vice president and senior manager of Central Bank, located on Broadway in Oakland. The bank served the medical community who worked around "Pill Hill" — a five-block area of Oakland dominated by three hospitals.

Nelson had noticed that surgeons in their medical greens were waiting in long lines for service. She began giving them preferential treatment, pulling them out of the lines to serve them at her desk. After all, doctors and hospital administrators accounted for 20 percent of the bank's customers but brought in 80 percent of the bank's business.

These customers responded so well to the personalized services that she thought it possible to open a bank just to serve that clientele. The thought remained dormant until the day when she and her employer disagreed over giving her employee a raise. The bank was born when her employer told her that she and her employee could command a much higher salary if there was a bank across the street.

Nelson approached a diverse group of businessmen and women and asked them to start a community bank. These individuals, representative of the community at large, became the organizers and board of directors of Summit Bank. The original board members included an auto dealer, an attorney, physicians, businessmen and women, developers, a former Oakland Raider, a certified public accountant and a banker. Capital was raised by the board who, along with Nelson, made substantial investments in the bank. They sold shares at $10 each to approximately 450 investors.

Two years after this dynamic board took on the challenge, Summit Bank opened its doors almost directly across the street from Nelson's former employer. Summit's first branch opened two years later in Walnut Creek, its second in 1986 in Emeryville, and its third in 1997 in Pleasanton.

As assets grew, Summit became recognized as one of the best-managed independent banks in the state, a premier performer, winning awards and accolades from industry watchdogs, trade journals, and its peers in the banking industry.

204

The banking world had become increasingly impersonal, increasingly automated. Gone were the days of knowing one's teller by first name, much less, the days when a teller knew a depositor's name. Nelson envisioned a more personal bank catering to the elite among the medical community — high-net worth medical and dental professionals. She insisted then, and does so now, that business is between people. The bank's success demonstrated that caring about people and conducting business accordingly result in profit and growth.

While the bottom line was important to Summit, more important was the goodwill gained from treating people and their money with respect. Nelson understood that people will, and do, pay more for excellent customer service. The bank provided a unique, intimate and personalized experience for its customers.

At Summit, service means more than a friendly smile, name and face recognition. Customers have a quick access to loans via pre-approved lines of credit, private offices for loan negotiations and on-site assistance with cash management. Customers are encouraged to linger for a cup of coffee, to lunch and chat with Nelson, to call her or any senior executive at the office or at home to discuss an investment, a business opportunity or to seek financial advice.

Such service has attracted loyal customers, and the client base has grown through personal relationships and word-of-mouth. Investors and borrowers are impressed by the bank's willingness to tailor loans. Some businesses need loans that consider the uniqueness of their situation. Few banks are willing to lend to a business or individual who does not fit into standardized lending slots. Summit, however, sees itself as the "make sense bank" — if a project makes sense, even if it is slightly unconventional, then the bank works with the client to see that it meets the regulatory requirements and structures the deal to work.

Summit goes beyond lending and managing money. Clients need someone to listen, to care about their businesses, to celebrate their victories with them, to help anticipate and counter challenges. The bank engages with its customers as partner, confidante, mentor — and friend.

The bank's atmosphere is serene, comfortable and warm. Summit's customers never stand in lines. They sit in burgundy, upholstered armchairs at private tellers' desks. In fact, if customers are too busy to come to the bank, the bank goes to them — via its couriers who pick up deposits.

Summit Bank reflects its founder — an enchanting, unpretentious woman who blends spontaneity and humor with sophisticated savvy and genuine interest in the people around her.

Today, Nelson, chairman of the board at Summit Bank and CEO, is involved in long-range planning and policy. She is one of only a few women bank CEOs in the state, much less the nation. With no college degree, and little knowledge of how the bank regulatory system operated, she dove in, learning quickly and letting her people

skills and intuition guide her through a male-dominated industry. Nelson relies on personal relationships to open doors and get things done — even to fund her civic and community projects.

The list is impressive, but most notably, Nelson co-chairs Sen. Dianne Feinstein's Women's Leadership Council and serves on the board of Harvard University's John F. Kennedy School of Government. The bank supports Oakland community activities, began a new Summit Bank community foundation and donates to schools and other nonprofit organizations. Nelson sits on the boards of several civic organizations, encourages employees to get involved in community activities and requires all bank officers to serve on the board of at least one civic or nonprofit organization.

While Nelson has given Summit Bank its charm, its success is also a function of the dedicated employees and supportive board of directors, a shared vision for personalized banking services to medical community businesses, and banking services to small businesses. The bank's founding, growth and its service to an exclusive clientele adds yet another dimension to the complexity and diversity of Oakland. ■

Summit Bank's original board of directors, c. 1984, (standing) Barbara J. Williams, Craig M. Cokeley, Robert A. Ellsworth and George H. Hollidge, (seated) Robert H. Mitgang, Martin C. Kauffman, Shirley Nelson, Jerald R. Goldman and Kikuo Nakahara, (not pictured) Thomas F. Louderback

205

Creative Wood

Creative Wood has been a successful producer of high-end contract business furnishings since its founding in 1986. It is aptly named, for the company's success hinges on its ability to offer a creative solution to the unique furnishing needs of architects and designers nationwide. Creative Wood's made-to-order solutions have included handsome, hardwood, fin-shaped reception stations with stainless steel accents, tower organizers featuring unique geometric designs and tilt-down work surfaces, and segmented conference tables with options such as brushed chrome accents and curly maple insets. One look at the variety of shapes and styles Creative Wood has produced reveals the company's exceptional ability to provide furnishing ideas to suit unique needs.

Joe Mendes purchased the majority of the corporation, then a fence post and odd-job company, with five other partners in late 1986. The product line was changed from millwork to fine wood office furniture and, during the first eight months, annual sales increased from $400,000 to $1,000,000. The company's success led to an increase in employees from eight to 26.

By 1989 Creative Wood's requirement for additional manufacturing space led it to move from its original South San Francisco location to 77th Avenue in Oakland. At its new location, the company had grown from 17,000 square feet to 28,000. Creative Wood grew so quickly, however, that it was soon operating out of a 36,000-square-foot facility, with 50 employees and sales reaching $5,000,000.

The Executive Oval Desk Unit embodies the utmost in beauty, simplicity and utility.

In 1987 Joe began the process of buying out their partners, and by 1992, he had become the majority owner of Creative Wood. The business continued to thrive. Four years later, sales had grown to $10,000,000 and, by 1997, it had reached $13,000,000.

Today Creative Wood employs 160 full-time employees, operates out of a 90,000-square-foot manufacturing space in Oakland and is still a rapidly growing, successful manufacturer of made-to-order, high-end business furnishings. The company's success rate is due to its high-quality, customized furniture and a management style that combines the best in modern innovation with economic good sense.

The strong, steady growth of Creative Wood has resulted in a financially sound organization that has overcome a number of obstacles since its inception. In 1993 Creative Wood withstood a very costly minority shareholder lawsuit along with other nuisance lawsuits, corporate IRS audits at "no change" each time, and other recurring tax audits. Despite such disrupting events, the company has always been able to meet the ever-changing demands of its customers by extending a 100 percent warranty on all products.

Creative Wood's standardized clients have included American Express and Wells Fargo, among a number of architects, interior designers and furniture dealers throughout the nation. The company's office units feature the rounded organic forms popular in modern corporate offices, with such unusual innovations as "floating glass" counters, ribbed glass, and "customized cubbyholes." Locally, Creative Wood has built interiors

One of Creative Wood's popular designs for the busy professional — the 2500 Series Executive L-Shape Wall Unit with Arc Desk Runoff

206

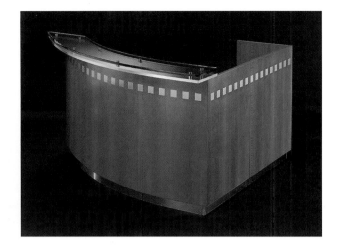

for the Oakland city attorney's office and the San Francisco and Santa Clara courthouses.

Creative Wood's graceful cabinets, desks, conference tables and other furniture are veneered with beautiful hardwoods, detailed with inlay and handcrafted edges to custom specifications, yet each job is produced with surprising speed. Creative Wood's secret is in the architectural-grade, veneered particleboard they use. This particleboard, a recycled material, has a very thin veneer of maple, oak, walnut or cherry wood firmly attached to both sides. In addition, carefully crafted hardwood edges are attached to each piece, providing the beauty of solid hardwood. This process makes limited use of natural resources and extensive use of recycled materials. Creative Wood has always complied with strict environmental guidelines in its production and recycled 100 percent of wood, paper and chemical wastes, despite the financial difficulties this poses when competing with less environmentally aware companies.

Though thoroughly modern, Creative Wood maintains a careful "if it ain't broke, don't fix it" mindset when it comes to technology. The factory contains an old planer made in 1912 that is used every day to regulate board thickness. The owners maintain that no modern equipment could do a better job. At the same time, the factory uses a "cutting edge" router that requires only the insertion of a floppy disk to tell the computer what sizes and shapes of tabletops to cut. In recent years, Creative Wood also acquired a straight-edge bander, a machine that takes the place of 18 workers and produces 20 different hand-finished quality, hardwood edges for tables, desks and cabinet doors. When such new machines are introduced, it allows more workers to concentrate on the delicate work of finishing and

sanding, which, due to the material's thin veneer, requires a practiced hand and gentle touch.

Joe Mendes considers Oakland the best city in Northern California for business and industry because of its excellent growth potential and labor pool. His company has been helping to build the city's future since its move to Oakland in 1989. Creative Wood has made charitable contributions to the schools and churches that its workers and their families attend and has contributed to a number of other philanthropic institutions in the Bay Area. In addition, Creative Wood is unique among furniture factories of its size, in that it offers all 170 of its employees and their families full medical benefits, 401K plans and profit-sharing.

Since its move to Oakland, Creative Wood has added 56,000 square feet of space to its factory and 8,000 square feet to its finishing room and is currently looking for additional work space. As business continues to improve, Creative Wood foresees buying additional high-end, computerized equipment from Germany that should improve efficiency and boost profits immeasurably.

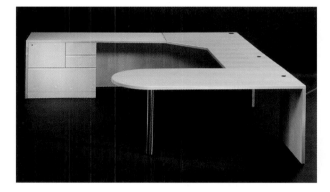

Business has always been good for Creative Wood, which offers almost unlimited overtime hours to its employees. However, the company's many years of success have not changed its principles. It still prides itself on quality workmanship, a demonstrated flexibility to adapt projects to customers specifications and short lead times. Creative Wood is a company that makes a point of constantly accepting the challenge of complex projects in order to continue to grow within the industry. Consequently, Joe Mendes' hard work over many years has created a company that is known locally for its innumerable contributions to the community, and nationally for its unparalleled service and unique designs. ∎

Sleek and unique, Creative Wood's Fin-Shaped Reception Station makes a bold statement.

This Executive U-Shape Unit features handsome blonde wood veneer and provides the maximum work area in a limited space.

207

Cost Plus World Market

For the woman who manages her home with the same efficiency she manages her career, shopping at Cost Plus World Market is an exciting reprieve from her busy life. She enters an exotic world enticed by its slightly peppery aroma not knowing what she will find, only that she will discover something new. She touches the nubby textiles and silky curtains, imagining how each might look in her home. She is fascinated by the colors of napkins, candles and accessories that would brighten her table. She lingers among the wines, the coffees and pastas and is transported to the broad valleys of the Loire, the open air market in Milan. As she reaches for an Indonesian basket, she smiles recognizing its beauty, its simplicity and its fine craftsmanship and decides it would add just the right touch of warmth and casual grace to her living room, beside the harvest mask from Ghana she bought on her last trip to Oakland's Cost Plus.

Forty years ago, the same sense of excitement may have sparked the birth of Cost Plus when a San Francisco businessman roamed the world and devised an ingenious plan for financing his treks. In 1958 he brought back a shipment of hand-woven, wicker furniture which he sold on the wharf out of a packing crate for cost, plus 10 percent. Long after the furniture had been sold, the idea and the name — Cost Plus — remained, and in the early 1960s the first Cost Plus store opened near Fisherman's Wharf in San Francisco, California.

Famed for its crowded aisles, Cost Plus offered distinctive collectibles, furniture and trinkets from nearly every country of the world at surprisingly affordable prices. The store, frequented by San Francisco's cosmopolitan residents, became a destination for tourists.

Cost Plus' Oakland store, opened in a warehouse near Jack London Square in 1973, contributed to the area's renaissance. By 1980, 33 stores existed along the West Coast. However, the expansion of Cost Plus did not come easily. Early challenges included spinning off its closest competitor, Pier 1 Imports, and struggling with the debt accumulated through the late 1980s.

In 1982 its headquarters moved to Oakland, where Cost Plus began to expand its retail market share. Its resurgence, credited to an ambitious national strategy, debt consolidation and public offerings, positioned Cost Plus to grow. Cost Plus had 48 stores by 1996 when it offered the public an opportunity to purchase its shares. Since 1997 it had averaged a 15 percent annual increase in profits. Debt-free, Cost Plus World Market strolled across America planting stores in metropolitan markets. At the century's end the number of stores had increased 20 percent a year to more than 100. It had 150 employees in Oakland, more than 3,000 employees nationwide, a $40 million credit line it had not used, and multimillion dollar profits.

From the mid-1960s to the mid-1980s, Cost Plus capitalized on changes in international trade, social behavior, technology, and cultural and environmental sensitivity. America's involvement in Vietnam sparked the curiosity of those who had tasted the flavor of Asia's mystery. Reopening of trade with China permitted the importation of previously forbidden goods. Cost Plus embraced both opportunities and established new Asian markets.

American lifestyles changed. Many had more leisure time and preferred living and entertaining more casually at home. They enjoyed cooking and delving into the world of gourmet foods. Cost Plus

Cost Plus distributes more than 500 wine varieties and more than 100 draft beers.

Dramatic displays of unusual collectibles attract the shopper's attention.

208

matched these social changes by expanding its home decor products, dining and kitchen wares, gifts and decorative accessories, and gourmet food and beverages. Cost Plus added home office furniture to accommodate the increasing trend toward telecommuting.

New technologies influenced how businesses operated and what products could be sold. The "slow boat to China" had been replaced by massive container ships traveling the oceans in days, rather than weeks. Containerization decreased breakage and increased the volume of shipped goods, enabling the stores to change inventory frequently and continue offering merchandise at low prices. Additionally, accessibility of airfreight and the ability to fly buyers to more remote places influenced the kinds of goods purchased and sold in the stores. Furthermore, Cost Plus had the added advantage of having its headquarters and distribution center located near the international ports of Oakland and Stockton.

Buying and arranging for merchandise transports had increased in speed and efficiency via the electronic age. By the late 1990s a rug buyer bouncing along on a four-wheel drive could use a cellular telephone to report her latest new find. Portable computers, e-mail and faxes had linked the stores with buyers and shippers.

Cost Plus had long-term relationships with vendors, and it imported goods from more than 50 countries. The trend toward off-shore production enabled Cost Plus to purchase directly from producers. Today nearly 60 percent of its goods are private label or made exclusively for Cost Plus. Its labels assure consumers of high quality and unmistakable value.

While buyers search for interesting items, they remain conscious of the social and environmental implications of their purchases. They seek, for example, wood products made from farmed trees rather than products that come from stripping old forests. Agents undertake extensive research to assure product authenticity and are willing to experiment with new merchandise. In addition, buyers and agents inspect factories regularly to ensure satisfactory working conditions. Because customers expect variety, 60 percent of its annual merchandise is new.

Cost Plus moved to adapt to these shifting social and technological currents, yet it never forgot its purpose to provide an array of distinctive products in a relaxed, attractive environment designed to captivate the shopper.

Store interiors replicate the original warehouse — concrete floors, open rafters, exposed fixtures. The backdrop creates an interesting atmosphere. Displays are colorful, provocative, teeming with multisensual experiences and stimulate a feeling that new possibilities exist around each corner. The overstuffed barrels and open shelves appeal to the typical shopper. She is well-educated, balancing family and career and wants to create an attractive, comfortable home. She enjoys beautiful furnishings and entertaining at home. She prefers a casual lifestyle, experiments with gourmet food and has a strong sense of her own eclectic style. She expects quality and value and eagerly spends an average of 50 minutes browsing through the store.

Cost Plus World Market is proud to be one of the Bay Area's homegrown companies that, during the last three decades, has built a new generation of national and international retail enterprises. It has worked hard to achieve a sound financial future, yet characteristically, it will maintain its irreverent spirit and entice shoppers to stroll through the world's bazaars. ■

Household furnishings, from Papasan chairs to wrought-iron tables to wood dining chairs and tables, constitute the basic product line.

The Marketplace, where Belgian chocolate meets Spanish wine, and where Italian pasta and South American coffee mingle

209

Metropolitan Contract Group, Inc.

The concepts — urban and classy, cultured and sleek — might lead one to think about richly burnished wood, sculpted glass, buttery leather, iron-on old brick. If one thought how these could be mixed irreverently with humor and utility, plastic and chrome, he or she might think about Metro Contract Group — furniture dealers and interior designers for the unconventional, the hip, the ethnically diverse future.

Metro began in 1989 from the dream of Dwight Jackson, a burned-out stockbroker who had a passion for design, a vision and the persistence to see it through. Metro's growth can be traced from a garden shed, tucked behind Jackson's home in the Oakland hills, to nearly 8,000 square feet of usable, beautifully designed office space near Jack London Square.

Within a few months of inception, Metro contracted with the City of Oakland and the East Bay Municipal Utility District to furnish its office spaces. With an army of independent contractors who designed and manufactured office furnishings, Metro soon attracted the attention of Herman Miller, one of the four major producers of high-end office furniture. In 1993 Metro became the East Bay's authorized dealer. The association drew large, corporate clients such as Bank of America, Silicon Graphics, Hewlett-Packard and AirTouch Communications. From its modest beginnings, Metro

Metro offices demonstrate the company's design versatility — fixtures, furnishings, carpeting and lighting tailored to client specifications.

grew from its first year's revenue of $25,000 to more than $10 million annually in only 10 years.

Metro began specializing in sports arenas in 1995 when it furnished the Oakland-Alameda County Arena, home of the Golden State Warriors. Metro's project included 72 suites, restaurants, owner's rooms, plants, outdoor furniture, artwork, back offices and dry-cleaning facilities.

Today sports and entertainment spaces including stadiums, arenas and large public facilities constitute a central component of Metro's business. Metro designers require detail craftsmanship and often incorporate team logos into the customized furnishings such as carpets and chairs intended to accommodate the shape of athletes, and other finishing touches.

Metro specializes in interior design, space planning and project management. It procures and installs furnishings, equipment and custom designs carpets and lighting fixtures. Metro professionals work with contractors and architects and provide asset management services including inventory, warehousing, transportation, and the sale and resale of equipment and furniture.

Because interior design evolves from the client's environment, Metro designers observe how people work to understand what interactions occur, how information flows between people and work units, and what aspects about day-to-day activity is essential to the client. For example, Metro clients include new, young Internet companies popping up throughout the Bay Area. Many of these small companies experience phenomenal growth, are unconventional and require custom design to fit the needs of an avant-garde corporate culture. For these companies, work is collaborative, work stations have two or three computers, and a 6-hour work day is the norm. Such challenges are met by Metro's creative affiliates — dtank — a group of designers who merge advanced manufacturing technology with creativity — and humor. Their designs are functional, inexpensive, ergonomically sound and "cool."

Metro's strategy for success includes reinvesting the profits into the company, into the people who helped the company grow, and staying attuned to new trends. Metro's offices — its "showroom" — display an intriguing blend of design and utility, and each wall, ceiling desk, fixture, chair or textured carpet demonstrates the company's versatility. Metro's investment in expensive software gave the company a design edge and enabled detailed project costing and tracking. Both investments expanded the company's capacity to handle more complicated projects. Metro also invests in its employees by supporting their personal and professional needs and encouraging them to grow with the company.

In 1999 Metro's ability to assess trends led to its newest venture — Metro @ home, a retail store featuring high-quality home furniture, lighting and accessories.

In recent years Oakland developments such as the bus terminal, Transit Center and Ferryboat Terminal made the East Bay connections to downtown San Francisco easier. With historically lower rents and a sunnier climate than San Francisco, developers began to refurbish and renovate older buildings into residential lofts. A loft-dwelling community emerged along a row of warehouses near Jack London Square. Today the loft-dweller community is expanding.

Metro @ home understood that loft living reversed the tendency of middle-class populations to migrate from city centers to the suburbs. The shift indicated changing sensibilities, values and aesthetic standards. In the forefront of new lifestyles, loft dwellers appreciated high-quality design elements — elements to blend the old and the new. Because of limited space, they sought innovative ways of combining form with function and expressed an increasing interest in cross-cultural designs, specifically designs incorporating strong Asian or African motifs.

Metro @ home emerged to reflect and help develop this burgeoning urban consciousness. The store blended Herman Miller classics with European imports — often light-years ahead of American design — and custom, one-of-a-kind items created by local and national artists and designers.

A central theme of the store is to provide an outlet for industrial artists, potters, glass blowers and others who rarely have galleries for their handcrafted designs. As Jackson notes, the Bay Area is filled with talented and ethnically diverse artists. Metro's goal is to support these local artists, to offer a gallery for displaying their cross-culturally inspired designs, and to use the

Team identity expressed through its logo, symbols and colors blended into carefully crafted design create a comfortable, tasteful service for the Golden State Warriors' fans.

store as a distribution outlet for locally produced and signed art.

In March 2000 Metro @ home launched an e-commerce division of its company, metroathome.com. The company offers an international catalogue of more than 100 product lines. Shoppers can scroll through designers' databases and purchase online or from the store directly. The site carries over 3,000 items, highlight an artist-of-the-week and offer the artist a worldwide presence and distribution network.

Although born in San Francisco, Dwight Jackson is a longtime resident of Oakland and is committed to the community through his direct involvement with various nonprofit groups.

Designed for loft-living, Metro @ home blends function and form.

In the short term, Metro aims to be the top dealer in office furniture in the East Bay within five years and duplicate Metro @ home in other major metropolitan markets such as New York, San Francisco and Seattle. Whether designing an office interior, a sports stadium or merchandising home furnishings, Metro Group, Inc. will continue to blend classic furniture and contemporary European style with the well-crafted designs and quality of local artists. Metro is at the forefront of defining a new urban consciousness, identifying new life and work styles, and shaping a new, exciting Oakland. ■

211

Piedmont Grocery

Nearly a century has transpired since Piedmont Grocery first opened its doors for business in 1902. Through earthquakes, fires and economic turmoil, it has remained consistent in its promise to deliver gourmet specialty foods from around the world and personal service that has endeared it to generations of families.

By the turn of the century, Oakland was the second-largest city on the Pacific Coast and enough of a metropolis to have its own suburbs. Nestled in the foothills of Oakland, Piedmont was one such suburb that began as a resort area aptly named Piedmont Park. Adventurous Eastern travelers swarmed to the natural mineral springs, while many San Franciscans came for day outings and summer vacations. As a playground for the rich, it was not surprising that Piedmont Grocery thrived as a specialty gourmet market — especially when items customers enjoyed while traveling abroad, such as Perrier water, could be found at their local grocer.

When co-founders Herman and Eugenia Sack expressed interest in a parcel of land on Piedmont Avenue, a real estate developer tipped them that the Key Route's transbay train system was coming within a block of the proposed site. The Key Route's electric trains traveled between San Francisco and the East Bay, bringing many wealthy commuters. Quickly realizing that the land was valuable, the Sacks bought the property on Piedmont Avenue and agreed to pay for the lot with groceries. After it was built, the Sacks resided above the store. In the early years, delivery-men went out in the morning to take orders and delivered groceries in the afternoon using horse-drawn carriages.

Oakland and its outlying districts experienced a housing construction boom after the 1906 earthquake. Many San Franciscans who summered in Piedmont decided that a permanent East Bay residence might be worth considering. In the 1920s, the demand for housing continued, spurred by postwar prosperity and the opening of new real estate tracks. Piedmont was among those areas that experienced the greatest growth, and business for the neighborhood grocer only got better.

Herman and Eugenia handed Herbert Sack, their son, shares to Piedmont Grocery on his 21st birthday. Four years later, the elder Sacks moved to a ranch in Concord, and Herbert and his wife Ida took ownership of the store.

A firm believer in organization, Herbert had the ability to pull together the right combinations to make sound business progress. He gained notoriety for being a leader in the food industry and was one of the organizers of Oakland's leading grocery-buying groups. The group made it possible for independent grocers to buy on the same basis as larger chains. Herbert never wanted to be the largest, just the best. He refused to lower principles or compromise quality, understanding that high standards needed to be maintained to meet and surpass his customers' expectations.

In 1921, at the tender age of 15, an ambitious Charles Larson began his career at Piedmont Grocery cleaning horse stalls. Recognizing his dedication and potential, the Sack family rewarded Charles with a series of promotions — from stablehand to delivery driver to buyer and store manager and, eventually, to general manager in 1935.

Prior to 1933, the store still offered counter service. Counter service meant that a clerk would pull sundries from the shelves at a customer's request. However,

The interior of Piedmont Grocery, c. 1910

when services were curtailed and prices frozen during World War II, economies of scale were a popular and necessary procedure. In response, Piedmont Grocery established its self-service grocery department, adjusting prices accordingly. Initially, the self-service concept was not embraced by its upscale customers. Over time, however, Piedmont Grocery's faithful patrons appreciated the price adjustments that made it possible to enjoy the same quality at reduced prices.

The Larson family bought controlling interest in 1956, never losing sight of the vital role their customers played in the success of the store. Piedmont Grocery continued offering a variety of fine foods and, perhaps more importantly, the personal service that captivated such prestigious customers as several California governors and one of the first chairmen of the Union Pacific.

Charles' son, Dave Larson, arrived at Piedmont Grocery in 1968 with a degree in food distribution from the University of Southern California. Dave certainly wasn't a stranger to the grocery business, having spent most of his childhood playing in and around the store. Dave became president in 1974, a year that marked the beginning of major lifestyle changes. Women began returning to the work force, and the days where mothers stayed home with their children — cooking pot roasts and mashed potatoes — were long gone. Piedmont Grocery accommodated these changes by introducing specialty items that could be prepared quickly and easily. New eating habits also emerged focusing on healthy living. Lighter, health-conscious foods were in demand, and Piedmont Grocery once again changed to meet the desires of its customers.

At one time, there were five Piedmont Grocery stores, including a gourmet food shop at the once-famous White House department store on Union Square in San Francisco. But in the gourmet grocery business, more was not necessarily better. Even when larger chain stores began popping up everywhere, focusing on high volume instead of quality, Piedmont Grocery didn't feel the squeeze of competition. Comparing it to a major chain was like comparing apples to kumquats — simply put, you couldn't.

Today, customers are greeted by a vibrant flower stand lining the outside entrance, filled with fresh-cut flowers, indoor and outdoor plants, as well as herbs. With the exception of a few updates, the interior reflects the Larson family's desire to maintain its niche as a neighborhood grocer. Employees call customers by name and, being that employee turnover is virtually nil, the same can be said in reverse order.

With specialty food items like peanut-braised tofu, Canadian veggie bacon and pear vinegar, it's easy to see why customers relish shopping at Piedmont Grocery. Featuring one of the most extensive cheese selections in the Bay Area, shoppers can choose from more than 300 hand-cut domestic and imported cheeses. Or, they can peruse the wine and spirit aisles to select the perfect domestic or imported wine, in addition to specialty bourbon and single malt scotch. With the widest variety of organically and hydroponically grown produce, customers will not have any trouble locating those hard-to-find items, ranging from 20th-century apple pears to black sphinx dates.

If the past is any indication of the future, Piedmont Grocery will continue to evolve to meet the ever-changing needs of each unique generation of shoppers, by offering unsurpassed quality, variety and personal service. ∎

(1904-1906) The Sacks resided above the store and depended on their dogs to keep intruders at bay.

Piedmont Grocery offered daily delivery service until 1958.

213

Douglas Parking

Sanford Douglas founded Douglas Parking in 1930. One of Oakland's oldest family-operated businesses, it is also one of the first parking companies in the country. According to family lore, Sanford Douglas started parking cars in 1930 after a motorist offered him a nickel to park cars one day at his Claremont Avenue service station in Oakland. Slowly, as more and more people drove to Oakland to shop at the city's bustling downtown retail stores, parking became the focus of the business.

Sanford's son, Leland, worked in his father's service station and parking lots after classes during high school and summers. He began working full time for the company in 1967. Prior to joining his father, Leland earned a degree in economics from the University of California at Berkeley in 1961, then served as an officer in the Army.

Currently, Douglas Parking is run by the third generation of Douglases — Leland's two sons, David and Steven, and their cousin, David Flett. Because Leland felt that an education and work experience outside of the family business had benefited him, he insisted that his children first graduate from college and work elsewhere for at least two years. This arrangement, he felt, would give his children the same opportunity to broaden themselves and to grow to appreciate the business that he had first enjoyed. He also felt it would allow his kids to decide for themselves if the parking business was what they wanted to do for a living.

Before joining Douglas Parking, David Douglas graduated from the University of California at Santa Barbara with a degree in business economics, then worked for a parking company in Ohio for two years. David's younger brother, Steven, earned a degree in broadcast journalism from Arizona State University, then worked for a large parking company in New York for two years. David Flett graduated from San Francisco State University with a degree in business administration. Currently, he oversees the company's off-airport facility, Airpark, at Oakland Airport.

Today Douglas Parking is a regional parking organization, operating more than 120 parking facilities in 27 Bay Area cities. The company offers a range of parking services that include parking and garage lot management, valet parking and shuttle transport. It is a progressive organization with an ethnically diverse work force.

Leland has served on the board of directors of the National Parking Association since 1975 and David Douglas became a member of the board in 1994. The Douglases are also active in their wider community, supporting a variety of philanthropic causes throughout the Bay Area. Leland is a member and past president of both the Lake Merritt Breakfast Club and the Executives Association of Oakland. He has also served on the Transportation Committee of the Oakland Chamber of Commerce and the Mayor's New Ways Business Leadership Forum.

David Douglas has been a volunteer with Big Brothers/Big Sisters of the East Bay and has served on the board of directors of the Rotary Club of Oakland. He has also served on the board of directors of the Central Business District Association. Steven is a member of the Guardsmen, a philanthropic Bay Area organization.

Located in a white, concrete building on Webster Street in Oakland, where it has been headquartered for the last 70 years, Douglas Parking could be called a pillar of Oakland's business community. ■

Douglas Parking main garage, 1936

214

The Fat Lady

Louis Shaterian, whose passion was Victorian-era antiques, opened The Fat Lady with his wife, Patricia, in 1970. Their intention was to create a homey, neighborhood establishment where local business people could meet for lunch and cocktails. It was to be somewhat secluded, a special place reserved for "those in the know." Accordingly, it was to be called The Rendezvous, but a young art student's painting would soon change all that.

A superior court judge and friend of Shaterian's knew the restaurateur was a passionate collector and introduced Shaterian to a recent painting done by his own son. It was a nude rendering of a pleasingly plump lady. Louis and Patricia liked the painting so well that it became the namesake for their new restaurant.

It was commonly known that The Fat Lady's building, built in 1884, had once been a house of ill-repute. The restaurant's founders could not resist the temptation to bring the painting to life through a bit of harmless mythology. As a result, "legend" has it that the large woman in the painting was none other than the madam of the building's former brothel. A woman of extravagant tastes, she is quoted on the restaurant's menu as having used as her personal motto, "It's much better to live rich than to die rich."

The Fat Lady is replete with artifacts such as colorful Tiffany lamps, beveled glass doors, bentwood chairs and ornate stained and leaded glass. There is glasswork from San Francisco's famous Fox Theatre and an ornate, turn-of-the-century backbar that was hammered out of the concrete at a defunct North Beach pool hall. Light fixtures have been acquired from Alameda mansions and stained-glass brewery signs from their original San Francisco locations. A chandelier was acquired from an old bordello in Northern California's gold country, and it illuminates the stairwell through rich, red globes. The colorful flowerboxes and outdoor seating also help to give the place a festive, New Orleans-style atmosphere.

The Fat Lady is the oldest establishment in Jack London Square to be continuously owned by one family. Louis and Patricia Shaterian's daughter, also named Patricia, who had been working in the family restaurant since her early 20s, purchased The Fat Lady in 1984 with her husband, Jerry Rossi. Jerry and Patricia have begun the process of passing on this family treasure by involving three of their four children in the business. In this way, three generations of Shaterians and Rossis have been born and raised in Oakland and taken some part in the life — and mythology — of The Fat Lady.

The early 1990s saw a banquet facility added to the restaurant's second floor. As customers ascend to the banquet room, they pass candid photographs of Jack London in various phases of his life, as well as historical photos of Oakland's once-thriving shipyards. The banquet room features ornate decorations, gilt mirrors, a carved, wooden bar and an antique, brass cash register.

Today The Fat Lady is a traditional meeting place for customers from all walks of life, and, due to its familiar atmosphere, has even been called the "Cheers" of the West Coast. Owner Patricia Rossi sees Oakland as "a city in the process of coming to full flower." Her vision is consistent with her experience, for The Fat Lady restaurant is now, and has long been, a dynamic part of that growth. ■

The Fat Lady Restaurant features indoor and patio dining in a warm, intimate, turn-of-the-century atmosphere.

215

Hilton Oakland Airport

When Conrad Hilton set out to buy a bank in 1919, he had absolutely no intention of investing in a hotel. Perhaps it was pure destiny that fateful day in Cisco, Texas. Regardless of the reason, the purchase of The Mobley Hotel was the first step to the end result of an empire known as Hilton Hotels — one of the most widely recognized corporations in the hospitality industry with over 1,900 properties and nearly 280,000 guestrooms available.

As part of this incredible legacy, the Hilton Oakland Airport began its operation on March 31, 1970.

The Hilton Oakland Airport is ideally situated just beyond the entrance of the Oakland Airport, deemed San Francisco's East Bay Gateway to the universe. With more than 20,000 square feet of meeting space and 363 spacious guest rooms, it accommodates the needs of a diverse community of guests, providing the ultimate setting for weddings, business meetings, galas and conventions. Business and pleasure travelers appreciate the array of in-room amenities, a heated outdoor pool, and a fully equipped fitness center.

Situated on 12 acres of meticulously manicured grounds, each guestroom is graced with opulent decor and thoughtful appointments.

Although the pace of activity in the lobby is frenetic, the Hilton Oakland Airport's courteous staff perfectly orchestrates the flow of traffic, creating a professional and tranquil atmosphere. Guests may even see Tom Hanks carrying a piece of luggage from the past while waltzing through the lobby.

Dining opportunities at the Hilton Oakland Airport are abundant, with three restaurants from which to choose. For gourmet fare, Stanley's Grill provides an intimate setting, while the Sports Edition Bar is a more upbeat atmosphere with the broadcasting of nonstop sporting events coupled with dance bands on the weekends. For a quick bite, Amelia's Café serves breakfast and lunch in an airy atmosphere.

Visitors have access to an unlimited number of nearby attractions, from a trip to the historic waterfront of Jack London Square to a sporting event or concert at the nearby Network Associates Coliseum and Arena. The world-famous sights of San Francisco are a mere 20 minutes away with traffic-free travel available through Bay Area Rapid Transit (BART). An enhanced ride by ferry may even be desirable.

Extensive marketing programs and renovations underscore the hotel's continued pledge to exceed each guest's expectations. The hard work and dedication of the staff was nationally recognized recently when the hotel received a prestigious award for the "Most Improved Hotel" in the Hilton Corporation. The Hilton Pride Award — 1998, speaks highly of the tremendous efforts by its team members to accommodate its guests.

The Hilton Oakland Airport is currently in the process of renovating its meeting facilities while working on the final plans for a complete exterior update, including a new outdoor pool and surrounding area.

The Hilton Oakland Airport will continue the heritage of innovation and quality that has made the Hilton name synonymous with first-class hospitality. ■

The manicured grounds at the Hilton Oakland Airport provide a perfect backdrop for weddings, galas and conventions.

216

Thai Kitchen

Seth Jacobson was contemplating entering law school when the hand of fate intervened in his life. In 1989 Jacobson was traveling in Asia and had planned to tour China when the Tiananmen Square political demonstration caused him to visit Thailand instead. There, the University of California, Berkeley graduate, who had worked for Pacific Film Archive and a computer research company, gained the idea of opening a Thai food business in the United States. Jacobson knew a few things about food — his family had a gourmet coffee store when he was a teenager — and he knew that Thai food, with its spicy, exotic and complex flavors, was popular in the Bay Area. After making several subsequent trips to Thailand, in late 1990 Jacobson decided to put his idea into action.

The most important thing about starting his own business was creating the Thai Kitchen brand. From the onset, Jacobson wanted to respond to the growing popularity of Thai food with authentic, high-quality, all-natural, healthy, staple products. He chose Oakland as the place to locate his business for three reasons: Pacific Rim/Northern California business ties, Oakland's expanding role as an epicenter of Asian foods, and its proximity to Southeast Asia, which provided good access to seaports. He launched Thai Kitchen locally in food markets such as The Berkeley Bowl and Whole Foods Market in Berkeley, Andronico's, The Pasta Shop, and Piedmont Grocery.

As a result of Thai Kitchen's dedication to quality, it is now the leading importer and manufacturer of authentic Thai food products in North America. Thai Kitchen has a commitment to make all its products with no artificial ingredients, preservatives or chemical additives: Thai Kitchen noodles are 100 percent natural, and Thai Kitchen instant rice noodles are made with rice flour and water — steam-cooked, slowly dried and not fried. Thai Kitchen coconut milk is freshly pressed from ripe coconuts, and its curry paste is milled from fresh herbs. Thai Kitchen's suppliers and growers use only the freshest and most carefully selected ingredients to capture the wonderfully complex and distinct taste of Thai cuisine.

Thai Kitchen products range from prepared dry noodles and flavored rice mixes to sauces, ready-to-serve soups and teas, and include such names as Lemon Grass & Chili Instant Rice Noodles, Jasmine Rice Stir-Fry Noodles, Original Recipe Peanut Satay Sauce, Coconut Ginger Soup and Thai Iced Tea. The products appeal to consumers who desire "quick and easy" foods, as well as those who want to prepare Thai food from scratch. One of Thai Kitchen's challenges is to help people learn basic Thai cooking; to this end, it offers recipes that use curry paste, coconut milk, fish sauce and other basic Thai ingredients.

Since Jacobson began bringing Thai food to America, both the Bay Area and other parts of the United States have seen burgeoning growth in the interest of Asian foods. The Thai segment of the Asian food category has posted double digit growth since 1990, and in 1998 sales of Thai food grew by 25 percent. In just over nine years Thai Kitchen's growing number and kinds of products have increased to the point that Jacobson now sells to every major market and thousands of specialty food stores in the United States and Canada. ■

Seth Jacobson, founder of Thai Kitchen

Washington Inn

George and Martha Washington — or rather, their stately profiles etched in glass in the double doors — greet every visitor to the Washington Inn. Beyond the doors of this landmark inn, opposite the Oakland Convention Center, one finds a part of Old Oakland's revitalized charm in the form of comfortable accommodations and fine dining.

Located on Tenth Street between Broadway and Washington in the Old Oakland Historic District — the city's first business area — Washington Inn was built in 1913 by locally prominent architect A.W. Smith in the Italianate style. Notable exterior features include

The full-service 495 Restaurant offers guests casual, romantic dining.

double-hung windows and a galvanized iron cornice featuring medallions above each bay and large-scale brackets. First known as the Hotel Ray, the hotel has changed hands many times over the years, even serving as a residence hotel during the 1950s. The inn has benefited from the design influences and fresh management approach of the Braun family, which has a strong commitment to excellence and clientele satisfaction.

In April 1987 an exterior "face lift," and interior refurbishing and restoration were completed, and in 1998 Washington Inn underwent seismic upgrading. Guests at the inn find that the upgraded rooms, in keeping with Edwardian charm, contain pedestal-style bathroom sinks, separate baths and either two twin beds or one queen-size bed. There are 47 guest rooms, including eight suites. A full buffet breakfast is included in the price of the room and the hotel management provides personalized service and attention to detail that makes a guest's stay both pleasurable and memorable.

Washington Inn's 495 Restaurant opened in 1998 after the former cocktail lounge/breakfast area was converted into a full-service restaurant. The restaurant's strong architectural design features rich mahogany wood paneling and pillars. These features, along with white tablecloths and warm candlelight, combine to create a casual-but-elegant atmosphere for a memorable dining experience. The restaurant can seat 50 people; the mezzanine will seat another 20. There are also private dining and banquet facilities for 10 to 50 people. The lunch-hour crowd is finding Washington Inn to be a popular dining setting in downtown Oakland.

The restaurant's chef holds a diploma from the California Culinary Academy, and the menu focuses on contemporary American cuisine with hints of international influences. Popular appetizers include Corn Crab Cake, Caribbean Coconut Prawn Salad, Ahi Tuna "Pokie" Tartare, and main entrees range from Moroccan Marinade Double Breast of Chicken to New Zealand Blue Nose Bass and Lemon Dill Papardelle Pasta. The restaurant also has an extensive wine list.

In addition to these amenities, the full bar has two televisions with a pool table in an adjacent area, and the hotel offers live music Friday evening. Washington Inn also has a conference room off the main lobby that will hold up to 70 persons. Today Washington Inn, in its convenient location opposite the Oakland Convention Center, serves many convention attendees. A federal building and major corporate offices nearby also attract many business travelers to Oakland, some of whom partake of Washington Inn's old-fashioned hospitality and enduring charm. ■

218

Waterfront Plaza Hotel

Buzz Gibb first founded what is now the Waterfront Plaza Hotel as a Boatel Inn in 1964. At that time, Jack London Square was already a bustling center of restaurants and cafes. Gibb's Inn featured 70 guest rooms and catered mostly to the business traveler. The establishment immediately began to thrive, soon becoming one of the Square's most prominent features. By 1990 the establishment had grown to 144 guest rooms and acquired local cache as one of the area's most well-appointed hotels.

The Waterfront's restaurant, once called Jack's Bar and Grill, has been revamped and is now the stylish Jack's Bistro. The Bistro features a modern exhibition kitchen, rustic accents, a collection of Art Deco prints, and unique wrought-iron furniture. Guests are entertained nightly with piano music, and weekends feature live bands. In addition, Jack's Bistro features a full bakery where all of the restaurant's bread is made fresh daily.

Most striking about Jack's Bistro is its beautiful, intricate mural work, completed in 1996 by Stephanie Taylor of Sacramento. Inside, the walls are adorned with larger-than-life paintings of plump tomatoes, onions and peppers. The vegetables seem to tumble across a wall over the cook's heads as they stoke the restaurant's own wood-burning pizza oven. Outdoors, the mural on Jack's Bistro's patio depicts a busy scene of patrons dining and waiters carrying colorful trays of crab, lobster and other seaside cuisine rendered in 3-D relief. The astute observer will also notice that to the left of the Bistro's entrance, within the mural's colorful, festive scene, hides a portrait of the owner, Buzz Gibb, serving the local fare, and one of Jack London himself, navigating with a sexton.

Since its early days as host to business travelers in Oakland's vital 1960s economy, through its continued growth in the intervening years, and now in its heyday as a corporate meeting place and wedding/bar mitzvah venue, the Waterfront Plaza Hotel has consistently given back to its community. The hotel's sales staff are active members of the Oakland Chamber of Commerce, and the general manager sits on the chamber's board of directors. The hotel regularly supports the Marcus Foster Institute, which rewards outstanding area teachers, the East Bay Symphony and Ballet and the Oakland A's. The hotel annually sponsors five local elementary school students on "Take Your Children To Work Day."

Across Jack London Square, a poem on the U.N. World Wall for Peace declares, "the stars that give night form... steer the dreamer." When the stars come out in Oakland, visitors at the Waterfront Plaza Hotel are found relaxing to the languid sounds of live music from Jack's Bistro, among greenery at poolside, or simply enjoying their comfortable accommodations. This familiar, well-appointed hotel has provided pleasant dreams for guests since 1964 and will surely do so for many years to come. ■

Jack London Square's unparalleled views of San Francisco Bay are one of the many attractions at the Waterfront Plaza Hotel.

Jack's Bistro is a popular place to dine, celebrate or meet informally with clients.

219

Yoshi's

Yoshi's began in 1973 as a small, North Berkeley sushi bar owned by a trio of struggling artists. Its founder and namesake, Yoshie Akiba, orphaned during World War II, came to the United States to study fine arts, dance and dance therapy. During her college years, Akiba began two things that have since changed her life: she began to practice a form of Buddhist meditation known as *zazen*, and with her two best friends — Kaz Kajimura, a journalist and carpenter, and Hiroyuki Hori, a painter and Japanese cook — she opened Yoshi's.

After its move to Claremont Avenue in Oakland in 1977, the sushi bar responded favorably to suggestions that it introduce live music. This commitment slowly evolved into Yoshi's becoming a respected music venue specializing in jazz. The partners built a bigger venue next door and soon developed an impressive reputation by featuring such greats as Joshua Redman, Branford Marsalis, Dizzy Gillespie and Oscar Peterson among hundreds of others.

Despite the new location's popularity, by the end of 1994 the extreme expense of keeping a jazz house packed began to take its toll on Yoshi's. The partners had sold their building and were beginning to sell off personal possessions in order to pay the bills. Yoshi's expected to close for good.

Just in time, the Oakland Redevelopment Agency and Port of Oakland offered help to the Oakland landmark. The city helped the partners to relocate to the newly remodeled Jack London Square.

The only space in the area big enough for the restaurant's acoustical and stage requirements was directly under a parking garage and near the Amtrak train tracks, so the partners, undaunted, began to design a venue that would have to overcome the vibration and noise of the trains and cars. Skilled architects and acoustical engineers worked with the partners night and day to solve the problems, and at the last possible moment, in May 1997, Yoshi's received city approval to open.

Opening night featured pianist George Shearing, who is blind and extremely sensitive to noise. A perfectionist, he has been known to refuse to play a gig if the venue doesn't meet his standards. Nobody was sure yet of the quality of the acoustical remodeling, so when a train passed during Shearing's rehearsal, none of the partners dared breathe. But the test proved their building worthy, for Shearing did not even notice.

Today Yoshi's gives back to the community that has supported it for so long by featuring a diverse spectrum of jazz shows and programs, providing a venue for emerging Bay Area musicians, and promoting Sunday matinees and educational workshops for children with visiting jazz musicians.

Yoshi's restaurant is well known for its sukiyaki, steamed sea bass, vegetable tempura and creative sushi combinations as well as its serene, nature-themed, Japanese decor. Due to the high-ceilinged, mini-amphitheater design, it has often been said about Yoshi's jazz club that there isn't a bad seat in the house. Though the room is large, the feeling is intimate. It is a fitting atmosphere because Yoshie, Kaz and Hiro have put so much effort into Yoshi's over the years that the trio feel like a family. It is this sense of warm hospitality that emerges to make Yoshi's one of the West Coast's premier night spots. ■

Owners Kaz Kajimura, Hiro Hori and Yoshie Akiba celebrate Yoshi's grand opening at Jack London Square.

220

Photo by Robert A. Eplett

221

Networks

Oakland transportation, media and other companies keep people, information and goods circulating throughout the region.

San Francisco Bay Area Rapid Transit District

A pioneer of the modern mass transportation era, the San Francisco Bay Area Rapid Transit District (BART), was the first rail rapid transit system to be built in the United States in almost 60 years. The last urban rail system before BART was built in 1907.

The central nerve system of BART is housed in downtown Oakland. The tranquil atmosphere inside the control center gives little indication of the organized hubbub taking place beyond its walls. It is here that the breadth and scope of the BART operation can be witnessed, as every employee focuses on the same goal — to make transportation throughout four counties as comfortable and efficient as possible for the nearly 330,000 people that ride BART daily.

Although the concept of BART officially took root in 1946, its inception can be traced back as far as 1920. Many of the world's top engineers were intrigued

BART train with San Francisco in view

by the challenge of constructing a transbay tube that would link San Francisco to the East Bay. Maj. Gen. George T. Goethals, who oversaw the construction of the Panama Canal, proposed to build the transbay tube. His idea was not pursued. Construction for the Bay Bridge began a few years later and was completed in 1936. Ironically, the transbay tube was built 45 years later, following almost the exact alignment outlined in Goethals' original plan.

The Jules Verne notion of an underwater tube resurfaced after World War II, as postwar migration and the automobile boom resulted in mounting congestion

on the bridges spanning the bay. In 1947 a joint Army-Navy review board decided that another connecting link between San Francisco and Oakland was needed, not only to ease traffic conditions, but also from a national defense standpoint.

As the population increased, so did the pressure for a traffic solution. In 1951 the California Legislature created the 26-man San Francisco Bay Area Rapid Transit Commission. The group was charged with devising a plan to address the long-range transportation needs of the Bay Area. Acting on the commission's recommendation, the state Legislature formed the San Francisco Bay Area Rapid Transit District in 1957. The District was comprised of five counties — Alameda, Contra Costa, Marin, San Francisco and San Mateo.

In the early 1960s the mind-set of the American people was considerably different than it is today. Aerospace technology was burgeoning, and the United States had just embarked on a space race with the Soviets. BART capitalized on space-age technology, allowing its visionaries to design a state-of-the-art system that would usher in a new era of rapid transit.

Throughout the planning and development stages, hundreds of meetings were held in district communities. In 1961 the final plan was submitted to the supervisors of the five counties for approval. San Mateo County Supervisors voted to withdraw their county, citing the high costs of the new system. Their withdrawal weakened the districtwide tax base, thus forcing Marin County to pull out as well. The five-county plan was quickly revised to a three-county plan. It was then placed on the ballot for the November 1962 election.

The plan required a 60 percent voter approval. It barely passed with a 61.2 percent vote districtwide. After the election, engineers immediately started work on the final system designs, only to be stopped in their tracks by a taxpayers' suit filed against the district. While the court ruled in favor of the district, six months of litigation resulted in $12 million in construction delays.

Despite numerous setbacks, BART continued to forge ahead. On June 19, 1964, BART construction

224

began with President Lyndon B. Johnson officiating at the groundbreaking ceremonies.

Four years later, an extraordinary feat in civil engineering was accomplished with the completion of the Transbay Tube. Assembled in 57 sections, 135 feet below the surface of the San Francisco Bay at its deepest point, the $180 million structure took less than three years to complete. Not only did the Transbay Tube receive numerous engineering awards, it had the power to capture the imaginations of people from around the globe. Thousands of curious visitors walked, jogged and bicycled through the tube before the installation of tracks and electricity.

BART first opened its doors for service on September 11, 1972. Throughout the next two decades, it continued to expand to meet the growing mass transportation needs of Bay Area commuters, by offering an alternative mode of travel that was both reliable and fast.

Then at 5:04 p.m. on October 17, 1989, the Loma Prieta earthquake rocked the Bay Area. A section of the Bay Bridge collapsed, and many other highways and bridges were shut down until their structural soundness could be affirmed. Within three hours of the record-setting earthquake, BART was up and running and was the only fully operational means of transportation in the Bay Area. Because it took several months to repair ravaged roadways, BART ridership went from 219,000 a day to a peak of 357,000 a day. BART became the Bay Area's shining star.

With one of the best safety records in the world, BART has carried more than 1.4 billion people over 16 billion passenger miles since it's inception. It continually strives to be at the forefront of technological breakthroughs and is developing an advanced, automatic train control system that will enable closer spacing between trains.

BART has also embarked on the largest construction program since the system was built. When in full operation, it will have grown the original 34-station, 71.5-mile system, to 43 stations and 103 miles of track with a fleet of nearly 669 transit cars. For the first time, direct service into San Francisco International Airport will be available.

Groundbreaking on the $1.513 billion extension took place in 1997. The four-station line will extend 7.4 miles from the Colma BART Station to Millbrae, with an additional 1.3 miles of track running east-west directly into the new international airport terminal currently under construction.

Most of the new line will be built underground with subway stations planned in South San Francisco and San Bruno. The airport station will be elevated and linked to the departure level of SFO's new international terminal. BART's new mainline station in Millbrae is designed to allow easy cross-platform transfers with Caltrain. Ridership on the BART-SFO extension is projected to reach nearly 70,000 trips daily by the year 2010.

Every day, BART serves a complex geographic area with acute attention to engineering and electrical innovation. With a proud past and promising future, it will embrace the tremendous challenges facing the mass transit demands of the Bay Area, with the same dauntlessness that created the system in the first place. ■

BART's Central Control Center at BART Administration Building

Passengers boarding BART train

225

East Bay Municipal Utility District

In 1923 the publicly owned East Bay Municipal Utility District, known as East Bay MUD, was brought into being by voters in portions of Alameda and Contra Costa counties. Previous decades, from 1866 to 1922, had seen a number of different private companies attempt to provide water for the region. Yet the East Bay's growing population still could not depend on water that was safe and plentiful.

Seven East Bay cities elected the directors of EBMUD, whose mission would be to find a quality water source and bring it to the region. In July 1924, they identified the Mokelumne River as the best source of water for the region. The Mokelumne, with its branches in the pristine Sierra snowfields north of Yosemite, could be dammed near the old gold-mining town of Lancha Plana. The estimated cost was $39 million.

At that point, George Pardee, a former mayor of Oakland and a former governor of California, used his political clout to become president of the board of directors of EBMUD and gain the district a $26 million bond issue. His leadership would become invaluable to the district.

In the following years, a drought and heat wave drained local reservoirs, and all eyes turned to the construction of Pardee Dam. Communities wondered whether it would be built in time to save them. Indeed it was. Built under budget, Pardee Dam was considered a masterpiece of engineering — the largest dam in the United States at the time, holding 68 billion gallons of water. It poured the first Mokelumne snowmelt into San Pablo Reservoir on June 23, 1929, just three weeks before the East Bay would have run completely out of drinking water.

It was an auspicious beginning, for a mere four months later the stock market crashed, signaling the beginning of the Great Depression. Although many stores and businesses closed down permanently and many people were out of work, EBMUD extended credit to its customers and began to form an alliance with the community that exists to this day. Works Progress Administration and Civilian Conservation Corps workers helped to reforest the all-important watershed lands and perform other necessary improvements. Because of volunteer effort, district engineers were able to continue to upgrade the water distribution infrastructure and plan a second aqueduct.

In 1941 America became involved in World War II and the population of the East Bay quickly increased to 200,000 as families came to work in East Bay war industries. The community consumed more than 113 million gallons of water per day, and the district's boundaries soon expanded as more cities petitioned for annexation to the water utility.

During the postwar boom, the problem of sewage accumulation along the East Bay shoreline became a public concern. As far back as 1936, *The Oakland Tribune* had noted "The odor at low tide can no longer be tolerated by a self-respecting community." Finally, in 1944, citizens in six cities pushed for a sewage treatment district. Because of EBMUD's excellent reputation, it was asked to shoulder the burden, and by 1951, a primary treatment plant was built that began to clean the water in the bay. This was the start of the greatest period of construction in district history and began EBMUD's commitment to protecting San Francisco Bay.

Between 1950 and 1970, the district completed six major projects: the second and third Mokelumne Aqueducts; a wastewater treatment plant in Oakland;

Mokelumne River water is collected in Pardee Reservoir in the Sierra foothills for East Bay communities. Pardee Dam is on the left; the spillway is on the right.

the Camanche and Briones dams; and the Walnut Creek Water Treatment Plant. It was good thinking, because during that time the East Bay's population swelled from 500,000 to more than 1 million, and water use had grown from 30 million gallons daily at the district's founding to 184 million gallons daily.

The growing population clamored for recreational use of EBMUD's carefully managed watershed lands. At first the district resisted, but after appealing for legislation ensuring environmental protections, large tracts were sold to a new East Bay Regional Park District. Yet public need for land use continued to mount. In 1958 Pardee opened to fishing and camping, and in 1966, Lafayette became EBMUD's first reservoir to offer public recreation. Today reservoir lands contain 80 miles of hiking trails and are home to much wildlife, including the endangered bald eagle.

EBMUD's growth had been so consistent throughout its existence, that by 1950 its employee base had more than doubled. Yet further change was imminent with the advent of civil rights, women's and environmental movements beginning in the 1960s. In the mid-70s, legislation added two more board seats and divided the district into seven evenly populated wards. Women, African-Americans and Asians began to serve on the board, helping EBMUD to better represent the diversity of the population it serves.

Over the years, EBMUD shifted its focus from building new facilities to developing environmentally focused programs. The district established committed stewardship of the environment as a cornerstone of its mission. In keeping with this commitment, the district implemented a wet weather program to process storm drainage, a wastewater power generation station to convert methane gas into energy, and a program for processing digested sludge for agricultural use. In 1972 the district created a program that reduced industrial toxics sent to sewers, and in 1977, the plant began "secondary treatment" of wastewater. Today, EBMUD maintains a nine-stage process which reduces pollutant discharge into the bay by 98 percent.

Due to its environmentally sound practices, EBMUD has become the only large wastewater facility to receive the EPA's National Wastewater Excellence Award three times.

In the mid 1990s, EBMUD began a 10-year Seismic Improvement Program to strengthen the water system against a major earthquake, and began long-term work to upgrade its aging infrastructure. Water conservation and water recycling were expanded as key components of the Water Supply Management Program (WSMP) to assure adequate high-quality water supplies for the future. The WSMP includes plans to tap the American River as a supplemental supply to protect East Bay communities from severe rationing during droughts.

East Bay MUD's mission is to manage the natural resources with which the district is entrusted, to provide reliable, high-quality water and wastewater services for the people of the East Bay and to preserve and protect the environment for future generations. Throughout the district's history, it has demonstrated this commitment again and again through a deeply held concern for the area's people, environment and future. ■

Conserve water. Grow flowers that use less

EBMUD offers rebates and free water audits to homes and businesses and promotes water conservation with free water-saving devices, brochures and colorful posters.

These are final settling tanks, or clarifiers — part of the secondary wastewater treatment process. Advanced technology and state-of-the-art scientific analyses aid EBMUD's conscientious efforts to protect San Francisco Bay.

227

The Oakland Tribune

The Oakland Tribune, the city of Oakland's metropolitan daily newspaper, turned 125 years old in 1999, celebrating a century and a quarter of covering Oakland news and events. The paper is honoring this milestone by moving back to its former home in downtown Oakland, the landmark Tribune Tower, at the corner of 13th and Franklin streets.

The move is significant, for the Tribune is committed to a revitalized downtown Oakland. Damage from the 1989 Loma Prieta earthquake forced the Tribune to leave the Tower in favor of Jack London Square, along the Oakland waterfront. While that move has been a successful one for the paper, Oakland's urban center is currently undergoing a major economic rebirth. As the city's daily voice, the *Tribune* is poised to play its part in that revival.

The historic landmark Tribune Tower, at the corner of 13th and Franklin streets in downtown Oakland, home of *The Oakland Tribune* and ANG Newspapers

Within the last several years, that role as the East Bay's leading daily newspaper has been dramatically enhanced under the Tribune's ownership by ANG Newspapers. By purchasing the Tribune in 1992 from Robert Maynard, ANG added its fifth East Bay daily newspaper to a stable of thriving suburban dailies, including *The Daily Review* in Hayward, the *Tri-Valley*

Herald of Pleasanton (with editions in the San Ramon and San Joaquin valleys), *The Argus* in Fremont and the *Alameda Times-Star*. Since then, ANG Newspapers has branched out to the peninsula by acquiring the *San Mateo County Times*, and to the North Bay, with the *Times-Herald* of Vallejo.

Under ANG Newspapers' direction, the *Tribune* has strengthened its coverage of local Oakland news and culture. The newspaper took a major step in 1999 by introducing two distinct editions to better serve its readers. One, the *Cityside* edition, reports on the news and events of urban Oakland, while the *East Bay Hills* edition focuses on the hillside communities neighboring the city, including Piedmont, Montclair and Berkeley Hills.

ANG Newspapers' corporate operations accompanied the return of the Tribune's news and business offices to the Tower in 1999, bringing over 350 employees to the heart of the city. Awaiting will be 60,000 square feet of office space, part of an $8 million renovation of the building, including major structural repairs, seismic retrofitting and wiring for high-tech usage. The 75-year-old, 21-story tower was designed by local architect Edward R. Foulkes and is capped by a distinctive, green copper roof and the four-sided neon TRIBUNE façade with four clock faces, each measuring 15 feet across each. It is, especially after nightfall, the signature landmark of the Oakland city skyline.

The *Tribune's*, and ANG Newspapers', concentration on local news reporting and presence is paying off. Fueled in part by the *Tribune*, ANG Newspapers was the only Bay Area daily newspaper company to experience gains in circulation during the first half of 1999. This circulation growth bucks a trend of declining newspaper readership nationwide. With rising readership in both Oakland and the Bay Area's rapidly growing cities and suburbs, the *Tribune* and ANG Newspapers continue to be the region's favorite local newspapers.

In Oakland itself, the Tribune's goal of bringing the news "closer to home" to the city's diverse population is succeeding. ■

228

Pacific American Services, L.L.C.

One of Oakland's biggest success stories, Pacific American Services (PACAM) has grown in a single decade from a start-up venture to an award-winning superstar of the warehousing and logistics industry. An even bigger surprise — its founders, Ronald Hothem and Linda Childs Hothem, were novices in the field.

A simple investment in a few warehouses turned into an unexpected business opportunity when a tenant in the Hothems' newly acquired buildings — a warehousing and drayage company — went bankrupt. On three days' notice, the Hothems decided to take over the company. This series of events gave birth to PACAM.

During the next decade, PACAM grew from a single 100,000-square-foot facility with annual sales of $750,000 to five locations, 1.5 million square feet of warehouse space, 150 employees and annual revenues in the millions. Most importantly, services were expanded to include a broad range of options for importers, exporters and domestic manufacturers.

Linda served as company president until 1996 when Ronald died in a tragic accident. Under her guidance as the new CEO, Hothem led the company in a program of expansion and diversification, resulting in a 240 percent increase in sales and substantial recognition in the industry.

Hothem explains PACAM's phenomenal growth with two words: customer service. "We never say 'no.' It's that simple. We pride ourselves on delivering total customer satisfaction, thanks to a creative and talented staff of highly trained individuals who stop at nothing to service our customers' needs."

Today PACAM offers a wide array of services, including bar coding, shrink wrapping, cold storage, specialized handling, distribution, drayage and logistics. On any given day, warehouses may be stocked with goods as diverse as wine and spirits, paper products, bulk foods, plastic food storage bags, computer monitors and footwear.

PACAM's flagship, Oakland Commerce Center, is a full-service, 500,000-square-foot complex, served by rail, and just seven miles from the Port of Oakland. Each building within the PACAM warehouse system is fully equipped with sprinkler systems and surpasses the requirements of U.S. Customs Cargo Security. All PACAM facilities are food-certified warehouses, managed with strict environmental controls to ensure compliance with the highest sanitation standards. State-of-the-art, computerized inventory control systems provide constant monitoring and accurate, timely shipping of customers' goods.

Within its Oakland warehouse complex, PACAM operates the Oakland Foreign Trade Zone. Often, products arrive from Europe or Asia to be repackaged or consolidated, then shipped elsewhere in the United States or abroad. In other cases, manufacturers may ship separate elements from several different international locations to PACAM for assembly. Quality control, cost savings, export duty deferral or duty elimination are cited as its customers' primary reasons for this strategy. PACAM also boasts the largest U.S. Customs bonded warehouse on the West Coast.

"The global economy is here, and it won't go away," says Hothem. "We enter the new millennium in step with importers, manufacturers and companies worldwide. Our unique capabilities and our proximity to the Port of Oakland make it all possible."

PACAM has been the recipient of numerous awards and continues to be recognized as an industry leader. ■

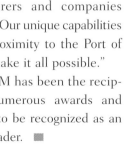

Among PACAM's numerous awards are: 1999 Top 100 Women-Owned Businesses #32, *San Francisco Business Times*; 1998 Top 100 Women-Owned Businesses #41, *San Francisco Business Times*; 1997 Top 100 Women-Owned Businesses #89, *San Francisco Business Times*; 1995 San Francisco Woman Entrepreneur of the Year, National Association of Woman Business Owners; 1995 Northern California International Business of the Year, Port of Oakland; 1994 Top 100 Fastest Growing Private Businesses, *San Francisco Business Times*; 1992 Vic Fernandez International Trade Award, Port of Oakland

Racks and rows: PACAM's facilities include over 1 million square feet of warehouse space.

U.S. Postal Service

When the Continental Congress named Benjamin Franklin the first Postmaster General in 1775, the United States was a weak confederation of colonies smattered along the eastern seaboard. The postal system created by Congress helped bind the nation together and resulted in a governmental branch that fuels the economy by delivering millions of messages and billions of dollars in financial transactions each day to 8 million businesses and 250 million Americans.

Since its beginning, the U.S. Postal Service (USPS) has helped develop and subsidize every new mode of transportation in the United States. As mail delivery evolved from foot to horseback, stagecoach, steamboat, railroad, automobile and airplane — with overlapping use of balloons, helicopters and pneumatic tubes — mail contracts ensured the necessary income to build the great highways, railways and airways that eventually spanned the continent.

In 1848 the pioneer movement to the West quickened in direct response to the Gold Rush. At the time, mail traveled by ship from New York to Panama, across Panama by rail and on to San Francisco by ship. Theoretically, it should have taken three to four weeks to receive a letter from the East. This goal was seldom attained. Californians felt keenly isolated from the rest of the union.

In an effort to speed the transfer of information, an American transportation pioneer, William H. Russell, advertised in the newspapers as follows: "Wanted: Young, skinny, wiry fellows not over 18. Must be expert riders willing to risk death daily. Orphans preferred." And thus, the Pony Express was born. The first delivery by Pony Express through the central route from Missouri to Sacramento took 10 and a half days, cutting the usual time by more than half.

In 1930 trains became the main form of transportation with more than 10,000 used to move the mail into every city, town and village. The Oakland branch of the U.S. Postal Service began its inception at the height of the Depression with the construction of the Oakland Main Post Office and Federal building in 1932.

The Oakland Civic Center, as it is known today, is a 60,000-square-foot building that earned a place on the National Register of Historic Places in 1980. The facility houses a post office, Superior courts, administrative offices and the office of the Oakland Postmaster. With nearly 1,000 employees and 19 retail stations, it proudly serves the diverse communities of Oakland, Piedmont and Emeryville.

On a global level, the USPS assists nearly 7 million retail customers each day. Such a large client base demands that its product line be the most comprehensive in the industry. In fact, if the U.S. Postal Service was a private company, it would be the 10th largest in the country. It relies on the most advanced, automated processing systems to handle more than 40 percent of the world's mail. The next largest is Japan at only six percent.

The United States Postal Service continues to make history as it helps lead the way to making the federal government more businesslike and responsive to customer needs — seven days a week, rain or shine. ■

The Oakland Civic Center Station was originally the Oakland Main Post Office and Federal Building.

230

Photo by Robert A. Eplett

231

Professional Services

ARCHITECTS, ENGINEERS, CONSULTANTS, ATTORNEYS AND OTHER PROFESSIONALS PROVIDE ESSENTIAL SERVICES TO THE OAKLAND AREA.

233

Y. H. LEE ASSOCIATES, Architects

If home is where the heart is, Yui Hay Lee has put down deep roots in Oakland, the adopted city he loves. After years of practicing architecture on the East Coast, in the early 1980s Lee and his family moved to Oakland where he started his successful architectural practice. Since then, Y. H. Lee Associates has worked on projects in and around the Bay Area and as far away as Florida, China and Taiwan. Lee values his regional, national and international work, but it is the projects in Oakland that mean the most to him.

Frank Ogawa Plaza —
Oakland, California
Photo by Hedrich-Blessing

Y. H. Lee Associates is an architectural and urban planning firm whose principal has had long experience in comprehensive urban design, housing projects, downtown planning, retail design and mixed-use developments. Key to Lee's design philosophy is his commitment to planning for the quality of life for the people who will be living and working in every project he works on. Lee approaches each commission from a fresh perspective, and all his designs evolve as solutions for specific problems in specific locations. He never imposes a signature style on his work but prefers to allow his buildings to speak for themselves in their appropriateness for their sites and situations. This philosophy has earned him a prestigious roster of satisfied and repeat clients.

For Oakland, Y. H. Lee Associates submitted the winning entry in the 1985 competition to design the Frank H. Ogawa Plaza at 14th and Broadway. The project was completed in the fall of 1998 and was immediately recognized as one of the region's most prestigious public spaces. Named after Oakland's first Asian-American city council member (and personal friend of Lee), the plaza is an urban oasis that surrounds Oakland's City Hall and administration buildings.

Lee is an architect with an international education. Born in China, he was raised in Hong Kong and spent two years at Chung Chi College. When he was awarded a scholarship to Miami University in Oxford, Ohio, he moved to the United States. In the summer of 1964 he studied at the Ecole des Beaux Arts in Fontainebleau, near Paris. He graduated with a bachelor's degree in architecture in 1965 and was awarded the Alpha Rho Chi Architectural Medal from Miami University. Then Lee received a scholarship to the Harvard Graduate School of Design and earned his master's degree in architecture and urban design in 1967.

While at Harvard, Lee studied under the renowned architect, Jose Luis Sert. Sert believed that architects should be more than creators of forms, that the spaces and the activities between buildings are often more important than the individual buildings themselves. Sert was interested, not so much in the shapes of buildings, but in how to improve the quality of life for the people for which they are designed. Lee's design of the Frank Ogawa Plaza is a tribute to Sert's philosophy, which he incorporates in all his work.

After Harvard, Lee was recruited by RTKL in Baltimore, a large, multidisciplinary architectural and planning firm that works on projects throughout the country. His 13 years with the firm allowed the young architect to practice on a wide range of projects while advancing in the firm. RTKL's comprehensive approach to downtown planning and urban mixed-use

234

developments has had a strong and lasting influence on Lee's architectural practice.

Early on in his professional life, Lee married his wife Suzie, who grew up in Taiwan and earned her bachelor's degree in architecture. Together the couple decided to move west, and Lee worked for a short time at a San Francisco architectural firm. Lured by the quality of life across the bay, the Lees moved to Oakland, and in 1981 Lee formed his own firm with Suzie as the general manager.

Based on his background, Y. H. Lee Associates was immediately commissioned to design large-scale projects, unusual for a small firm. Lee's first commission was Brickell Key in Miami, a 300-unit, 600,000-sqare-foot, bayfront high-rise housing development, and he went on to design several large-scale waterfront luxury housing projects in Florida. One of his most exciting Florida projects is Ultimar, a luxurious three-tower, 400-unit condominium community in Clearwater where he developed the master plan, designed all three phases of the residential towers, provided the landscape design of the open spaces and designed the interior public spaces. The broad scale of the project was deeply satisfying for Lee, a design-conscious architect interested in every aspect of a large project.

In Northern California, Y. H. Lee Associates has worked on many prominent projects around the Bay Area, including Lion Plaza, Berryessa Villas, Murphy Villas, Pacific Rim Shopping Center and Lion Estates in San Jose. For San Francisco, Y. H. Lee Associates designed the interior of the Taiwan Consulate and the renovation of Dr. Sun Yat-Sen Memorial Hall. The firm also designed the Royal Village and Mission Square

Shopping Center in Fremont, and in Oakland the firm has collaborated on the Swan's Market, the Oakland Garden Hotel and the Golden State Warriors Arena.

Lee devotes a large part of his time to civic affairs. He has served as president of the East Bay Chapter of the Organization of Chinese Americans, a national civil rights advocacy group for Asian Americans, and as vice president of the Oakland Asian Cultural Center and the Oakland Consolidated Chinese Association. He was the chair

of the Oakland Asian Pacific American Redistricting Task Force, and in 1993 he was influential in the creation of the city's first Asian plurality district. In 1991 Lee was appointed to the Oakland City Planning Commission and was elected its chair for the year 1993-1994. For Lee, it is immensely gratifying to be actively involved in the professional, political and cultural life of the city that means so much to him and his family. ▪

235

Crosby, Heafey, Roach & May

More than a century ago, Peter Crosby Sr. moved his law practice from the farming village of Union City to the dynamic, growing town of Oakland. When he nailed his "shingle," a brass sign, to the Victorian office building at 10th and Broadway in Oakland, he had no idea that he launched a firm that his two sons and their colleagues would expand into one of the largest law firms in California — Crosby, Heafey, Roach & May.

When wooden sidewalks and horse-drawn carriages gave way to street lighting and automobiles, Peter Crosby began to play a prominent role in the community. The son of Irish immigrants, Crosby, who studied law at the University of Michigan, was able to do so only

Peter Crosby Sr. (1872-1938)

with the financial help of his relatives. As a young man, he became an active member of the Republican Party and had been a delegate to the Republican National Conventions in 1916 and 1928. He also served a term as president of the State Bar of California from 1931-32. Having become a successful attorney, he was able to send his two sons, Carlisle and Peter Jr., to law school at Stanford University. Carlisle first joined his father's firm in 1921, served as a deputy district attorney from 1923 to 1924, and then joined his father in the firm of Crosby & Crosby.

In 1933, when Peter Crosby Sr. was appointed to the Superior Court bench, Peter Jr. joined his brother in the firm. Six years later, the firm became Hagar, Crosby & Crosby, when Gerald Hagar, a respected Oakland attorney, joined the practice. Gerry Hagar, himself, served as president of the State Bar of California (1939-1940). He also had a deep commitment to excellence in higher education and became president of the University of California Board of Regents. Today the firm, committed to excellence in education, continues to provide legal services to several prestigious institutions of higher education located in the Bay Area.

Meanwhile, another prominent community figure, Edwin A. Heafey, had started practicing in Oakland during the Depression years. Heafey came from an Oakland family that owned several important properties in the city. He, too, had served as a deputy district attorney in the 1920s. His private litigation practice flourished, and he eventually became a partner in the firm known as Clark, Heafey & Martin. He served as president of the Alameda County Bar Association from 1936 to 1937 and was president of the State Bar of California from 1957 to 1958.

Like Peter Crosby Sr., Edwin Heafey had two sons who went on to become attorneys — Edwin Jr. and Richard. Rather than joining his father's firm after graduating from Stanford Law School in 1955, the older Heafey son became an associate at Hagar, Crosby & Rosson. A few years later, he was able to persuade a law school classmate, Justin Roach Jr. to join him as an

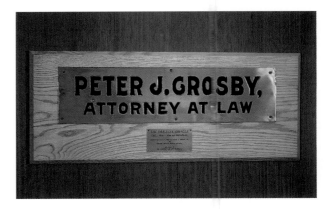

Original shingle mounted by founder Peter Crosby Sr. when he moved his practice to Oakland in 1900. The shingle, presented to Crosby, Heafey, Roach & May by Peter J. Crosby Jr., was restored by Crosby partners Mel McKinney and Ron Rosequist.

236

associate at Hagar Crosby. Although born in Nebraska, Justin had come to Oakland as a youth. He was loyal to the city and decided to practice law there. Richard, Edwin's brother, also joined the firm.

Edwin Jr. and Justin had bigger ideas than just practicing law. After a while they became partners at Hagar Crosby, and Justin became the managing partner. Their vision was to create a major law firm in Oakland: a first-rate firm that provided a wide range of legal services — a firm that could become one of the most influential legal institutions in the Bay Area. By 1968, they had arranged a merger between Hagar Crosby and Clark Heafey. Their vision quickly began to take shape as they scouted for new talent. Another merger brought Paul May, a business and probate lawyer with a significant reputation. Other well-known trial lawyers were brought into the fold. The firm had grown to 14 lawyers, and in 1969, it incorporated as a professional corporation. Its name — Crosby, Heafey, Roach & May, as the firm is known today — emerged.

In the ensuing years, attuned to the changing nature of business and alert to the changing needs of its clients, Crosby Heafey has grown steadily and stepped boldly into new arenas. Today it has almost 250 lawyers, operates from its Oakland headquarters beside Lake Merritt and has offices in San Francisco, Los Angeles and Century City. Over time, its client base has shifted from individuals to small businesses, and national and international corporate clients.

Crosby Heafey has a long tradition of involvement with Oakland's civic and legal organizations. At various times, the firm's attorneys have been active and held leadership positions in civic projects for the Oakland Chamber of Commerce, the Oakland Museum, the Marcus Foster Institute and the Oakland Symphony, among many others. In the early 1990s, in the wake of the Loma Prieta and Northridge earthquakes, Crosby Heafey established a private foundation to assist in rebuilding the community. Today the foundation focuses on educational projects.

Crosby Heafey's greatest challenge over the last couple of decades has been growth — how much, how quickly, in what direction, and in what service areas. The firm's approach to change reflects the values and characteristics shared among those who constitute Crosby, Heafey, Roach & May. These values include a commitment to excellence in legal services, a commitment to

Peter Crosby Sr. tried his cases at the old Oakland Courthouse, built in 1875.

keep pace with its clients' needs, and its commitment to maintain an internal culture of collegiality through camaraderie rather than competition.

Oakland is one of the most diverse cities in America, and the firm is proud to reflect this diversity at all levels. The firm's percentages of women partners are among the highest in the state — as well as in the nation. Peter Crosby Sr. would have been proud to see the firm moving ahead, embracing change, adjusting its work to reflect, and respond to, the needs of its clients. Crosby, Heafey, Roach & May will remain alert to possibilities, maintain excellent standards of service and continue its commitment to Oakland's future. ■

The Lake Merritt Plaza, one of the most beautiful buildings in the Bay Area, is headquarters for Crosby, Heafey, Roach & May, 1999. *Photo by Valrie Massey/Vasily Vandouris*

237

RINA Accountancy Corporation

Our Focus is Your Future

Contrary to some popular misconceptions, Oakland did not need the Loma Prieta earthquake or the Oakland Hills fire to be put on the map. In fact, progress has been more noticeable on the east side of the Bay, punctuated by the Port of Oakland, Jack London Square, downtown redevelopment and the overall increases in business and industry.

In 1946 World War II had just ended and conversion to a peacetime economy was underway. Young veterans were returning from overseas, a number to the East Bay where Oakland, at the hub of the Bay Area, was poised for business and industrial growth.

In the post World War II years, Oakland prospered. Business and the profession that serves it are inextricably linked. One grows with the other. It was no coincidence therefore that a new accounting practice, subsequently known as Rooney, Ida, Nolt and Ahern Accountancy Corporation (RINA), shared the fortunes of the developing companies in Oakland and its neighboring communities. Not those of Kaiser Industries, the Port of Oakland and American President Lines, but the fortunes of smaller businesses that built houses, sold clothing and furniture, baked pastries and distributed plumbing supplies.

Current Oakland office

RINA quickly became Oakland's most significant local practice because its partners understood that, among professional firms, it is the accountants who best understand the functions of business, its organization, systems, controls, profitability, and financial and tax reporting.

Like the city it serves, RINA's practice started modestly, with a desk and phone in the corner of the library of Mark Hardin's law firm in Oakland. These were unusual times and they required extraordinary people. The first four partners of RINA included a navy flyer, an air force flyer, a soldier who fought under Gen. Patton in Europe, and a Japanese-American who had recently endured internment in the United States. Three of these men became attorneys as well as CPAs. As the firm grew it continued to attract individuals with varied talents and interests: a U.S. Treasury Department auditor; a Santa Clara University basketball

President James R. Kohles

star; a graduate from the master's program at Cambridge University. Others followed with backgrounds in business, both as entrepreneurs and employees, and as homemakers. They weren't all mavericks; some had reached their professional status along traditional paths. The collective result however was a reservoir of talent, experience, energy and imagination unmatched in local and regional accounting firms.

The new and expanding businesses in Oakland and adjoining cities demanded extensive support and services: financing, organization, marketing, systems and accounting. This expansion included many small companies with a heavy concentration in warehousing and distribution, light manufacturing, retail and land development, and home construction. East Bay growth spilled over into the neighboring areas from Fremont to Richmond, and in Diablo Valley from Martinez to Pleasanton. RINA discovered that it could best serve its local clients by being prepared to cover their interests outside of Oakland; hence the opening of additional offices — Sacramento in 1975, Walnut Creek in 1991, Fremont in 1996, and San Francisco in 1998. On June 1, 2000, RINA moved its Sacramento office to Roseville.

238

As the conduct of business and its methods became more sophisticated, external advisors have had to respond to ever-increasing demands for economic guidance, direction in tax matters, and help in achieving and maintaining profitability. It is an axiom that change is constant. The public accounting firm has had to shift its attention and focus continually to keep pace with advances in technology and in business methods. Consider some of the developments during the last 50 years, not all of them good:

- Manual recordkeeping has virtually disappeared.
- Communication has become instantaneous — e.g., facsimile, e-mail, telephone and teleconferencing.
- Benefits for employees have been expanded to include retirement, medical, dental and other insurance.
- Employees frequently work irregular hours; flex time is no longer associated with low productivity.
- Outsourcing for a variety of services has become more prevalent. Microcomputers and micro-processors have become a way of business.
- The Internet has become a way of life.
- Interstate and international travel has increased and sped up. One has to consider the legal ramifications of almost everything one does.

Staying abreast of this kind of "progress" encourages the professional into continuous re-education as it entails broadening the scope of a firm's services including the full spectrum of management advisory services, information systems, planning, profit enhancement and litigation support.

Progress might be somewhat hollow if it were business only. Oakland has witnessed significant cultural developments within its boundaries, including The Oakland Symphony and Ballet, The Oakland Museum and the events it organizes, and The East Bay Zoological Society. There are also other ways of benefiting society — Children's Hospital of Oakland has become world renowned as a trauma and surgery center. What role has RINA played with each? The firm has acted as professional advisor or sponsor for all of these institutions.

To further augment its capabilities, RINA harnessed the resources of a large number of experts, first by becoming an active member of Midsnell Group

RINA's first office was in the Central Bank Building on 14th Street in Oakland.

International (MGI), an international group of accounting firms operating throughout the world, and secondly by forming alliances with other professionals including brokers, attorneys, and retirement plan and human resources specialists. It might be further noted that working in a community with a diversity of races and cultures calls for a response on ethnic and cultural levels. RINA mirrors this diversity and within its ranks offers fluency in numerous languages other than English including Spanish, French, Russian, Hindi, Hebrew, Cantonese and Mandarin.

Networking by design has been motivated by the fact that, whether large or small, businesses now face complex requirements dictated by laws, operating methods and social issues. A collective expertise must be applied as it was recently with the Oakland Communications Technology Cluster, sponsored by RINA amongst others, to assist particularly in matters affecting start-up businesses: choice of entity, systems, internal controls, and use of research and development credits.

RINA, now with five offices and 60 certified public accountants, paraprofessionals and administrative assistants, along with its network of experts in a variety of professions and its international membership and connections, looks forward to serving a revitalized Oakland and Bay Area. ■

239

ABC Security Service

The president and CEO of ABC Security, Ana Chretien, is one of the most well-known Hispanic entrepreneurs in the Bay Area. A native of Nicaragua, who moved to Los Angeles at 18 and attended adult school, Chretien earned a bachelor's degree in accounting. She then moved to the Bay Area and in 1979 went to work for ABC Security. The owner was Jim Ellis.

Chretien began to learn the security business from the ground up. As the only woman then at the firm, she could have felt intimidated, but not Chretien, who has six older brothers. The business became like a family to her, and so two years later, when ABC Security found itself owing the IRS, she made a loan to Ellis from her personal assets. When Ellis could not repay the loan, Chretien settled for an 18 percent interest in the firm. She then began to buy out the other partners.

In 1989 Ellis died. By then, Chretien had accumulated a 48 percent share of ABC Security. She used the collateral in her home to secure a loan from a bank to

Chretien's door is always open to all of her employees. She is more a friend to them than an employer.

purchase the remaining interest in the company from the Ellis family. It was difficult to raise the needed capital. She tried to obtain it through the Small Business Administration, but it would not help. With her characteristic, can-do-anything persistence, she

was finally able to buy the business with the help of a local bank. Her relationship with that bank is, today, one of the things she credits for ABC Security's longevity and spectacular success.

As full owner of ABC Security, Ana instituted a few major changes. One was a restructuring of the entire organization, creating several new management positions including departments for quality control and sales. Another was not renewing contracts with accounts she considered high risk or not cost-effective. As a result, she no longer provided armed guards.

These decisions were the result of several factors. With personnel carrying firearms, the insurance was three times as costly. In addition, many of the armed posts were for rock concerts and she feared that these promoters could write a bad check and leave town. But her paramount concern was for the safety of her employees. If a post really needed armed guards, then by definition it was too dangerous.

Others wondered if ABC could survive without the option of armed guards. But the test of time proved the decision was a wise one. Her work force nearly doubled over the next five years and the increase in revenues was proportional. In 1990 ABC Security was recognized and awarded the Small Business of the Year Award from the Oakland Chamber of Commerce. Then, in 1993, the company's small business status changed after reporting gross sales of more than $5 million.

It is, and always has been, Chretien's policy to ensure that the atmosphere at ABC Security is a supportive and friendly one in which employees from all cultures and countries are comfortable. Chretien has a barbecue in the summer and a dinner at Christmas to thank her employees for their part in making ABC Security a leader in the industry and to keep their spirits high. She has great faith in her staff and encourages them to make their own decisions.

Chretien is known as a no-nonsense businesswoman — someone who expects results. She is also known as a generous patron who loans her employees money to make ends meet and even, on occasion, to

240

buy a home. She enjoys close relationships with all of her employees, both past and present, and demonstrates her concern by being at the office every day to meet with them in order to keep track of how they and their families are doing and how they feel. Chretien takes pride in knowing each of her employees by name and relating to them more as a friend than as an employer.

ABC Security provides security officers for businesses and government agencies throughout the Greater Bay Area and even as far north as Sacramento. It has major contracts with Pacific Bell, PG&E, the Oakland International Airport, the San Mateo Transit District, The Golden Gate Transit District, the city of Oakland, the county of Alameda and many, many others, including being the prime subcontractor for the area's AT&T sites. It currently employs about 450 men and women to whom it provides a profit-sharing plan, excellent wages and many benefits.

Currently a major expansion into Sacramento is underway with the establishment of a branch office. But Chretien executes changes slowly, carefully and methodically. She runs her business conservatively, being just as wary of expanding too rapidly as she is of its opposite evil of too slow a growth. With this philosophy, the company had a controlled expansion of $4 million to $5 million between 1992 and 1993.

And as part of her firm's commitment to encouraging others in the community to follow her example in making their own way through life, her company is hiring a number of welfare-to-work applicants and is participating in a program with the Salvation Army to employ homeless people who are then given a place to live for 30 days until they can get back on their feet.

Because of her active involvement in numerous civic organizations, Chretien has become a fixture in the community. Though she values her privacy and strives not to draw attention to herself, her drive to make Oakland and the entire Bay Area a greater place to live and work for persons of all backgrounds has inevitably thrust her into the foremost ranks of community activists. Among many other awards, recognition and positions of trust, she co-chaired the planning committee for the Airport Area Business Association and is now its

president. In addition, Chretien is a board member on the Greater Oakland Chamber of Commerce; secretary of the Hispanic Chamber of Commerce; was chosen the Business Person of the Year by the State of California Hispanic Chamber of Commerce; is a member of the Business Budget Advisory Committee for the city of

Chretien owns the building that serves as ABC Security's corporate office.

Oakland; received the Business Leadership Award from the Business Women Leadership Foundation at the National Summit on Hispanic Women in Business in 1997; and her company is recognized as one of the 500 largest Hispanic-owned businesses in the entire country. Chretien is also a sponsor of both the Bobby Sox Softball League and a scholarship for local high school students and contributes to the San Francisco Police Activities League. She is a member of the Chicano Foundation and the Mexican-American Association and the list continues to grow.

Although Chretien is known for her strictly businesslike demeanor and her cautious yet aggressive approach to business, she is aware that many security companies are run in an almost military manner. She opposes this style of management. She sees to it that ABC Security maintains a family-oriented atmosphere where the employees know that the boss, though expecting professional behavior, really cares about them as people. This, then, is Chretien's company at the beginning of the millennium — energetic, confident and poised to take on whatever challenges the future may hold. ■

241

Harza Engineering Company, Inc.

Since its founding in 1920, Harza Engineering Company, Inc. has completed assignments in numerous fields of engineering, in more than 90 countries around the world. Harza uses its diverse talent and strategic investments to be a preferred global provider of clean water, reliable power and great engineering. The company's capabilities cover project phases from planning to design to construction, in such fields as water resources, power systems, infrastructure and environmental services.

Harza's expertise in multiple engineering disciplines has earned the company an international reputation and numerous awards for excellence. Harza's success is due in part to the ethics of its founder, Leroy Harza, and to the employees who have continued to carry his vision to new levels. Since its founding 80 years ago, Harza has comprised a staff of talented and dedicated individuals who embody creativity, technical expertise and commitment to meeting clients' needs. The company has sustained its reputation for excellence and innovation by providing outstanding services using the right technology for the project at hand, and by a commitment to excellence, client relations, integrity, fairness and financial strength.

Harza's Oakland office is its flagship office in California. With the 1992 acquisition of Kaldveer and Associates, Harza established a California base of operations to provide regional experience in geotechnical, water resources and environmental services. To date, Harza has expanded its California network of offices to include Concord, Los Angeles, San Diego and Sacramento.

The strong and growing Oakland office specializes in roads, bridges, streets and business parks, commercial development and public works projects for municipalities. Growth has also meant expanded capabilities in special inspection and materials testing. In 1999 the company opened a new soil and materials testing laboratory to increase efficiency and technical capabilities. The lab contains a SATEC Universal Testing Machine with a 400,000-pound testing capacity and is fully equipped to provide clients with the latest in materials testing technology.

Harza's California projects have included Pacific Gas & Electric pipeline expansion in the Sacramento area; BART structures, tunnels and bridges; East Bay regional parks; and renovation of more than 50 Oakland public schools. The work capitalizes on Harza's expertise in the geosciences, including site investigations, materials testing, foundation design and seismic risk assessment.

Recently, Harza supported the Port of Oakland's "Vision 2000" program, the

Harza was responsible for all geotechnical investigative work on Oakland's Elihu Harris building.

Harza's engineers laid the groundwork for construction of Chinatown's Pacific Renaissance Plaza.

242

merger of Oakland's Naval Supply Center and harbor facility. Other work on the Oakland skyline has included geotechnical investigation and analysis on the Elihu Harris building, as well as the Pacific Renaissance Plaza in Chinatown. Through these and other projects, Harza has demonstrated its ability to deal with the unique geotechnical and geological challenges of the Bay Area.

Other Harza projects include Pier 39 in San Francisco, Lawrence Berkeley National Laboratories, environmental sampling and geotechnical monitoring for landfill sites, and seismic retrofit of bridges. In addition, the company has consulted on the development of the Oakland YMCA facility, Peralta Towers on Lake Merritt, the 20-story 20th & Webster office building, the Merritt Hospital expansion, and several East Bay Municipal Utility District projects.

Harza routinely provides services to a mix of public and private sector clients. These include the City of Oakland, Port of Oakland, San Francisco Public Utilities Commission and the City of Berkeley, as well as cooperation with a variety of developers and other civil, structural and architectural design firms. Harza values long-term relationships and seeks to partner with its clients on every project that they jointly pursue.

Harza is a privately held organization, entirely owned by its full-time employees, who place great importance on their ability to listen to clients, provide appropriate technology and act with fairness and integrity. Harza employs some of the most technically astute architects, engineers and scientists in the industry. Its geotechnical engineers have formed a "best practices" group to share experience across geographic regions. Harza is proud to be a leader in the transfer of technology to people worldwide, working side by side with

local engineers to provide the best technology. Because of its extensive experience in the Bay Area as well as internationally, Harza draws top engineers from Bay Area colleges and around the world.

Harza has thrived in the welcoming business environment of Oakland that provides numerous advantages in serving global, national and regional markets. The company has enjoyed a long-standing relationship with the Oakland community and will continue to support such programs as Habitat for Humanity, Boy Scouts of America, Give Something Back, Special Olympics, Goodwill and Adopt-a-Family.

Vision, innovation and a commitment to excellence are a standard part of the engineering process at Harza Engineering Company. With confidence in the talents of its employees, Harza is committed to providing the best client service possible for the new century and beyond. ■

Oakland's Elihu Harris building

Dr. Refaat Abdel-Malek, president and CEO, and Nicholas Pansic, regional manager

243

Charles F. Jennings Architects

Charles F. Jennings Architects is a full-service architecture firm, established in 1984, which provides architectural and planning services to commercial, corporate and institutional clients. A diversity of experience enables the firm to design and coordinate a broad range of project types and scales.

Commissions for architectural design, renovation and master planning have been completed ranging from small remodeling to projects in excess of $20 million. Building types have included sports facilities, banks and high-rise buildings, newspaper and cable TV facilities, hotels and convention centers, and corporate and governmental offices for clients that include the Golden State Warriors, Saint Mary's College of California, CivicBank of Commerce, Lesher Communications, Bay Cablevision, Marriott Hotel, Kaiser Center, Maxim Integrated Products, the state of California, Alameda County and the city of Oakland.

Charles Jennings began his career in Oakland working on the Oakland Airport and local schools while still attending the University of California at Berkeley. He graduated with degrees in architecture and engineering from UC Berkeley and has taught architecture at UCLA. Prior to establishing his firm, Charles Jennings was a senior design architect for major projects with the renowned San Francisco office of Skidmore Owings and Merrill. There, he designed projects for IBM, Bank of America and Bechtel.

In 1988 Charles Jennings relocated from San Francisco to Oakland to design the West County Times Building for Lesher Communications. This 26,000-square-foot building houses the newspaper's business, editorial, circulation and advertising offices as well as a community room, library, photo studio and other support functions.

In 1989, following the Loma Prieta earthquake, Charles Jennings designed improvements to the Kaiser Center Mall. Recently the firm completed renovation of the Kaiser Center Building lobby, which uses new travertine stone walls and indirect lighting to create a lobby room. The existing escalators were enclosed in stone and a new fountain added within a cylindrical opening of stainless steel.

One of Charles F. Jennings Architects' most notable projects is the award-winning corporate office and training facility for the Golden State Warriors, sponsored by the city of Oakland and Alameda County. It is located above the existing Oakland Convention Center adjacent to the Marriott Hotel in downtown Oakland. This two-story, 58,000-square-foot facility includes offices, two practice courts, team facilities

with lockers, a training room, weight room, conference/video room and adjacent parking. The coaches' offices have windows that overlook the courts and a balcony for the coaching staff. The remainder of the floor is dedicated to marketing, communications and management offices that have panoramic views of downtown San Francisco, Oakland and the San Francisco Bay.

Charles Jennings is a member of the Oakland Metropolitan Chamber of Commerce, UC Berkeley Alumni Association and is a sponsor of the Lincoln Child Center. Dedicated to participating in the revitalization of Oakland, Charles Jennings' future plans include an expanding practice with experience in sports and entertainment projects, and providing multi-unit housing in the downtown area. He also intends to diversify regionally with projects already under way in Contra Costa, Santa Clara and San Mateo counties. ■

Golden State Warriors Training Facility

West County Times

Kaiser Center Lobby

244

Law Offices of John L. Burris

John L. Burris, born in Vallejo, California, and raised by working-class parents, once lived the relatively quiet life of a young accountant. But that all changed in the late 1960s when the winds of the civil rights movement blew across the land. Inspired by people marching in the streets, sitting at the lunch counters and boycotting buses, Burris made a personal commitment to social justice.

After deciding that law was the most effective tool for changing social conditions, Burris attended the University of California at Berkeley, School of Law, and upon graduation, joined a law firm in Chicago. He soon joined the Cook County State Attorney's Office, where he became a criminal prosecutor working among some of the finest legal minds in the nation. Life was good.

Although facing a bright future in Chicago, Burris decided to risk his career and leave the professional ties he had foraged in Chicago and return to the Bay Area, moving to the East Bay to work with the Alameda County District Attorney. He liked the diversity he found in Oakland, where the quality of life for some could be quite high. He found a significant black, middle-class population, excellent transportation and access to the greater Bay Area.

But while at the District Attorney's Office he became restless. In 1979 Burris entered private practice with colleagues Elihu Harris, who subsequently became mayor of Oakland, and David Alexander, who went on to serve the Port of Oakland.

As a criminal defense attorney, Burris' talents and trial skills — honed from high-energy, aggressive cases — did not fulfill his sense of place in the world, his sense of participating in socially redeeming endeavors. His commitment to Oakland and his determination to challenge and expand the concepts of social justice led him to investigate a police shooting of a 14-year-old African-American boy.

Over time, his practice shifted to police misconduct and abuse cases. By 1985, when he created his own firm, he specialized in civil rights. Having no tolerance for public policies differentially applied to racial and ethnic groups, he set about to hold institutions accountable for the harm resulting from discriminatory, abusive or dangerous policies. He challenged law enforcement practices such as the use of deadly weapons, pepper spray and stun guns. He questioned police training and internal affairs investigations, compelling the police to examine the propriety of established practices. He represented victims of toxic torts, the disabled facing discrimination and participated in consumer class actions. He found the work rewarding, because he forced institutions to review and adjust their policies, and to take responsibility for their actions.

John L. Burris

As co-counsel on behalf of Rodney King, whose videotaped beating riveted the residents of Los Angeles in 1991, Burris was no stranger to the press. He became a media commentator, guiding audiences through complicated legal issues, or the courtroom tactics of high-profile proceedings such as the O.J. Simpson murder case.

While his commitment to civil rights continues (he recently authored a book titled *Blue vs. Black: Let's End the Conflict Between Cops and Minorities*), Burris has also turned toward international issues, focusing on the rights of individuals injured by acts of terrorism against the United States.

John Burris' legacy resides in his personal commitment to highlight socially relevant issues affecting Oakland's quality of life. He will continue to serve individuals and seek a just society for all. ◾

245

C.J. Tyler Architecture

When Carylon Tyler ("C.T." to her friends) told her high school teacher she wanted to become an architect, his response was, "That's a hard thing for a girl to do." However narrow-minded, such a comment was probably well-meaning for the times. To Carylon, it was a challenge that galvanized her determination to be exceptional. Demonstrating great talent in her architectural and mechanical drawing classes, she won a scholarship, earned her architectural degree at The University of Texas at Austin, packed her bags and headed for California.

Carylon served her internship in architecturally rich San Francisco and Los Angeles during the late 1970s. She got a taste of large, traditional architectural firms as well as small, energetic studios. Carylon seized the chance to work as an associate architect for a respected

"C.T." Tyler consults her protégé, Derrick Barron.

firm in Santa Monica, where she demonstrated her versatility on projects ranging from Orange Julius franchise locations to NEC's facilities in Torrance.

After five years in Los Angeles, Carylon concluded that she needed to develop her project management skills, and returned to San Francisco to work for a company well known for its interior design. The project manager who hired her was so impressed with her drafting and interior design skills that he became her mentor, and as fate would have it, an integral part of her future as an independent architect.

Carylon resisted efforts to categorize her talent in such a large firm because she feared being lost in a sea of nameless, faceless specialists. She needed to be free to try new ideas; to wear many hats and test her limits. A former associate architect of the firm opened a studio of his own and enthusiastically recruited her. Carylon found the experience of responsibility in a small firm exhilarating, and she hungered for even more autonomy.

Soon, she convinced her mentor to join her in starting their own studio, taking a coveted Bank of America account with them which formed the foundation of the new enterprise. Carylon became a registered architect in the states of California and Hawaii, and the partnership flourished. After two years, and with considerable success to show for it, the partners went their separate ways and C.J. Tyler Architecture opened for business in January 1993.

The eldest of five "Air Force brats," constantly moving from base to base, Carylon never felt the urge to grow roots until she was drawn to — the city of Oakland. A resident since 1992, she tolerated the bay commute for years until the day she spotted a billboard that read, "Oakland Welcomes... the Shorenstein Company" — and the final piece fell into place. She attended city planning meetings and gatherings, the dedication of the Oakland Civic Center, the transformation of Jack London Square and learned what a great future lay ahead for the city. Carylon moved her studio to its 17th street location on Halloween 1997.

Contributing to the renaissance of Oakland is a driving force for Carylon and her assistant, Derrick Barron. The studio has provided architectural and interior design services gratis for a minority youth center and a Life Ministries Church. Carylon feels deep gratitude for the opportunities she has enjoyed and now continues the tradition of mentoring.

Carylon's project list is heavily weighted with renovation and design of living, working and learning environments for both public and private clients throughout Oakland and the Bay Area. Carylon readily accepts requests to speak at career day events, always hopeful that she can inspire Oakland's youth in their formative years with her story of success and her passionate vision of prosperity for her adopted city. ■

246

Consumer Credit Counseling Service of the East Bay

The booming post-World War II years changed how people purchased consumer goods. Whereas once people paid with cash, they began consuming on credit, encouraged by stores issuing credit, then by banks making credit cards easily available. Easy credit led to big debt, which led to bankruptcy and, for some, to destitution. How people manage their money can destroy marriages, burst dreams and haunt them for years. Learning to play the money game can free people from worry and empower them to control their money for their own benefit. Helping people master their money and achieve financial peace of mind has been Consumer Credit Counseling Service of the East Bay's (CCCS) mission since 1966.

CCCS is a nonprofit credit counseling and money management education community resource that began when Oakland bankers and business owners saw their customers and employees floundering under the weight of hefty interest payments and decided that people needed to know how to use credit wisely. CCCS began offering free and low-cost services.

Free services include counseling, where individuals and families develop an action plan to meet their financial goals. CCCS conducts a series of workshops designed to teach people budgeting, home buying and basic investment skills, wise credit use and debt elimination. Additionally, CCCS has a phone bank where more than 100,000 people call annually to ask credit and debt questions.

For a nominal fee, CCCS helps people repay their credit obligations by negotiating interest rate and payment reduction schedules with creditors. CCCS staff members also provide credit report reviews — giving members a copy of their credit report, teaching the client to read and understand the report and developing an action plan to get the credit report into shape.

CCCS also has a first-time homebuyers program to help people understand how credit is evaluated by lenders, about the types of loans available, and the loan process. CCCS works with many organizations to accomplish its mission including lenders, mortgage companies, large and medium-sized employers, city and county organizations, churches, civic groups, colleges, schools, libraries, bookstores and other nonprofit organizations. CCCS is certified by the Department of Housing and Urban Development (HUD) and accredited by the Council on Accreditation.

Since its inception, CCCS has grown from two employees to a staff of 52 paid employees and 17 volunteers. From one office serving Alameda County, it now has 13 satellite offices serving residents of Contra Costa and Solano counties as well. Computer programs allow counselors to "run the numbers" for clients wishing to buy a home, and a network enables counselors to remain in contact with their clients from any location.

Consumer Credit Counseling Service of the East Bay will continue to educate people so they can decide their own money issues, to seize control of their finances, and in the process, offer peace of mind to thousands of people struggling to make ends meet. In so doing, CCCS will enable people to enjoy Oakland's rich resources without jeopardizing their future. ■

"It was actually a relief to go to CCCS... they contacted my creditors, negotiated with them and arranged a comfortable payment schedule." — Kathleen, Livermore, California
Photo by Jim Dennis Photography

Residents of the East Bay receive assistance at free money management workshops.
Photo by Jim Dennis Photography

Ted Jacob Engineering Group, Inc.

Ted Jacob Engineering Group, Inc. (TJEG) is an Oakland-based engineering consulting firm with offices in Pasadena. TJEG specializes in mechanical and electrical engineering design for health care facilities, laboratories and high-technology buildings on national and international scales.

TJEG refurbished an Art Deco/Neoclassical building on Broadway that it now owns and fully occupies. Fully integrated computer systems make operations as automated and foolproof as possible and allow engineers to monitor projects in remote locations.

Health Care

Ala Moana
Entertainment Center

Notable health care projects include: Tower II, a world-class 450,000-square-foot facility for The University of California, Davis Medical Center, Sacramento, that accommodates a bone marrow transplant unit, isolation rooms and a radiology department; and 800,000-square-foot Kaiser Los Angeles Medical Center, the flagship hospital for Kaiser medical centers in Southern California. Other notable projects include Summit Medical Center, San Mateo County Health Center, and Children's Hospital, Oakland. On an international scale, TJEG is working on hospitals in Kuwait, the United Arab Emirates, India and Sri Lanka.

(Right)
UC Davis Medical
Center Tower II

(Below)
Gallo Research Center

Laboratories/Research

TJEG has developed the Standards and Master Plan for a 1.5 million-square-foot laboratory/research space for The University of California, San Francisco. For Kaiser Berkeley Regional Laboratories, TJEG designed a 105,000-square-foot laboratory expansion, an 80,000-square-foot facility in Emeryville, California, for Gallo Research, a 40,000-square-foot project for Roche Diagnostics, a Lawrence Livermore Laboratories project, Chiron and an EPA laboratory research building in Richmond.

High Technology

TJEG's agreement with Oracle Corporation includes high-technology projects for all Oracle expansions and remodels throughout the United States. Other high-tech projects include a prototype for MCI WorldCom in San Jose, as a model for other data centers throughout the nation. TJEG is designing multimedia recording studios and classrooms for Ex'Pression, and a computer laboratory for EMC². A unique TJEG entertainment and commercial project is the 1 million-square-foot, five-star hotel in Oahu, Hawaii.

TJEG looks to future expansion of its business each quarter with its firm reputation as health care, laboratory and leading-edge, high-technology design experts. ■

Fern Tiger Associates

To understand the work of Fern Tiger Associates, it is necessary to understand the goals of its founder, Fern Tiger. A native New Yorker, Tiger was trained in fine arts at Pratt Institute during the highly charged era of civil rights, peace and women's movements, when the creation of art for museums and collectors seemed remote from pressing social issues. Following postgraduate studies at Pennsylvania State University and Carnegie Mellon University, Tiger taught at Penn State University and Washington University, seeking ways to link her writing, photography, design and art skills with her commitment to social change. In 1977 Tiger moved to Oakland to document in words and images the energy and activities of residents and neighborhood organizations. She was especially interested in what communities were doing for themselves and the impact of government policies on them. With funding from Oakland's Office of Community Development, she created the book *Oakland 1979*.

In 1978 she founded Fern Tiger Associates (FTA), a professional firm focused on the needs of nonprofit and public sector organizations. The firm utilizes its multidisciplinary, creative skills to produce materials and media that promote the work of diverse nonprofits

for Los Angeles. In 1991 the firm developed a manual to train nonprofits to understand marketing and outreach strategies. FTA has documented self-help housing projects and created *Oakland Assets* to promote the city's cultural, historical, architectural and environmental landmarks. For more than 15 years the firm has worked to advance issues related to child care and family services. *Making a Difference*, a publication emphasizing the role of child care in preventing abuse, was distributed to licensed child care workers throughout California. *Ages & Stages*, which has been used nationally by early childhood educators, helped parents and providers understand typical child development activities. FTA has also focused on the problems faced by low-income families seeking affordable child care. Recently, FTA launched a capital campaign to expand Saint Vincent's Day Home, the oldest and largest child development center in Alameda County, and prepared *The Child Care Portfolio*, a county-by-county analysis of child care needs in California.

For its only corporate client, Bayer Biotechnology, FTA developed a strategy that enabled the company to receive special zoning rights in Berkeley, while linking the company to community groups and nonprofits. The process resulted in a precedent-setting Development

and enable these organization to explain complex public policies to lay audiences. For 20 years, FTA has undertaken projects on topics as diverse as child care, the environment, public education, adoption, philanthropy, youth development, senior housing and economic development. The firm has received awards from a variety of professional organizations, including the Public Relations Society of America and the International Association of Business Communicators.

FTA created Greenstreets, an award-winning street tree plan for Oakland, as well as a similar plan, Treeways,

Agreement between the company and the city, and the creation of a biotechnology training program, Berkeley Biotechnology Education Inc. (BBEI) for at-risk high school students.

Despite the firm's long-standing interest in Bay Area organizations, it has increasingly taken on statewide and national projects, as well as projects as far away as Hawaii, Alabama and Arizona. The firm has a commitment and philosophy that is shared by clients. A 12-person, interdisciplinary staff works to select projects that can have an impact on communities, families and society. ■

For 20 years, Fern Tiger Associates has undertaken noteworthy projects on topics as diverse as child care, the environment, public education, adoption, philanthropy, youth development, senior housing and economic development. *All photos © Fern Tiger Associates*

249

Jordan Woodman Dobson

The architectural/engineering firm of Jordan Woodman Dobson (JWD) is Oakland's equal in global importance. JWD is an award-winning firm whose history is firmly rooted in the development of the Port of Oakland, and the firm has always taken an active role in the community. It is proud to send international clients home with positive impressions of Oakland.

Founder Michael Jordan, who helped revolutionize the shipping industry by designing the structure for the world's first dedicated container crane, opened an office in 1964 to provide engineering design for the new container cranes and terminals. Richard Woodman joined him the following year, adding his planning and civil design expertise, and the company evolved into a firm specializing in the design of container terminals. Combining Jordan's detailed nuts-and-bolts engineering and Woodman's planning experience earned the new firm an industrywide reputation for innovation and integrity.

In 1972 Frank Dobson, a past president of the East Bay chapter of the American Institute of Architects, founded an architectural firm in Oakland. The two firms merged in 1974, and their architectural/engineering services expanded to include master and operational planning and computer-based simulation analysis. JWD designs ports and container terminals as well as commercial, service, retail and industrial buildings and campuses.

JWD's work includes remodels such as Oakland's historical Breuner Building, Jack London Square's parking structure, the Spaghetti Factory, and hundreds of offices, manufacturing plants, and dining and retail establishments scattered around the Bay Area. Container terminals and their buildings can be seen in the ports of Oakland, Long Beach, Los Angeles, Seattle, Houston and Virginia, and internationally in Korea, China, Thailand, Taiwan, Pakistan Australia, Brazil, Holland, Israel and Canada.

JWD's work is a high-profile presence in the Port of Oakland. A collection of landmark JWD-designed facilities is near the end of Seventh Street, including the internationally acclaimed and award-winning TraPac Terminal at Berth 30 and many of the earliest container terminals and buildings. Among its 1999 designs are the master plan for the port's Vision 2000 project — a huge development incorporating the Navy's decommissioned Fleet and Industrial Supply Center — and the new Hanjin Terminal at Berth 55/56, with three major and several minor buildings.

With JWD's diverse experience, it can offer its clients the complete services necessary to make fully informed decisions. JWD provides design alternatives and quantitative analysis, allowing clients to make objective evaluations and informed choices. The planning and analysis service is tailored for clients planning to purchase, develop or operate a property. Services include detailed due-diligence reviews, assessment of user's needs, examination of traffic patterns and physical constraints, animated 3-D computer views of alternatives and detailed cost analyses.

JWD is quick to react to changing business climates. During the early 90s recession, JWD dramatically changed its management structure by bringing in new partners, among them Sugi Loni, an engineer with 10 years' experience, who became president in 1992. In reflection of the city's diversity, JWD is minority-owned. JWD's long-term commitment to the community is integral to the company's mission, and it invites a young, diverse staff to share in the future of the organization and in the city of Oakland. ■

TraPac Administration Building and Gatehouse, Berth 30, Port of Oakland

250

Liftech Consultants Inc.

Michael Jordan, Liftech's founder, sees today's world as a global factory with goods moving from port to port on board ship. Before the 1960s, loading cargo was tedious and time-consuming. Then a new idea speeded up the process — containers that detached from truck chassis were packed full of goods and turned into giant shipping boxes. This seemingly simple idea revolutionized international commerce and brought down the cost of shipping. Loading and unloading could be done in one-sixth the time, but it wouldn't have worked unless engineers designed a crane big enough to move the huge containers.

Michael Jordan was part of the team that developed the concept of those cranes. Their patented container crane designs set the standard for the industry, and today Jordan's firm, Liftech Consultants Inc., is a leading designer of container cranes and terminals in ports around the globe. In addition to Oakland, Liftech's clients include ports in Long Beach, Portland, Seattle, Tacoma, South Carolina, Virginia, Korea, Australia, Guam, Argentina, Taiwan, Manila and Israel.

Jordan's firm was fortunate to be in Oakland during the mid-1960s because the Port of Oakland was the first on the West Coast to recognize the importance of the new containers and to build the cranes and terminals that would bring increased traffic and revenue to the city. The port's management had the foresight to understand the importance of the revolutionary development, and by the end of the 1960s the Port of Oakland had become the second-largest port in the world in container tonnage and terminal acreage. Since then, the city has spent more than $700 million building 680 acres of marine terminals to handle containerized cargoes, and Liftech has been involved in all aspects of their design.

Liftech originated as Jordan Woodman Dobson and became an independent consulting group, still mutually supportive, to focus on the container cranes, heavy lift cranes, specialized rigging and waterfront terminals. Arun Bhimani, a structural engineer and one of Liftech's founders, has been president since 1977. Liftech is a structural engineering firm providing highly specialized services to owners, engineers, operators, manufacturers and riggers worldwide. Liftech offers complete engineering services for the design of new container cranes and the modification and relocation of existing cranes. The firm is also expert in the design and review of wharves, industrial and commercial buildings, rail installations, silos and unusual structures.

The firm's services include procurement, technical review, construction, quality control review, structural maintenance programs, design and analysis, upgrades, remodeling and transportation. Liftech has invested

ZPMC cranes from China heading for the Port of Oakland

heavily in engineering design tools and created sophisticated custom software for use in simulation studies. In addition to its specialized structural engineering, Liftech performs conventional engineering, including structural design for buildings and civil engineering for port-related work.

Founder Jordan is quick to credit Oakland for being an important factor in the firm's success. Being there during the transportation revolution, Jordan and his firm enjoyed the advantage of working with the port's progressive leadership. Providing Oakland with the tools to make it a world-class port enabled Liftech to become a leader in designing the technology that keeps the pace of global commerce moving efficiently. ◼

251

West Office Exhibition Design

Since 1985, West Office Exhibition Design has provided master planning and exhibition design services for museums and other educational institutions. As one of a handful of companies worldwide that provides such services, it specializes in integrating design, education and entertainment, and has mastered effective techniques for communicating diverse concepts to museum visitors. Utilizing state-of-the-art computer technology, West Office develops stimulating interactive exhibits, multimedia presentations and computer-related activities to create unique learning experiences.

The company's converted warehouse studio, located in Jack London Square's historic district, functions as a creative think tank for its staff of 25. The West Office approach brings together people with expertise in all aspects of exhibition design — from research and writing, graphic and 3-D design, exhibition planning and model making, to multimedia development. The success of the company is due in large part to this dedicated and creative staff, which enables the office to take on large, complex projects.

West Office's ability to offer comprehensive museum design services has yielded diverse clientele and projects around the world that include science and technology museums, maritime museums, children's museums, cultural museums, history and natural history museums, as well as traveling exhibitions and corporate education centers. In the science realm, topics range from that of the basic sciences of chemistry and electricity, to the applied sciences of communications technology and petroleum production, to the life sciences of physiology and health. Historical and cultural projects focus on such diverse topics as the history of Washington state, wine and food in America, the contemporary maritime community of Puget Sound, and the historical and contemporary culture of the Plains Indians.

West Office's renovated warehouse in Jack London Square's historic district

"The World Through Animal Eyes" — one of more than 200 science and technology exhibits designed by West Office for The Hong Kong Science Museum

Looking to the future, West Office plans to build on the experience and knowledge of the past 15 years and continue to create high-quality, innovative designs for meaningful visitor experiences.

West Office projects include: The Plains Indian Museum, Cody, Wyoming; The American Center for Wine, Food and the Arts, Napa, California; The Louisville Science Center, Louisville, Kentucky; The Science Museum of Virginia, Richmond, Virginia; The Hong Kong Science Museum; Odyssey: The Maritime Discovery Center, Seattle, Washington; The Saudi Aramco Exhibit, Dhahran, Saudi Arabia; The National Taiwan Science Education Center, Taipei, Taiwan; and the Los Angeles Zoo. ■

252

Photo by Robert A. Eplett

253

Quality of Life

Educational, medical and religious institutions, as well as community organizations, contribute to the quality of life enjoyed by Oakland area residents and visitors.

La Clínica de La Raza

A doctor's patient is a Spanish-speaking woman, 54, overweight with hypertension, high blood pressure, and a pre-diabetic condition. How does she get her patient to lose weight?

If she provided health care through La Clínica de La Raza, she would call upon her health services team members to help create a plan of action. The community health educators would introduce her to the clinic-initiated salsa aerobics class at the local elementary school and send the patient there. The nutritionist would teach the patient how to prepare food for her family in a way that maintains the flavor of traditional Latino cooking while incorporating nutritional, low-fat alternatives. The team might teach the patient how to get the neighbors to cook differently and to join her at salsa aerobics. They might also teach the patient how to organize those neighbors to improve their health, and if along the way, her neighbors need to change the community-at-large, then the team teaches her how to do that, too.

The team would do all that and more, for La Clínica is more than a clinic — it is a way of life in Oakland's ethnic neighborhoods.

For nearly 30 years, La Clínica de La Raza-Fruitvale Health Project, Inc., a nonprofit organization, has served the medically indigent and ethnic populations of Oakland. La Clínica soared into being in 1971 when a group of students and health professionals from the University of California at Berkeley walked through the heart of Oakland's Latino neighborhood in the Fruitvale District and talked to the people about their needs. Beyond the smell of familiar spices, the sound of familiar music, and banter of familiar Spanish words, the students found a vibrant community with increasing poverty and illness and few health care services. While Alameda County provided health services at distant facilities, the Latino community found their access barred by language, lack of transportation, and the cost of care.

La Clínica's founders, steeped in the community activism of the 1960s, saw the need for a health care facility in their own Latino neighborhood, staffed by people who spoke their own language and who were familiar with, and respectful of, their own culture. Armed with a philosophy — healthy communities generate and nurture healthy individuals, and healthy individuals in turn create healthy communities — the founders embarked on an extraordinary adventure. With a crew of medical volunteers and a sprinkling of donations, the founders opened a free clinic on Fruitvale Avenue — the first of several, which later became the neighborhood medical complex. There, the Latino community received immunizations and basic public health.

Patients who used the clinic, articulated the need for health services far beyond those initially envisioned. Staffed solely by volunteers, La Clínica added family medicine, dental care, mental health and optometry. In the exhilarating days of its beginnings, enthusiastic volunteers used their innate resourcefulness to face each challenge as it arose. Health professionals intent on using every precious inch of their cramped facilities devised ingenious solutions such as the hinged table top, that when lowered, converted a bathroom into an eye examination room.

La Clínica drew enthusiastic community support as donations increased and volunteers flocked to help. In 1977, Raymund Zala Nevel and Xochitl Nevel Guerrero, renowned Latino artists, painted a mural on a wall of the Dental Clinic. The images from Mayan and Aztecan cultures, in bright primary colors, depicted Latino people and symbols of strength and unity. Together, the mural and La Clínica became landmarks of the neighborhood. In a street environment covered

A mural painted on the side of the Dental Clinic depicts Latino cultural motifs blending traditional and modern health remedies. The mural's restoration celebrated the doubling of the Dental Clinic's capacity, and was rededicated in April 1999.

256

with graffiti, the mural and La Clínica buildings remained virtually untouched for years.

While volunteers and donations continued to support the clinic, in 1973 Alameda County granted La Clínica its first Revenue Sharing funds to establish a model health care program for the Latino population in Oakland. The grant stabilized La Clínica's budget, thereby freeing staff to expand facilities, services and programs. With federal dollars, La Clínica moved its operations to another site on Fruitvale Avenue and began buying buildings to house its clinics. At the same time, La Clínica became integrated as a full partner in the county's public health care system.

The community clinic movement grew nationally, and by the mid-1980s federal funding programs sought the mergers of like health care centers with overlapping programs. Simultaneously, La Clínica, serving the Latino population in Fruitvale, and the San Antonio Neighborhood Health Center, serving Asians, Eritreans, Ethiopians, African Americans and other ethnic populations in East Oakland, had discussed merging its operations. In 1984 San Antonio became La Clínica's first satellite.

La Clínica provided services to all persons, regardless of their ability to pay, within culturally sensitive contexts. By doing so, La Clínica recognized the influence of social and economic conditions on the mental and physical health needs of the patient population. As La Clínica monitored the health and socioeconomic status of its neighborhoods, it adapted its services to address emerging needs.

For example, La Clínica staff recognized that reluctant teen-agers avoided seeking sensitive services at the main clinic fearing exposure by family and friends among the other patients. In 1987 La Clínica established its third satellite center serving teen-agers exclusively. An in-house pharmacy joined the medical clinic in 1991, and in 1993 a school-based clinic opened at one of Oakland's elementary schools. La Clínica de La Raza operates from eight sites:

La Clínica's Fruitvale Avenue medical complex offers family medicine, pediatrics, women's health including OB/GYN, health education and nutrition, women, infant and children (WIC) services, pharmacy, social services, dentistry, mental health and eye care.

San Antonio Neighborhood Health Center continues to serve an ethnically diverse population with one-third of its patients being Asians. The center provides primary health care, including prenatal, social services, family planning, laboratory services, health education and nutrition, and WIC.

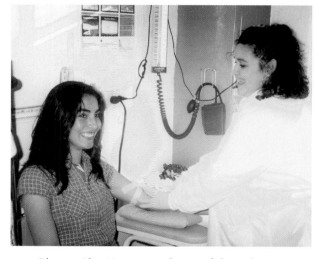

At Clínica Alta Vista, nearly 1,000 teen-agers a year receive health care focused exclusively on their needs.

Clínica Alta Vista provides confidential access to nearly 1,000 teen-agers a year. The clinic provides education and information, counseling, family planning, anonymous HIV testing and counseling, general medicine, sexually transmitted disease testing, diagnosis and treatment, and social services. The teen programs have expanded to include the "psychosocial" services needed by youths experiencing stress from violence or gangs. The Teens and Tots program provides services to parenting teens and their babies. Teen-agers can also obtain the full array of other services offered to adults.

At Hawthorne Elementary School, a basic in-school clinic offers preventive well-care services, immunizations and acute care for the K-6 patient population and accepts patients from nine other elementary schools as well. Children needing physical examinations to attend public school can receive an examination on site. Rather than taking sick children out of school for a long series of bus rides to receive medical care, parents can obtain medical needs and follow-up directly at the school.

In Oakland La Clínica operates a full-service Optometry Clinic situated in a local shopping center and a radiology department that serves both patients from La Clínica and outside physicians.

In 1999 La Clínica opened two, full-service medical and dental sites in Pittsburg, California, to serve the Latino and other working uninsured populations of neighboring Contra Costa County.

257

Doctors with admitting privileges at local hospitals, continue to see their hospitalized patients and assure treatment in their patient's language. Doctors, nurses, health educators, nutritionists and social workers form an interdisciplinary team to assure high-quality care. Medical students and residents from nearby teaching

La Clínica offers a wide array of health services including dental care.

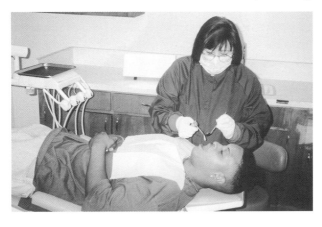

programs such as University of California at San Francisco receive on-site training, from La Clínica professionals. Bilingual health care workers trained at La Clínica, often move on to private health care providers where they are much in demand.

In addition to health services, La Clínica designed and operates a series of model health programs intended to educate and, more importantly, empower the community to advocate for a healthier social and economic environment. Beneath the umbrella of Casa CHE (Community Health Education), La Clínica operates four programs based on the Brazilian writer Paulo Freire's philosophy of popular education, empowerment and action.

Casa en Casa (CHE in the Home) began more than 15 years ago when Casa CHE health educators went to people's homes to moderate discussions about immunizations, family planning or other health concerns. Often, discussion spilled over to social issues such as renters' rights. Health educators encouraged individuals to address their health issues, organize among themselves and take action. In one instance, a group of residents concerned about hypertension identified the need for affordable fresh fruits and vegetables, and began a cooperative that phased out when a local produce store opened.

Parenting teens and their babies receive expert care through the Teens and Tots program.

Escuela Para Promotores (School for Promoters) evolved to teach residents the philosophy of community action around health issues. Health promoters, often residents who have hosted the Casa en Casa discussion groups, attend classes in group dynamics, leadership, needs assessment, program organization and evaluation. The promoters frequently become the catalysts who spark community projects. The program has been replicated for English-speaking populations and has been used as a model by the University of California at Berkeley.

Casa en las Escuelas (CHE in the School) reaches out to youth in the elementary, middle and high schools to teach a youth-oriented version of the Casa en Casa program. Health topics such as conflict resolution, pregnancy prevention, tobacco usage, family life, etc., focus on self-esteem and cultural identity. The classes are eagerly attended, and teen-agers consider the curricula relevant and powerful components of student life.

The Youth Brigade puts theory to practice. Under the guidance of adult mentors, teen-agers take to the streets to address a community health issue. These projects occur in the summer and combine training such as that available to the promoters, tailored to teen-agers 12-19. In the mid-90s, for example, a group of students working with the local police and licensing agencies undertook a local tobacco "sting" operation and demonstrated how easily underage children could obtain tobacco products from local merchants. The students documented their approach and findings so well that local businesses immediately complied with legal requirements, and the project drew national attention.

In 1999 the Zellerbach Fund, LaFetra Family Foundation, and the city of Oakland's Cultural Arts Division commissioned a new mural to be painted over the original deteriorated by weather and age. The new mural depicted brightly colored symbols of traditional health, Asian remedies and Native American medicine, side by side with modern medicine and dentistry.

Over time, several trends affected the operation of La Clínica. Most recently, the move toward managed care has forged linkages between La Clínica and established health insurers resulting in a diversified patient base. Passage of state

258

Proposition 187 affecting services to undocumented residents has frightened even legal residents from seeking services, while welfare reform and the rising numbers of uninsured working people have driven the demand far above the clinic's capacity.

In response, La Clínica is seeking to offer urgent care in every clinic and expand its hours and facilities.

Within a few years La Clínica will have a new facility located in the midst of an urban Transit Village. A local community development corporation in partnership with the Bay Area Rapid Transit (BART) district, the city of Oakland and La Clínica recognized an opportunity to improve the economy of the neighborhood around the Fruitvale Station. The mixed-use development incorporates housing, commercial retail and community services. La Clínica's facility will integrate pediatric, family medicine, OB/GYN and dental services. Patient support services such as child care and a senior center will be located within a few steps of the clinic's doors.

Today La Clínica is governed by an 18-member board of directors, two-thirds of whom are drawn from the patient population. Patients have direct input into the operations of La Clínica through board membership, focus groups, surveys and suggestion cards.

In 1999 its budget neared $16 million. It became one of the largest community health clinics in Alameda County and has expanded services to Contra Costa County. La Clínica employs more than 250 people, owns 10 of the 12 buildings that house clinics and serves approximately 17,000 people. Annually, the La Clínica staff assists over 400 births and encounters approximately 85,000 medical visits.

La Clínica is a well-respected health care center, a leader in the community, and an expert in Latino health care issues. It is an active member of the Alameda Health Consortium, a coalition of community health centers, a founding member of the Community Health Center Network, and a partner with Summit Medical Center. La Clínica is an asset to the quality of life of the city of Oakland. It has contributed to the economic resurgence of the community, provides employment and enhances neighborhood facades and the general appeal of the neighborhood.

Promoting healthy alternatives to smoking is one example in which Casa CHE's staff and health promoters reach out to educate community members in their homes, at community events and on the street.

Its future challenges will be to maintain the community's ownership and governance of the clinic and to balance between providing health care access in a colorblind, culturally and linguistically sensitive manner while adopting mainstream medical systems.

La Clínica has changed the way health care is given to the community by providing care evolving from the needs of the people rather than imposed from without. As a result, La Clínica continues to establish higher standards of care replicated by other health care institutions serving all people across the spectrum of ethnicity and income in the East Bay.

La Clínica's involvement in the community has traditionally exceeded the provision of health services. It has empowered the people to take control of their own health, and the social and economic health of their community. It has advocated for, and participated in, the development of ethnic communities in Oakland.

La Clínica de La Raza will continue to break molds, create new programs and serve as a model for community health centers in general, and for community empowerment, in particular. After all, change is endemic to the nature of La Clínica, a characteristic of its birth, and a fundamental component for delivering relevant, culturally appropriate health care to the diverse populations living in Oakland. ▪

Transit Village at the Fruitvale BART station — La Clínica de La Raza will anchor the economic resurgence of the Fruitvale area. The Village contains offices, community services and residences along with retail stores.

259

California State University, Hayward

California State University, Hayward, opened its doors in 1959 with four schools that flourish today — the schools of Science; Arts, Letters and Social Sciences; Education and Allied Studies; and Business and Economics. From the start the university was dedicated to providing quality education through hands-on learning, a caring and involved faculty, a solid curriculum and sensitivity to the educational needs of each generation of students. These worthy ideals still hold true today. The university, which currently offers 37 baccalaureate majors, 63 minors, and master's degrees in

More than 68,000 Bay Area residents are graduates of Cal State Hayward.

CSUH professor Julie Glass of Oakland was named the 1999 California Professor of the Year by the Carnegie Foundation for the Advancement of Teaching. Glass hosts a cable television program devoted to college algebra, writes math-oriented children's books and co-founded a math and science day camp for school-age girls.

26 fields, was ranked among the top eight regional public universities in the West in the 1999 *U.S. News and World Report America's Best Colleges* guide.

A Global Campus

Cal State Hayward was chartered to serve Alameda County and the greater East Bay area. Forty-two years later, the university has a total enrollment of approximately 13,000 students, with many enrollees transferring from Merritt and Laney colleges. Nearly one-fourth of the student body are graduate students, many of them enrolled in the MBA program.

The main Cal State Hayward campus, situated on 342 park-like acres in the Hayward hills, affords a panoramic view of almost the entire Bay Area. Instructional facilities include 150 classrooms and teaching laboratories, and 177 specialized instruction rooms. The university

library's collection of more than 1 million items is accessible through its online catalog. Other campus facilities include a 500-seat theater and a 8,400-square-foot television studio complex.

The Contra Costa campus, in Concord, provides full instructional and student-life support for more than 1,500 upper division and graduate students. The university also is the most active participant in the Higher Education Center in downtown Oakland. The university has established research and exchange programs with Russia and countries of the Pacific Rim and Europe, executive MBA programs in Moscow, Hong Kong, Vienna and Beijing, and an international MBA program through a Paris university — making Cal State Hayward a truly global campus with an international student body.

The university's commitment to educational excellence for a diverse society has become manifest, for the demographics have changed significantly during its four decades of existence. Women students now outnumber men. Minority students make up more than half of the population, with Asian-Americans numbering 31 percent; African Americans, 14 percent; and Hispanics, 13 percent.

Cal State Hayward is well-known for the quality of its faculty. In 1997 professor Stephen Benson was named the top biology instructor in the California State University system. Recent winners of the university's Outstanding Professor Award include economics professor Nan Maxwell, history professor Henry Reichman and educational leadership professor Linda Lambert.

A Strong Local Presence

Cal State Hayward is a major economic force in the region. Combined spending of the university, the CSUH Foundation and the student population exceeds $205 million annually. Economists estimate this spending generates $466 million in economic activity and supports more than 5,500 jobs.

Cal State Hayward faculty, staff and students are involved in the ongoing life of the Oakland community. They work with many Oakland agencies, including

260

those serving children, senior citizens, victims of abuse and the homeless. Cal State Hayward has created partnerships with many local institutions and the public at large.

Forging New Paths

Cal State Hayward was the first university in the United States to offer a master's degree in multimedia to serve the employee needs of the 2,000 multimedia companies in the Bay Area. The success of this program results from students and faculty from the sciences, arts, business and education working together in a multi-disciplinary approach to education.

Cal State Hayward is on the cutting edge of computing technology in equipment and teaching methods. Every student has guaranteed access to a computer, with electronic mail connections to professors and links to the Internet.

Interactive distance learning technologies, originally designed to connect the Hayward and Contra Costa campuses, have been expanded to accommodate a variety of needs. For example, a scientist has been able to teach genetics to biology students from his lab at Lawrence Livermore National Laboratory. The engineering program uses the technology to link with engineering departments at California Polytechnic State University (Cal Poly), San Luis Obispo and San Jose State University.

Anyone, from a high school student to a world-renowned scientist, may send a specimen to the university's electron microscope laboratory. The image can be manipulated and magnified from a remote location. This is another way telecommunications enables Cal State Hayward students to master research techniques without leaving the lab.

Teacher Education

One of Cal State Hayward's goals is to provide well-prepared teachers. The university produces 6 percent of the state's credentialed teachers, and these alumni work in Oakland schools more than anywhere else in the Bay Area. More than 300 Oakland teachers have earned their credentials through the Partnership Credential Program, created in 1994 to address the teacher shortage. Currently, more than 230 Cal State Hayward teacher candidates are working in Oakland schools.

Cal State Hayward has one of the most diverse student populations of any California State University. *Photo by Tony Avelar*

Cal State Hayward is in the forefront of the CalState TEACH program, the California State University system's ambitious project to develop thousands of new elementary schoolteachers in the Bay Area. Cal State Hayward works to recruit minority teachers for Oakland and also supports them in the early years of their classroom work.

The university is working to increase the number of students who enroll directly from Oakland schools. Cal State Hayward trains its students to serve as reading and math tutors for Oakland high school and middle school students. Oakland high school graduates who need to strengthen math and writing skills to qualify for university admission may spend six summer weeks at the university to improve English, math and computer literacy skills.

In 1997 the university began the Presidential Scholars program, designed to attract the brightest students graduating from local high schools. The goal is to have more than 200 presidential scholars in this program by 2001, with $2,000 annual scholarships provided by the university, local business, professional organizations and alumni.

From full-time freshmen to working students seeking degrees at night to presidential scholars and graduate students, Cal State Hayward students receive a first-class education that enriches their personal lives and prepares them for professional success. ■

261

Alameda County Medical Center

Alameda County Medical Center comprises Highland Hospital, Fairmont Hospital and the John George Psychiatric Pavilion, and five ambulatory care centers — in Oakland, San Leandro, Hayward, Alameda and Newark. With 483 licensed beds, Alameda County Medical Center is one of the major health care systems in the Bay Area. The medical center accommodates several hundred thousand patient visits each year across its varied service areas.

Alameda County Medical Center (ACMC) traces its roots to several independent hospitals and health centers, including Fairmont Hospital, which opened its doors in 1864, and Highland Hospital, which opened in 1926. For 135 years, the medical center has been committed to offering compassionate care to all who seek its services, regardless of patients' ability to pay — a mission not shared by any other hospital in Alameda County. ACMC provides comprehensive, high-quality medical treatment and a continuum of care for wellness through all stages of life through a fully integrated system of hospitals, clinics and health services, and a dedicated staff that is responsive to the county's diverse cultural needs.

The Three Campuses

Fairmont Hospital campus, a 173-bed facility in San Leandro, hosts one of Northern California's foremost rehabilitation programs, including specialized occupational/physical therapy and speech-audiology therapy services. Fairmont provides 123 beds of skilled nursing; a palliative care program to provide comfort and pain management for terminally ill patients; seniors' programs; and a range of primary and specialty care clinics.

The John George Psychiatric Pavilion, built in 1991, also in San Leandro, is a modern, 80-bed facility that provides intensive mental health outpatient and short-term hospitalization.

Highland Hospital campus is comprised of the original hospital, constructed in the 1920s; the clinics building, erected in the 1950s; and the nine-story acute services tower, built in 1967. The 230-bed facility includes the designated Level II Trauma Center for

Northern Alameda County. This acute care hospital offers emergency, medical and surgical, critical care, nursery, obstetrics and ambulatory care services.

Highland Hospital has also been a teaching hospital since its inception. In 1988 the hospital formalized a medical education affiliation with the University of California at Davis. Top neurosurgeons, thoracic surgeons, hematologists and pathologists from schools such as the University of California at San Francisco, Stanford University and Harvard Medical University are available as teachers and consultants to the medical staff.

The original Highland Hospital buildings are of historical and architectural interest. Highland, the first planned comprehensive health care system in Alameda

County, opened its doors in 1926, and by the 1930s was regarded nationwide as one of the best examples of public health care facilities. The three-story administration building, situated at the crest of a hill, was designed by Henry W. Meyers and built in the Spanish Baroque style with ornamented twin towers, a tile roof and exterior decorative details of terra cotta. The interior foyer includes marble flooring, wainscoting and columns, metal grillwork and vaulted ceilings, and brass chandeliers. The hospital grounds were entered through two wrought-iron gates.

The Hospital Authority

Until last year, the Alameda County Board of Supervisors acted as trustees for the medical center.

The original Highland Hospital was regarded nationwide as one of the best examples of public health care facilities.

262

On July 1, 1998, this board transferred governance of the medical center to a new, 11-member Hospital Authority Board whose trustees are singularly focused on and dedicated solely to the medical center.

The Hospital Authority Board is a critical ingredient for the ACMC's continued success at a time when rapid change is taking place throughout the health care environment, both locally and nationally. While mergers and acquisitions, hospital closures and consolidations have become common across the land due to the increasingly competitive managed-care marketplace, ACMC has remained a strong, viable institution. The new governance will provide the continued independence the medical center needs to function more like a community hospital without abandoning its mission of providing high-quality, compassionate care to all county residents.

Expanded Programs

ACMC has set into motion new approaches to health maintenance and begun new building construction in order to be at the forefront of managed health care. In May 1998, Eastmont Wellness Center, the most recent addition to the medical center, opened its doors in a beautiful and efficiently designed facility, bringing needed health care to an East Oakland community that has been medically underserved — and an entirely new concept of giving patients the tools they need to keep themselves well.

On March 29, 1999, ground was broken on the Highland Hospital campus on a new, five-story, 143,000-square-foot Critical Care and Clinics Building and 390-stall parking garage, slated for completion in 2001. It will replace the 1950s clinic building and the 1920s wing buildings, which are outmoded, do not meet seismic standards and can not be upgraded to the needs of current medical practice. The expansion on the Highland campus will allow the medical center to focus on the continued development of the trauma center, oncology care and the Bright Beginnings Family Birthing Center.

The new facility is positioned for increasing trends toward outpatient modes of treatment. Highland's nationally recognized trauma center will have state-of-the-art resuscitation and monitoring equipment, an outpatient imaging department, a pharmacy, a phlebotomy lab, and an outpatient surgery center with pre-operative and post-operative areas.

The Primary Care floor will include 65 examination rooms, areas for pediatrics, women's urgent care and OB/GYN, and adult general medicine. The Specialty Care floor, with 83 exam and procedure rooms will house medical and surgical specialty clinics with dedicated areas for adult immunology, ophthalmology, oncology and orthopedics.

The Breast Cancer Early Detection Program at Highland aims to reduce mortality from breast cancer by providing screening to uninsured, underinsured and low-income women 40 years of age and older.

Since 1980, more than 40,000 babies have been delivered at Highland. ACMC's health services for women, newborns and children are second to none. ACMC has long been a leader in creating and implementing innovative programs that meet women's health care needs, such as the midwifery program, created in

ACMC is building for a healthier community — Highland Hospital's Critical Care and Clinics Building, to be completed in 2001
Designed by RBB ARCHITECTS INC.

1988. The Bright Beginnings Family Birth Center carries forth the medical center's commitment to providing comprehensive quality care by offering low-cost birthing packages and inviting families to attend births.

In addition to all these innovative programs, the Alameda County Health Care Foundation is busy building bridges with the community. While working to raise $5 million for medical equipment and furnishings for Highland's new facility, and $1 million to begin an endowment for the medical center's future needs, the foundation generates awareness of ACMC's health care clinics and other community-based health care programs. ■

263

Golden State Warriors

The Golden State Warriors — first known as the Philadelphia Warriors — is one of three charter members of the National Basketball Association still in existence, joining the Boston Celtics and the New York Knicks. The league began play in 1946 as the Basketball Association of America (BAA) and expanded into 17 teams in 1949, when it was renamed the National Basketball Association (NBA).

From 1946 to the end of the 1961-62 season, the Philadelphia Warriors dazzled its fans and produced legendary players like Wilt Chamberlain, Joseph Fulks,

Owner Christopher Cohan has placed community involvement as one of the top priorities of the organization since purchasing the team in 1995.

Paul Arizin and Neil Johnston en route to capturing two NBA championships. Under the guidance of head coach Eddie Gottlieb, the Warriors claimed the first-ever BAA title, beating the Chicago Stags in the championship series. It claimed its second title in 1956, beating the Fort Wayne Pistons and going from last place in the Eastern Division in 1954-55 to first place a year later.

During the 1959-60 campaign, the Warriors gained Philadelphia native Wilt Chamberlain, a 7-foot-1-inch, 275-pound giant with tremendous power and grace who would change the face of the game instantly and forever. During the 1960-61 season, Chamberlain's reputation drew huge crowds wherever the

The state-of-the-art, refurbished Arena in Oakland features 72 luxury suites and is one of the country's top venues.

Warriors traveled. The following season, "Wilt the Stilt" set records (a 50.4 scoring average and 4,029 total points) that have yet to be challenged. On March 2, 1962, Chamberlain scored an unprecedented 100 points in a game against the New York Knicks.

The Move to the West

Warriors owner Eddie Gottlieb sold the team in 1962 to an investment group from San Francisco led by Diner's Club and Franklin Mieuli. A year later, Mieuli became principal owner and president of the team. San Francisco was placed in the NBA's Western Division, and in 1970, when the NBA divisions were realigned, the team was placed in the new Pacific Division.

In 1971 the San Francisco Warriors moved to the Oakland Coliseum arena for its first season as the Golden State Warriors. During the memorable 1974-75 season, the Warriors advanced to the NBA Finals, where they swept the Washington Bullets (4-0) and captured its first NBA championship since moving to the West Coast.

Inspired Leadership

Christopher Cohan assumed control of the Warriors franchise on January 19, 1995, with a three-fold vision — to guide the team into the 21st century, provide Warriors fans with a comfortable and convenient facility, and create an NBA championship-caliber organization, both on and off the court.

264

The team has played in a state-of-the-art arena since November 1997, when the Arena in Oakland's refurbishing project was completed, solidifying the Warriors commitment to remain in Oakland for 30 years. In 1998, the Warriors moved into its new two-story, 58,000-square-foot training facility in the Oakland Convention Center. The $7.5 million structure, designed by Charles F. Jennings Architects, provides space for corporate offices, practice courts, media and team facilities. It was named the national winner in the 1999 American Institute of Steel Construction Engineering Awards of Excellence for projects up to $10 million in construction value.

Throughout his career, Cohan has remained committed to the community through the arts, charities, public radio, children and sports. Through his leadership, the Warriors' active participation in community programs has become exemplary. Warriors H.O.O.P. (Helping Out Other People) is a program designed for Warriors staff members to donate their time to various charities, clubs and organizations throughout the Bay Area. Another innovative program created in 1998, Warriors Golden Moments, is designed to affect lives positively through the element of surprise and random acts of kindness. With Warriors H.O.O.P., the sponsorship of the nationally ranked Road Warriors wheelchair basketball team, the child literacy program "Tall Tales" and many others, Cohan and the Warriors continue to broaden the Warriors' reach into Oakland and the Bay Area.

Retired Numbers and Other Honors

Many great players have donned a Warriors jersey, but only four have had their number retired — Tom Meschery (14), Alvin Attles (16), Rick Barry (24) and Nate Thurmond (42). Meschery averaged 12.9 points and 8.5 rebounds per game during six seasons with the Warriors. He played in the 1963 NBA All-Star Game and had his number retired on October 13, 1967.

Attles averaged 8.9 points during 11 seasons as a player, and coached the Warriors to the 1975 NBA Championship. He finished his 14-year coaching career with a 555-516 (.518) record and had his number retired on February 10, 1977. He has served as vice president and assistant general manager since 1987 and his relationship with the Warriors as a player, coach and administrator has grown into a legacy.

Barry averaged 25.6 points during his eight years with the Warriors. He was the NBA Rookie of the Year in 1966 and was voted to the NBA All-Star team eight times. Barry was selected as the MVP in the 1975 NBA Finals and had his number retired on March 18, 1988. Thurmond averaged 17.4 points and 16.9 rebounds during his 11 seasons with the Warriors and was selected to the NBA All-Star team seven times. He is the team's all-time leading rebounder (12,771) and had his number retired on March 8, 1978.

NBA All-Star 2000

As the Warriors forged into the 21st century, it played host to NBA All-Star 2000. The weekend (February 11-13, 2000) featured the NBA Jam Session, NBA TeamUp Celebration, All-Star Saturday activities and, finally, the 49th annual NBA All-Star Game. The nationally broadcast TeamUp Celebration brought NBA stars together with film, television and music celebrities to highlight the importance of youth community involvement. Throughout the weekend, an estimated 100,000-plus fans visited the NBA Jam Session in Oakland, which was the league's premier interactive fan event, featuring dozens of basketball activities, games and exhibits. The All-Star Saturday events at the Arena in Oakland featured the Schick Rookie game, NBA 2Ball competition and the AT&T Long Distance shootout contest. The weekend concluded with the All-Star game on Sunday, featuring a matchup between the league's best players from the Eastern and Western conferences. ■

The Warriors hosted the NBA's top players from the Eastern and Western conferences during NBA All-Star 2000 on February 11-13, 2000.

265

Matilda Brown Home

The notorious O'Leary cow did more than start the Great Chicago Fire. It gave birth to an oasis of dignity and elegance — a home for older women, with serene gardens, beautiful antiques, safety and security located in the heart of Oakland, California.

The Matilda Brown Home is a not-for-profit, fully licensed, residential-care facility for elderly women. In more than a century of existence, the home has retained the aura and characteristics of its founders — a small group of tenacious women, who faced each obstacle with implacable grace. Their efforts ignited the imaginations of Oakland's early leaders. The yellowed pages of the home's annals document assistance from: Elijah Bigelow, Samuel Merritt, James de Fremery and many others whose vision sparked Oakland's development.

The home's debut began in 1872, when President Ulysses S. Grant appealed to women's clubs of America to help thousands of people who survived the Chicago fire, but faced destitution and a harsh winter. In response, a dozen Oakland women formed the Ladies' Relief Society, today known as the Ladies' Home Society of Oakland. Women from all social strata and religious denominations, together sewed and sent 13 boxes of warm clothing.

Before these foreign endeavors had been completed, the society turned its efforts to meet local needs of aged women, abandoned babies and orphaned children living among the 10,000 or more people in Oakland. The society ladies filed incorporation papers and adopted a constitution. In 1872 the society began operating a Home for Aged Women and providing accommodations for over 100 children.

To support the home, society ladies walked down rutted, dirt streets and knocked on every door, first collecting dimes, then larger donations: three cows; a pig; chickens; fruit; bundles of clothing and furniture; cemetery plots; and land located on the Berkeley Railroad line for a building. A permanent residence for elderly women was completed in 1882.

The society met the constant challenge of funding with fortitude and by conceiving ingenious methods of raising money — from special events to convincing the police to turn over half of their fines to support the facility. In the face of each difficulty, the society's ladies garnered their talents, lifted their skirts and marched forward to keep the home alive and functioning. In the spirit of courage and earnest endeavor, the society intended to create a model of service for the state — and it did so. Today the society is renowned as a predecessor of Northern California's philanthropic organizations.

Under the dynamic leadership of Matilda E. Brown, the society's president for 30 years, the board of directors expanded and contracted the home's operations to meet the needs of a changing Oakland. By World War I, the number of residents increased from 20 to 30. Any infant in Alameda County could receive care at the Infants' Shelter. Vegetables grown on its farm supplied its kitchens. In 1923 the Home for Our Sisters in the Autumn of Life replaced the original structure. The home survived the Great Depression, and the children and elders ate well and had clean clothing. In 1935, following her death, the residence was renamed the Matilda Brown Home. After World War II, with the advent of foster care programs, the Children's Home closed.

Nearly 130 years after its inception, the society continues to operate a comprehensive assisted-living care facility for up to 36 "ladies." The Matilda Brown Home provides a variety of assistance to women 62 or older, allowing them to age in one place, within a nurturing, safe environment. Women seeking relief

Matilda Brown Home, built in 1882, designed by McDougall & Son of San Francisco, constructed by A. Herbst and located on three acres along a line of the Berkeley Railroad

266

from the burdens of maintaining a private home, find living in a community of other ladies an attractive alternative to social isolation often experienced in the community.

For many residents, moving to the home improves the quality of their aging. Private rooms allow residents to enjoy their solitude surrounded by photographs and personal items. Group dining, classes and daily events offer social outlets. Staff assistance with dressing, bathing, housekeeping and monitoring medications helps the ladies prepare for daytime activities while assuring their safety. The staff provides concierge services arranging transportation and activities that enable residents to participate in Oakland's community.

The home is serene and beautiful. The existing building renovated in 1996 to accommodate needs of the contemporary older women, maintains its historic and architectural character. Tall curved windows, airy rooms, carpets and drapery accent the antiques and upholstered furniture, which bring to mind a charming hotel. The building contains a sun room, beauty parlor, Jacuzzi and laundry facilities. The dining room staff serves a nutritious cuisine prepared on the premises from scratch to stimulate appetites or meet special diets. The structure is surrounded by 2.5 acres of lush gardens crowned by a mature magnolia tree and all watered from an on-site well. Fountains, sheltered patios and a gazebo are all visible from within.

Directors, staff, residents and relatives function much like an extended family. Directors, 54 in number, provide a portion of the operating costs, actively raise other funds and devote several hours a month working with the ladies or at the facility. The average tenure of an employee is 12 years. Commitment often extends beyond mere requirements as illustrated by the East Bay Hills Fire of 1991 when the staff — even those on leave or off duty — went to the home prepared to evacuate the residents if necessary. Skilled staff teach certification courses for other elder-care facilities and provide on-site training to Merritt College students, who are studying nursing, geriatric care and physical therapy. Residents themselves are involved in the life of the home, helping their more frail "sisters," suggesting activities, volunteering in the community at large, or participating in ongoing research on osteoporosis or women's health care issues. Residents' families are welcome at the residence and openly appreciate that the staff and board do not minimize their roles and involvement.

Changes in life expectancy and physical well-being have and will affect how the home serves older women. In 1872 the average life expectancy of women was 45 years. Then, a woman with memory loss or who was nonambulatory would not have been considered for residence. Modern women live to their mid-80s and, in the coming decades, may live well into their 90s. Today the home accepts residents who are more frail, use walkers, or have some form of memory loss. As health technologies and science change, the home will, as it has in the past, incorporate those advances to serve the needs of older residents.

The home will also accommodate changing interests of residents as in 1950 when three ladies installed television sets in their rooms supplanting the traditional pastimes of quilting and canning. Likewise, today's tea and cookies may give way to tomorrow's high-tech amusements. While the Matilda Brown Home is poised to combine Old World charm with modern innovations, it will continue to provide gentle hands, patient listeners and gracious smiles in a comfortable and familiar environment. ■

The carpeted, antique-filled atrium invites residents to linger and chat.

267

St. Mary's Center

St. Mary's Church, Oakland's oldest Roman Catholic parish, and St. Mary's School, staffed by Sisters of the Holy Names, had served the needs of local families for more than 100 years. After the school closed in 1973 due to financial difficulties, people living in the downtown west Oakland area were surveyed about their needs, and the church's staff members decided to dedicate themselves, the parish and school resources to meeting the needs of this low-income community.

Even while the school existed, a vibrant summer youth program had attracted many Latino and African-American youths. In 1973 this was expanded to a full-year program. At the same time, the staff went door to door surveying those who lived in the surrounding neighborhoods, downtown apartments and SRO hotels to better understand their needs, dreams and hopes. It was thus that St. Mary's Center came into existence, involving people of all ages, cultures and backgrounds. It truly became a community center that embraced all and fostered leadership, resiliency, education and fun.

Soon a Parent/Infant Education Program began, which later became the current Preschool. In 1974 older adults began the Senior Companion Program and outreach to those living in SRO hotels. Senior dinner programs that brought people together around food and companionship also began.

In the mid-1970s, St. Mary's Parish sponsored St. Mary's Gardens, 100 units of low-income senior housing to replace housing demolished by the construction of Interstate 980. St. Mary's Center helped with the development of programs at St. Mary's Gardens and provided transportation for its residents to its center and community events.

New programs appeared in the 1980s to meet growing needs. The Food for All Ages program started by providing a bag lunch for people on the streets. Staff members prepare lunches for the preschool children, a weekly supplemental grocery bag to 40 families and 70 seniors, and more than 350 Christmas baskets donated by local churches. It also provides daily coffee and pastries for homeless seniors, and six senior dinners each week. For many, St. Mary's Center provides their only hot meal for the day and their only chance to socialize.

The center also began responding to a disturbing trend: seniors showing up on the streets, homeless because of the closing of low-cost residential hotels — a trend that increased greatly after the 1989 Loma Prieta earthquake. St. Mary's staff found housing for many of these seniors.

In 1992 St. Mary's Center incorporated as a separate nonprofit public benefit organization, and two years later, it moved to its present site at 22nd Street and San Pablo.

St. Mary's Center Preschool is now a five-day-a-week educational enrichment program for 30 poverty-level children ages 3 to 5 years. The primary goal is to prepare children for success in elementary school and beyond. Each school day provides an exciting literature-based curriculum with a balance of academic and development activities: physical activities to develop large and small motor skills; an art period; time for hands-on mathematics; computer time on donated computers; science explorations; music time; creative free play and language development.

At the preschool, children are either African-American or Asian-American, mostly Chinese, Vietnamese and Filipino. Many come unable to speak or

St Mary's is proud of its numerous meal programs that feed the homeless, seniors and families.

268

understand English and needing translation and special language help. All are from families whose income is below the poverty line, including families with two working parents. Some live in a nearby housing project where drug dealing and gunshots are commonplace. Violence touches their lives deeply, and often, St. Mary's Center is their only experience of a safe place.

Sunday dinners are prepared and served by a different organization each week, including local and suburban churches, corporations and civic groups. This program enriches the giver as well as the receiver. Volunteers have an opportunity to interact with people very different from themselves and learn about some of the causes and effects of poverty.

More than 750 seniors are served annually by St. Mary's Outreach and Advocacy Program, which helps the frail elderly live as independently as possible. The staff coordinates care with medical professionals, gives referrals to resources, provides telephone reassurance, home visits and emotional support, assistance with filling out forms, shopping escorts and other services. The goal is to render basic services to help seniors "age in place," comforted by familiar surroundings.

St. Mary's Center is the only agency in Oakland with programs exclusively designed for homeless seniors. Many have lost trust in everyone, and it often takes an outreach worker months of frequent contact on the streets before a homeless person is willing to come to the center. Once a homeless senior has enough trust to come to St. Mary's Center, a case manager in the Senior Homeless Program locates temporary housing and then begins the careful, slow process of working with the senior to find permanent housing and the most appropriate plan of action to address medical, financial, social and psychological needs.

Homelessness is a severe health hazard for anyone, but especially so for elderly persons. St. Mary's Community Nursing Program helps respond to their particular needs. St. Mary's is an approved clinical site for San Francisco State and California State University,

Hayward, universities. Several faculty and student nurses from each campus come one to three days a week to provide health assessments. They also monitor medication, change dressings, accompany seniors to clinics and provide health education.

If seniors are addicted to alcohol or drugs, St. Mary's finds them temporary housing and requires that they complete the Recovery 55 program before being placed in permanent housing. This is a daily, eight-week outpatient alcohol and drug abuse recovery program to assist seniors to stop or lessen their dependence on alcohol and/or drugs. Daily group meetings focus on

The Preschool serves up to 40 neighborhood children with a comprehensive early childhood education program.

One of the many seniors helped by St. Mary's stands near the center's main entrance. All photos by Steve Fisch

dealing with emotional issues such as anger and stress, and grief over the many losses in an older person's life. The meetings also focus on the effects of alcohol and drug abuse.

From December 1998 to April 1999, St. Mary's opened its first winter shelter for homeless seniors. The shelter provided a safe place to sleep out of the cold and rain for 20 seniors each night, while also serving them a hot dinner and breakfast. In addition, many of the seniors who used the shelter were helped to find permanent housing and mental health counseling.

For nearly 30 years, St. Mary's Center has responded to the dire needs of community members who were faced with the loss of their homes, the hardships of poverty and the need for early childhood education. In a cityscape that can often seem harsh and unfriendly, thousands of people have come to know St. Mary's Center as a community of loving concern. ■

University of California

The University of California (UC) traces its roots to Oakland with the founding of the College of California in 1855. Thirteen years later, college trustees transferred its assets, including land north of Oakland, which they named Berkeley, to the state for the establishment of the University of California, the state's only land grant institution.

When it opened in 1869 in Oakland, UC included 10 faculty members and 40 students. Today the university, with nine campuses and a 10th campus under development in the San Joaquin Valley, educates approximately 174,000 students — 90 percent of whom are California residents — and has a work force of 140,000 and a $12 billion budget.

The College of California in downtown Oakland gave impetus to the creation of the University of California.

A public university with campuses in Berkeley, Davis, Irvine, Los Angeles, Riverside, San Diego, San Francisco, Santa Barbara and Santa Cruz, UC is recognized as one of the world's most acclaimed institutions of higher learning. The 10th campus, UC Merced, is expected to open as early as 2004. The university's central administration, the Office of the President, moved from UC Berkeley to Oakland in 1989 and relocated to new quarters on Franklin Street, across from the university's original Oakland location, in May 1998.

Under California's Master Plan for Higher Education, UC is the state's primary academic agency for research, providing undergraduate, graduate and professional education. The top 12.5 percent of California's high school graduates are eligible for admission to the University of California under the plan.

Instruction on UC campuses covers all fields of human knowledge, including the arts and humanities, social sciences and physical sciences, representing one of the broadest ranges of study of any institute of higher education in the world. Six UC campuses have been elected to membership in the prestigious 61-member Association of American Universities; no other university system in the country has more than one campus as a member.

Under the state constitution, a Board of Regents governs the university. The board consists of 26 members: 18 are appointed by the governor for 12-year terms, subject to Senate confirmation after consultation with an advisory committee; one is a UC student appointed by the regents to a one-year term; and seven are ex officio members — the governor, the lieutenant governor, the speaker of the Assembly, the superintendent of public instruction, the president and vice president of the Alumni Associations of the University of California, and the president of the university.

The university is a powerful economic engine for California and its residents. The state provides core support for UC's mission of teaching, research and public service. In return, UC brings in billions of dollars in nonstate funding, reinvesting this money in California, primarily through research, which leads to new technologies, new products and jobs. UC and its three affiliated national laboratories — Ernest Orlando Lawrence Berkeley and Lawrence Livermore national laboratories in California and Los Alamos National Laboratory in New Mexico — produce more research leading to patented inventions than any other public or private research institutions. UC researchers have been awarded 35 Nobel Prizes since 1939.

UC has awarded more than 1 million degrees and has approximately 970,000 living alumni worldwide. ■

270

Oakland Museum of California

The Oakland Museum of California is a multi-faceted jewel in Oakland's crown. The city-owned museum was created when voters passed a $6.6 million bond issue in 1960 to construct a new complex covering four city blocks near Lake Merritt. Initially, the museum brought together the collections of three separate small museums — the Oakland Public Museum, containing city curator Charles L. Wilcomb's American Indian collections; the Oakland Art Museum; and the Snow Museum of Natural History, built to house the natural history and conservation collections of big-game hunter Henry A. Snow.

Esther Fuller led the search for a distinguished architect, believing that Oakland should have a great building for its new museum. The chosen firm, Kevin Roche, John Dinkeloo and Associates, designed the museum to fit into the urban landscape comfortably and to be a place where people felt welcome. Its interior park — designed by Daniel Kiley and Geraldine Knight Scott — is open to everyone. The innovative, three-tiered structure, with a series of terraced, landscaped gardens each formed by the roof of the gallery beneath, was opened in 1969 and named a city landmark in 1994. Ada Louise Huxtable of *The New York Times* called it "the most thoughtfully revolutionary building in the world."

The Oakland Museum also has a "thoughtfully revolutionary" role in Oakland's everyday life. It serves as a place where diverse communities can meet and share traditions, and as an education center for Oakland's children. Its excellent collections and changing exhibits accurately reflect its name, the Oakland Museum of California. One of America's largest regional museums, it has brought the best of the past — and the present — to fully represent the complex story of California's natural sciences, people and art.

The building's first level depicts the state's environments and ecology, and the second level shows the evolving character of California, from the earliest human inhabitants, Spanish conquest and Gold Rush eras to the influx of immigrants in recent decades and the high-tech culture engendered by Silicon Valley industries. The art gallery on the third level displays a wide range of fine arts, from master painters such as Albert Bierstadt and William Keith to present-day creators of works in painting, sculpture, photography and mixed media. With the displays of California's natural habitats, the rich mixture of diverse cultures and the fascinating confluence of art at the Oakland Museum of California, there is something for everyone!

The Oakland Museum is justly proud of its changing exhibits and educational outreach programs that interpret the story of California. As an outgrowth of the Gold Rush sesquicentennial exhibitions in 1998, the museum and California teachers created a new curriculum that expands the teaching of California history from fourth grade into the 11th grade. Although funded by Oakland's taxpayers, the museum could not carry out its exciting programs without the significant financial support and leadership of two important groups, the Oakland Museum of California Foundation and the Oakland Museum Women's Board, which have raised millions of dollars over the years. This public-private partnership has created one of the most exciting cultural institutions in the country. ■

The museum's gardens and terraces were designed by renowned landscape architect Daniel Kiley.
Photo © Aaron Kiley

Fourth-graders from Montclair School at a museum Gold Rush program in 1998
Photo © Joe Samberg

271

Black Adoption Placement & Research Center

The Black Adoption Placement & Research Center (BAPRC) story is one that serves a perfect analogy for the plight of children languishing in foster care. While it is a story of faith, vision and perseverance, it is also one of hope and a belief in a better reality for children who wait.

In the late 1970s and early 80s, the Oakland community was deluged with dismal statistics about the crack cocaine epidemic, its effect on the African-American community and frightening predictions about the number of children born who were either exposed or affected by this drug. On the heels of the reports came requests from the local public child welfare agency to the African-American community to come forward and serve as adoptive or foster parents to the growing number of children entering foster care

Executive director
Gloria King, M.S.

because of the drug epidemic. After countless numbers of people saw their efforts to come forward thwarted by bureaucracy, insensitivity and other barriers, a group of dedicated people came together to develop another option to solve this growing crisis. After much thought, the consensus was to create an adoption agency that sought to meet both the needs of the children in foster care and the needs of the families who hoped to parent them. Thus, BAPRC was born.

Now, about 17 years later, BAPRC remains faithful to its vision and mission. BAPRC is a private, nonprofit adoption and foster family agency whose mission is to recruit, train and certify families for the placement of African-American children and all children waiting for permanent homes. BAPRC places an emphasis on advocating on behalf of children with special needs and for those families who step forward to provide a safe, nurturing and healing environment for them. BAPRC assists families through each step of the process, which includes a two-hour orientation, in-home family assessment, 30 hours of pre-placement training, the home-study process, and ongoing support, training and education services after training.

BAPRC is licensed to serve families and children in 14 Northern California counties. BAPRC's three programs are adoption, fost/adopt (which places a child with a family willing to adopt once the child becomes legally available) and "Bridge to Permanency," which could mean family reunification with the birth parents or adoption.

BAPRC has long regarded its partnership with public agencies and linkages with other community-based organizations as critical to its success in child and family advocacy. Over the years, the BAPRC staff has developed and nurtured several innovative and effective public-private collaborations, resulting in the placement and finalizations of approximately 250 children with special needs and major system changes in the child welfare field.

According to BAPRC's executive director, Gloria King, one of the agency's most spectacular accomplishments was the placing of a "five sib" group — that is, five children from the same family with one adoptive family.

A proud "complaint-free" member of The Better Business Bureau, BAPRC is the recipient of numerous awards and recognition, including the prestigious John R. May Award from the San Francisco Foundation.

The BAPRC story is one of which the Oakland community should be proud. It chronicles the efforts of one small visionary group of individuals who have left a wonderful and lasting legacy. ■

Blue Cross of California, State Sponsored Program

Blue Cross of California, one of the largest public health insurance companies in California, started in Oakland in 1937. Formed by a coalition of Bay Area hospitals, it grew and prospered, and although its headquarters moved to Southern California, its presence is still very much a vibrant part of Oakland's life. While Blue Cross quietly pursues its mission to manage health care for uninsured and low-income populations, its Community Resource Center (CRC) has embarked on an unusual collaboration with the city of Oakland to improve the health of all its residents.

Early in 1997 the CRC staff discovered that injury and death from fires had a tremendous impact on the health of Oakland's residents and cut across income, race and social strata in the city. Fire is an important issue to Oakland residents, more so since the East Bay Hills Fire in October of 1991 took lives and destroyed

thousands of homes. Even so, the fire department's budget limited its ability to educate residents and initiate fire prevention activities despite its estimate that 20,000 homes had inadequate or no smoke detectors. The CRC staff decided that Blue Cross' community health strategy had to include fire safety — a topic not normally considered a traditional health issue.

To address the fire safety concern, Blue Cross approached the Oakland Fire Department with ideas to augment the department's fire safety education program. In 1997, during Blue Cross' grand opening of its new offices in downtown Oakland, amid the jovial festivities

complete with clowns, balloons and booths, Blue Cross donated 2,000 smoke detectors to the fire department, and has done so every year since.

Subsequently, Blue Cross provided staff to work with the fire department in designing, planning and coordinating a fire safety program. In collaboration with the fire department, Blue Cross kicked off a city-wide fire safety education program in the schools, including the widely successful Fire Safety Poster Contest. Blue Cross established an oversight committee, which includes both police and fire department representatives, and hosted a series of meetings and luncheons in preparation for taking the fire safety message to the community.

The program intends to create a "catchment area" around the 25 firehouses in the city, wherein residents would develop an escape plan, receive free smoke detectors and batteries and be educated about fire safety, extinguishers and other fire safety matters. The intention was to establish the program as an ongoing function of the city that can be replicated by other communities.

To date, its efforts have led to an increase in the fire department's budget for community education and its smoke detector distribution program. Blue Cross and the city of Oakland have established Toward Year 2000: the City of Oakland, A Fire Safe City, to ensure that every residence has adequate numbers of smoke detectors. To achieve that goal, Blue Cross and the Oakland Fire Department will conduct a citywide survey of residents, tapping once again into the 60 elementary schools in Oakland. Additionally, Blue Cross will assist the oversight committee to seek foundation funds and corporate donations to support the program.

Blue Cross established an innovative collaboration with the city of Oakland that may continue long after the goals of the fire safety program have been met. The Blue Cross Community Resource Center will remain in the forefront — addressing health issues that affect all Oakland residents. ■

The 1998 Fire Safety Poster Contest grand-prize winner of the contest sponsored by the Oakland Fire Department and Blue Cross (left to right) Shirley Lim, 10, a fifth-grader at Lincoln Elementary School in Oakland, Shirley's teacher Elgine Rotzin and John Monahan representing Blue Cross.
Oakland Tribune,
Photo by Dino Vournas

273

Mills College

The oldest women's college west of the Rocky Mountains, Mills College traces its history back to 1852, the era of California's Gold Rush. In 1865, it was taken over by Cyrus and Susan Mills, who set about creating a school modeled on Susan's alma mater, Mount Holyoke College. Cyrus Mills, an amateur botanist, planted more than 5,000 eucalyptus trees to form shaded walkways on what grew to be a 135-acre campus. Outstanding examples of Victorian architecture, as well as handsome Spanish Revival buildings designed by Walter Ratcliff Jr. and others by Julia Morgan (of San Simeon fame) were created to house students and faculty, classrooms and offices.

Once country where Ohlone Indians hunted, then part of a grand Spanish rancho, the beautiful, park-like Mills campus remains an island of green peace in the bustling Oakland that has grown up around it.

(Inset left)
For most of its long life, Mills has been a center for the fine arts in the Bay Area, welcoming the public to outstanding concerts of music and dance, art exhibitions, plays, lectures and other events.
©*Rick Rappaport*

(Inset right)
"We made it!" The class of 1999 joins the long, long line of graduates who have left Mills to make their mark in the world, many of them choosing to live and work in Oakland itself — the city that is home to their college, Mills.

Over the years, Mills College has attracted a broad range of talent in faculty, students and distinguished visitors. Jane Addams, Booker T. Washington, Martin Luther King Jr., Dean Rusk, children's rights advocate Marian Wright Edelman and Congresswoman Barbara Lee (a Mills graduate) have all spoken at Mills. Noted art historian Alfred Neumeyer and internationally famous French composer Darius Milhaud have taught at Mills (the latter for 30 years). In addition, musicians John Cage and Anthony Braxton have performed there, as have dancers Merce Cunningham and Martha Graham. The college also counts legendary jazzman Dave Brubeck as a former Mills graduate student.

From the beginning, Mills was designed as a dynamic, intellectual environment that would contribute to Oakland and the Bay Area, rather than just an enclave where young women would be sent to retreat from the world. Mills takes an open-minded approach to what a liberal arts college should be and how it should prepare students to best achieve their long term goals. Since the early 1960s, Mills students have been encouraged to work within the community — as interns in the Oakland mayor's office, for example — as a part of their studies.

In 1974 Mills became the first women's college to offer an undergraduate major in computer science. That same year, out of concern about the low numbers of young women pursuing math-based and science-based careers, Mills College became the catalyst for the founding of the Math/Science Network. More than half a million young women in grades 6 through 12 have attended the Network's Expanding Your Horizons conferences, which expose them to female role models in fields like engineering and technology. And with the help of a grant from the National Science Foundation, the college's department of education has been responsible for innovative teacher-training methods that have fundamentally changed the science curriculum in every elementary school in Oakland.

Included among Mills' graduates are three U.S. ambassadors; a state governor; a congresswoman; a scientist who developed a treatment for sickle-cell anemia; Emma Plank, who created a method of teaching chronically ill or injured children in hospital environments; and choreographer Trisha Brown, recipient of a MacArthur Foundation "genius" Fellowship. The variety and stature of their achievements reflect the interdisciplinary strengths of the liberal education Mills offers.

Mills awarded its first graduate degrees in 1920; today it has 775 undergraduate women, and 350 male and female graduate students. In 1990 despite pressures to become coeducational, Mills re-dedicated itself to its founders' belief in the lasting value of a college where education focuses on women's perspectives, values and concerns. ■

Samuel Merritt College

Oakland is home to an extraordinary educational institution with a long, proud history of leadership. For more than 90 years Samuel Merritt College has educated students for a life of highly skilled and compassionate service in health care. Today it is the premier source of health science professionals in the East Bay. Samuel Merritt College offers Bachelor of Science degrees in nursing (a joint degree with Saint Mary's College of California) and in health and human sciences. Samuel Merritt's eight master's degree programs prepare physical therapists, occupational therapists, general and specialty nurses, and physician assistants for health care careers.

The story begins in 1890 with the death of Dr. Samuel Merritt, the first mayor of Oakland. He left his estate to his sister with instructions to establish a hospital in Oakland. This bequest led to the founding of Samuel Merritt Hospital and its nursing school in 1909. Over the years, changes in health care and higher education transformed the hospital and the school. Summit Medical Center and Samuel Merritt College stand as the 21st-century legacy of Dr. Merritt's original bequest.

Today Samuel Merritt College thrives, with over 750 students almost equally divided between undergraduate and graduate programs. Many are adults who have chosen a health profession as a second career or already hold an undergraduate degree elsewhere. Their diversity of age, ethnicity and experience enriches the Samuel Merritt education.

Known nationally for its innovative and personalized approach, the college is located on "Pill Hill" campus. Along with access to this major medical center, the college provides state-of-the-art facilities that include specialty laboratories for nursing, physical therapy, occupational therapy and anatomy. The college's health sciences library — the East Bay's largest — offers extensive multimedia resources and computerized search facilities. The college's rich and varied clinical curriculum involves more than 500 partner agencies throughout the United States. Students gain hands-on patient care experience through clinical courses and internships in outpatient centers, hospitals, home care agencies, community clinics and physician offices. Employers consider Samuel Merritt College graduates some of the best-prepared health care professionals in the industry.

Health care organizations and consumers throughout the Bay Area feel Samuel Merritt College's impact. Its graduates are leaders and serve on the front lines of health care in California. Student, faculty and staff participation in educational and charitable work enhances Samuel Merritt College's contribution to good health in the Oakland community.

The 1999 California Governor's Golden State Quality Award — Level One (Commitment) recognized Samuel Merritt College's pioneering work in applying quality improvement principles and practices in higher education. Samuel Merritt College is the first institution of higher education to receive this award. ■

275

The Scottish Rite Temple of Freemasonry

The Scottish Rite is one of the largest of approximately 100 orders of Freemasonry, which are thought to have developed during The Crusades. Formerly aligned with the "Knights Templar," a group dedicated to protecting holy pilgrims, the Freemasons suffered persecution from both the Pope and monarchies of Europe and were forced underground until 1717, when the fraternal order resurfaced as the "Grand Lodge of England."

Today the Scottish Rite order of the Freemasons is a nondenominational fraternal organization open to men of all races and backgrounds. The few requirements consist of good moral character and belief in a Supreme Being. The organization is dedicated to the promotion of brotherhood, charity and the improvement of the character of its members.

One of the tenets of Freemasonry is that all members swear to support the wives and daughters of fellow masons who may die unexpectedly. It is for this reason that a great many "forty-niners" from the East Coast joined the organization before embarking upon the gold rush, many leaving their families behind. In this way, Freemasonry was brought to Northern California.

The Scottish Rite Temple — an Oakland landmark since 1927

The Scottish Rite Temple in Oakland was first organized in 1883 with 31 members, and in 1896, a former synagogue on 14th Street was converted into the first Scottish Rite Cathedral west of the Rocky Mountains. The Temple's popularity in the early 1900s led to the construction of yet another cathedral, "built for a lifetime," on Madison Street. A post-earthquake population boom ensured that within 20 years the Scottish Rite simply had to create a temple so grand, so magnificent and so modern that it could never be outgrown.

On December 12, 1927, a lavish ceremony dedicated the new Scottish Rite Temple, the focal point of 14th Street, located on Lakeside Drive in the heart of the area's sumptuous "Gold Coast." Oakland businesses, their owners often Freemasons themselves, were responsible for the elaborate interior painting, ironwork, millwork, embroidery and furnishings.

The temple's cast-bronze exterior doors open onto a two-story foyer with a richly decorated, medieval-style ceiling. The lobby is flanked by broad stairways and opens onto the Grand Ballroom with its Italianate ceiling, stage and capacity of 1,500. Also opening onto the lobby is a beautiful, spacious ladies parlor, well preserved in the Art Deco style. The building's chief point of interest may well be the fourth floor auditorium, with its vast circular space, dome ceiling, curved choir balconies, and red velvet curtains

The Scottish Rite Temple demonstrates its belief in charitable works by maintaining a free clinic dedicated to eradicating childhood language disorders such as aphasia and dyslexia. The center was established in 1982, and has since helped thousands of children to overcome difficulties that could have otherwise had educationally crippling effects. The Temple also offers a scholarship foundation that sponsors students from Northern California public high schools all the way through their college careers.

Although the popularity of the Scottish Rite's fraternal order has dwindled in recent years, its landmark Oakland edifice preserves that heritage with its legendary beauty, now made available to East Bay citizens for formal events. The building's artwork proudly features Scottish Rite symbols, and its administration is still solidly that of Freemasons, upholding the principles that the fraternal order was based upon more than a century ago. ■

276

Photo by Robert A. Eplett

277

Technology

DIVERSE BUSINESSES HAVE GATHERED TO MAKE
OAKLAND ONE OF THE COUNTRY'S LEADING CENTERS
OF TECHNOLOGY INNOVATION, DEVELOPMENT,
MANUFACTURING AND EMPLOYMENT.

Endymion Systems, Inc.

Once, Fred Phares, an avid science fiction reader armed with a math degree, made a choice between selling pharmaceuticals, light bulbs and working with computers. With an aptitude for computers, he leapt into the strange, fascinating world of technology. After years of shepherding his knowledge, he became a consultant. In 1991, with a fellow consultant, he founded a consulting company known as IDEX Technologies, Inc., and from this zygote, Endymion Systems, Inc. (ESI) emerged in 1998.

Phares and his partner knew voice and network systems inside and out. As competing consultants, they established communications systems for clients mystified by technology, or clients who had embraced technology at a pace far quicker than their staff or infrastructure could handle. These companies needed outside help to guide them through the universe of possibilities.

Although their expertise overlapped, the demand for communications consultants flourished. Yet both understood that credibility and ultimate success would be hampered by the absence of a formal business structure. They pooled their talents. Phares and his partner wanted to give clients top-notch communications services. They also wanted a workplace where individuals were treated in a professional manner, where consultants had an opportunity to grow and to be intellectually challenged — without sacrificing family time or income, and without burning out.

Their business decision proved fruitful. The company attracted more customers, demonstrated the reliability of the principals and illustrated that it could maintain and improve the quality of its services.

The company's first client had defined a communication problem and a solution and wanted Phares' company to work out the feasibility issues. The analysis found the solution anything but feasible. Rather than leave the client with a "no-go," Phares' staff identified a cost-effective alternative that would address the problem. The extra effort set the tone for future work.

ESI is driven by its clients. Over the last six years of its journey, it jumped from one staff member and two partners to more than 200 employees — never once stopping to advertise. Yet it took the time to build long-term personal relationships with its clients, a key to bringing in new business.

Initially, the business revolved around network services and infrastructure. It eventually provided the closet equipment, operations system, cables and mainframes. The staff members became "technology enablers" because they helped clients put their own business platforms on top of that infrastructure, linking the physical world with the electronic world.

Despite the company's growth, a gap existed between providing cables and establishing workable processes for accessing and using technology afforded by that cabling system. This vacuum, along with changing technologies, precipitated a restructuring of the business, which occurred in 1998. The cabling function remained with IDEX predominantly, while ESI consolidated the technical consulting component.

ESI is based in Oakland, California, because the business-friendly city had reasonable rents for start-up companies. Accessibility to the rest of the Bay Area, a traveler-friendly airport and multiple transportation options all made Oakland the ideal business environment. ESI also has offices in Wilmington, Delaware, and Seattle, Washington, and more than 100 full-time employees. Its clients are distributed among the banking and finance, retail, health care agribusiness, manufacturing, distribution and services industries.

ESI supplies technology consulting — strategies and planning, applications development, project management, voice and data-network support, systems integration, cabling design and management — and has a host of alliances related to the industry. The company is organized into consulting practices that focus on distinct business lines.

Enterprise Solutions, the newest of its practices, began in 1999. It was created when Steve King joined Phares at ESI to bring his applications experience and unique vision to the company. Enterprise Solutions explores how to meld Enterprise Resource Planning packages, data warehousing and the Internet and forge linkages between new business opportunities

280

and new technologies. ESI helps clients discover entrepreneurial opportunities by taking them into the electronic marketplace.

Technology build-out services merge traditional brick-and-mortar disciplines with the technology needs of the future. From installing cables to designing systems for "smart buildings," ESI works with architects, contractors and designers to ensure that furniture, connection points, firewalls and other essential requirements are coordinated.

Space-planning teams help both mature and incubating companies advance to their next phase by creating an environment that expresses their newfound status and stability. ESI identifies essential functions and key themes, then collaborates with furniture and design firms to bring these to life through customized and attractive interiors.

ESI's relocation teams move companies from one facility to another — without major headaches. Experts in protecting data and sensitive equipment, they create a seamless transition that limits downtime and lost revenue. They get companies back online and in business quickly by anticipating and planning the entire process from initial design to final plug-in.

ESI provides ongoing support for businesses needing technical experts. Support ranges from one engineer needed to help during a staff shortfall, to a team of experts to solve migration problems, set up network stations or operate help lines.

The company establishes long-term relationships with its clients, providing help along the way, anticipating needs, and understanding every aspect of its client's operations and growth. In essence, ESI becomes its customers' state-of-the-art technology partner.

ESI would not exist without the explosion of the Internet, where voice and data are converging, where even the most sophisticated companies must learn entirely new data-networking technologies. It brings to the table a core of technologically competent players who understand how to merge large and complex networks into cohesive, useable solutions.

As technology matures, it will become more of a commodity. It will spread to every facet of people's lives. There will be less need for engineering expertise because the state-of-the-art will become more consistent. Miniaturization will continue. The world of instantaneous information will become more friendly, functional, less expensive and everywhere — even in people's bodies. Interfaces will become seamless paths to communication. As technology becomes less expensive and more standardized, it will be easier to install and replace. The evolution is dramatic and forms the underpinning of ESI's maneuver into the "new world" of applications.

It is difficult to remember that, despite the excitement and possibilities technology offers, ESI is a people-based company. Its challenge is to figure out how to grow the company and serve its long-term clients without losing the personal relationships its growth is based on, or losing the ability to maintain and control the high quality of its services.

Fred Phares (left), founder and CEO of ESI, and Steve King, president and COO

Endymion Systems, Inc., a modest champion of technology, slightly irreverent and intensely principled, leaps from the present to the future with ease. It will continue to move toward higher levels of technology, into the applications realm, leading its clients safely through the firmament of the Internet and teaching its clients how to tame the technology beast. ■

281

Versata, Inc.

The story of Versata is a story of growth so rapid and goals so ambitious that the company surpassed its own expectations within its first years of existence. Vision Software, now Versata, was co-founded by Naren Bakshi and Kevin Fletcher Tweedy in 1995. From its inception, it has been a venture-backed, employee-owned, private company that has recently gone public. Versata established as its mission the desire to create a truly technology-driven software company that would dramatically change how applications are developed.

Versata's original location on 14th Street in Oakland was selected for the availability of excellent software engineers brought to the area by other local companies that were establishing the Oakland/Berkeley area as a "hot spot" for technology-driven enterprises.

Versata's primary visionary, Val Huber, established the company's initial ambition: to create technology that enables custom applications to be developed through business rules automation technology that was technologically independent, instead of through traditional programming methods. This means that changes to a program may be made through changing the business rules rather than through the time-consuming traditional process of rewriting programmer's code.

Detractors called it an absurd idea, and even Versata's founders knew that the project was incredibly ambitious. If possible, the technology breakthrough of business rules automation would deliver custom applications in one-tenth the time or more compared to applications developed by writing code. This gives the user the ability to respond quickly to business change, resulting in previously unheard-of agility.

Against the odds, Versata quickly became so successful and active that it expanded four times in 1995, each time outstripping the capacity of its current facility. The company began with only five people in January 1995, and by the end of the year it employed 50. In 1996 Versata moved to a building on Webster Street, where it now resides. The move was well timed, as 1998-99 became an even bigger year for growth, where the company grew from 53 employees to more than 150. And in 2000 Versata has grown to over 500 employees in more

than eight countries. Versata has always experienced low employee turnover, which has helped it to rapidly add to its pool of technological and market expertise. As a result of this expertise and Versata's unparalleled business growth, the company now has field operations in over 14 U.S. cities, Europe and Asia.

In addition to its business-rules automation technology, Versata offers a Professional Services organization to ensure customers' project success. This organization, also located at the Oakland headquarters, provides a full range of consulting, training and mentoring services for Versata's customers. It helps clients and partners develop their own internal skills to take full advantage of the important changes Versata has brought about in how applications can be developed.

The Versata E-business Automation System delivers rapid time to market advantage and gives the customer

the ability to change deployed applications overnight. The resulting application integrates a company's existing computing system into a new, flexible solution running on the Internet.

The "absurd claims" of tenfold or more time to market advantage made by Versata in 1995 have been thoroughly realized by Versata's 500-plus customers, whose businesses have increased dramatically. In 2000 Versata added over 200 customers to its base.

Versata management team (front row): Manish Chandra, Jon Bond, Rahul Patel, Prakash Bhaskaran (back row): Mike Stangl, Mike DeVries, Val Huber, Jack Hewitt, Peter Harrison (missing): David Segleau
Direct Images
Photo by Bill Knowland

282

For example, an early Versata customer, Pacific Bell, used Versata's software to develop a customer call center for a new digital video services business in Los Angeles. Executives projected it would take two years to develop the system by modifying a packaged application. They came to Versata and, in a mere 13 weeks, the system was up and running. Pacific Bell then changed the system five times in six months — a near-impossible task for traditional, handwritten software applications — and sent their developers to Java training.

Throughout the region, several different companies have used Versata's software automation software to similar advantage. An Oakland company, Infoworks, is using the technology to build an Internet mortgage services company.

Versata's basic mission was well established in the marketplace by 1998. The company is continuing its rapid growth in 2000, with its primary focus on the Internet and e-business applications. As a consequence, Versata sees itself as a solution for start-up Internet businesses, as well as established companies who wish to use Versata's rules-based technology to develop e-commerce applications for business-to-business e-trade.

Versata still maintains the same mission of using business-rules automation to develop and deploy applications, but the platform is now targeted to the Internet. Versata continues to operate on the same concept — customers are able to build and then deploy to an n-tier computing infrastructure with their applications connecting to databases, other legacy packages and custom applications developed for clients' own environments. These new Internet custom applications can respond rapidly to business change, enabling Versata customers to achieve competitive advantage through continuous business innovation.

Versata sees itself as an important provider for software that companies simply cannot do without in this age of rapid change and growth. The Crossroads Survey of Fortune 1000 companies reports that over 50 percent of companies change their business consistently, yet only six percent of those companies have the technology to support that pace of business change. On the Internet, change occurs even more rapidly, and business rules automation may be the only way for companies to keep up with Web time.

The company completed the ninth-largest initial public offering on Nasdaq in 2000 (Nasdaq:VATA) and continued to grow 50 percent quarter to quarter. Versata has always looked to exceed expectations and succeeded. As a result, local businesses, large and small, share their success through increased versatility, productivity and the ability to engage in dynamic e-business through the Versata E-business Automation System. ■

The Versata Professional Services organization offers training to empower its customers.
Direct Images
Photo by Bill Knowland

Versata's Oakland, California, Training Center
Direct Images
Photo by Bill Knowland

Tucker Technology, Inc.

Tucker Technology, Inc. provides full-service telecommunications and information technology solutions for its customers' voice and data applications. Tucker Technology performs two primary types of services — central office installation for dial-tone providers and major long-distance carriers, including both switching and transport equipment, and installation of customer premises-based equipment such as PBX systems and personal computer networks. Additionally, Tucker Technology handles inside wiring for residential and corporate business customers, installs voice and data cables, and provides maintenance for the equipment it installs.

Tucker Technology was established in 1994 by Frank Tucker, who has 25 years experience in the telecommunications industry. Tucker, a native of the Bronx, worked 10 years for New York Telephone, Pacific Bell and AT&T, and in an executive capacity for other telecommunications companies. Founded and headquartered in Oakland, Tucker Technology has seen such a meteoric rise in business that in just five years it has grown from a four-employee company operating in the East Bay to a company with more than 150 employees and satellite offices in Kansas City, Baltimore, New York City and Washington, D.C.

Tucker credits his company's success partly to the proliferation of the Internet, increased competition in the telecommunications industry created by the Telecommunications Act of 1996, and a robust economy. An expanding infrastructure, with increased need for ISDN line and cable installation, has provided more projects for companies such as Tucker Technology as local telephone companies have been hard-pressed to keep pace with demand. This has consequently brought more workers into the industry. Frank Tucker also believes his company's success is due to the partnerships it has formed with major players in the telecommunications industry, including the Regional Bell Operating Companies (RBOCs), other telephone service providers, and long-distance carriers in handling their engineering, installation and maintenance of major construction projects.

Tucker Technology is also affiliated with Communications Workers of America (CWA), the primary union of the telecommunications industry. Tucker Technology employees are union members, which sets it apart from companies that supply contract labor to meet peak demands. The company is a Minority Business Enterprise (MBE) certified with Oakland and the state of California. It is also certified as an 8(a) enterprise by the federal Small Business Administration.

Tucker Technology has a commitment to the Oakland community and the inner city communities wherever it does business nationwide to foster employment and industry growth. Tucker believes that Oakland can surpass Washington, D.C. as the telecommunications center of the nation if human resources are properly developed in this area. To that end, Tucker Technology has taken the lead in working with the city of Oakland and local community-based organizations such as WEAP (Women's Economic Agenda Project) to train young people in the telecommunications industry and to create meaningful employment for them. Tucker Technology has fostered partnerships with CWA and Cisco Systems to train WEAP constituents in telecommunications jobs. Trained workers can quickly advance from making $9 an hour to $50 an hour with three or four years' experience — in an industry with a future. ■

Frank Tucker and the professional core staff of Tucker Technology

284

Photo by Robert A. Eplett

Technology

bibliography

Chapter One: Claims, Characters and Commerce

Bagwell, Beth. *Oakland: The Story of a City.* Novato, California: Presidio Press, 1982; reprinted by Oakland Heritage Alliance, 1994.

Bixby, William. *Track of the Bear: 1873-1963.* New York: Van Rees Press, 1965.

Brookes, Douglas S. *The Oakland Waterfront: 1850-1940.* Master's thesis. Orinda, California: John F. Kennedy University, 1983.

Brooks, Maria. Orinda: The Unquiet Spirit." *WNews Magazine,* February 7, 1999, p. 8.

Conomos, T.J., ed. Pacific Division, American Association for the Advancement of Science. *San Francisco Bay: The Urbanized Estuary: Investigations into the Natural History of San Francisco Bay & Delta with reference to the Influence of Man.* Lawrence, Kansas: Allen Press, 1979.

Dobrin, Michael. "Iron Will and Arctic Ice: The Life and Times of Captain Christian Theodore Pedersen." *Up Here: Life in Canada's North,* August-September, 1992, pp. 26- 28.

Harlow, Neal. *The Maps of San Francisco Bay from the Spanish Discovery in 1769 to the American Occupation.* San Francisco: The Book Club of California, 1950.

Merlin, Imeida. *Alameda: A Geographical History.* Alameda: Friends of the Alameda Free Library, 1977.

Moore, James R. *The Story of Moore Dry Dock Company.* Sausalito: Windgate Press, 1994.

Mutnick, Dorothy Gittinger. *Horace W. Carpentier: A Man of His Times.* Lafayette: Monograph by the author, 1977.

Oakland Museum of California. "A Walk Along the Water: Oakland's Dynamic Waterfront." Exhibition text by various authors. 1996.

Shepard, Irving, ed. *Jack London's Tales of Adventure.* New York: Doubleday & Company, Inc., 1956.

Staniford, Edward. "Horace Carpentier — the lord of the legal land grabbers." Berkeley: *The Independent & Gazette,* June 22, 1980, p. 3.

Weber, David. *Oakland: Hub of the West.* Tu sa: Continental Heritage Press, Inc., 1981.

Chapter Two: Traces of the Peraltas

Arredondo, José. Interviewed by Chiori Santiago. Oakland, April 2000.

Bradford, Amory. *Oakland's Not For Burning.* New York: David McKay Company, 1968.

Camarillo, Albert. *Chicanos in California.* Sparks, Nevada: Materials for Today's Learning, Inc., 1984.

Martinez, Arabella. Interviewed by Abby Wasserman. April 19, 2000.

Oakland Tribune. "City Asked to Act in Zooter War/Pachucos in Oakland Jail." June 11, 1943.

Oakland Tribune. "12 Youths Held in Brawl." November 23, 1943.

Ruiz, Vicki L. *Cannery Women, Cannery Lives.* Albuquerque: University of New Mexico Press, 1987.

Chapter Three: The Politics of Invention

Hinkel, Edgar, and William E. McCann, eds. *United States Work Progress Administration, Oakland 1852-1938,* Vol. II. Oakland: Oakland Public Library under the auspices of the Works Progress Administration, 1939.

League of Women Voters. "A Guide to Local Government." Oakland: League of Women Voters, 1990

Martinez, Arabella. Interviewed by Abby Wasserman. Oakland, April 19, 2000.

O'Donnell, Father Bill. Interviewed by Brenda Payton. Berkeley, March 3, 2000.

Rothrock, Kate. "Taking It to the Streets: The Oakland General Strike of 1946." *The Museum of California,* Vol. 20, No. 4, Fall 1996.

Stow, Marietta. "Women's Republic." *Women's Herald of Industry,* c. 1880.

"West Oakland: A Place to Start From." Oakland: CalTrans brochure, 1994.

Wyman, Bill. "Roots: The Origins of Black Politics in the East Bay." *East Bay Express,* Vol. 9, No. 43, August 7, 1987.

Chapter Four: Artistic Harvest

Albright, Thomas. *Art in the San Francisco Bay Area, 1945-1980.* Berkeley and Los Angeles: University of California Press, 1985. Boas, Nancy. *The Society of Six: California Colorists.* Berkeley and Los Angeles: University of California Press, 1988.

Clark, Garth, ed., *American Ceramics: 1876 to the Present.* New York: Abbeville Press, 1987.

Jones, Caroline A. *Bay Area Figurative Art, 1950-1965.* San Francisco: San Francisco Museum of Modern Art and University of California Press, Berkeley, 1990.

Jones, Harvey L. *Twilight and Reverie: California Tonalist Painting, 1890-1930.* Oakland: The Oakland Museum, 1996.

Heyman, Therese Thau, ed. *Seeing Straight: The f.64 Revolution in Photography.* Oakland: The Oakland Museum, 1992.

Karlstrom, Paul J., ed. *On the Edge of America: California Modernist Art, 1900-1950.* Berkeley: University of California Press in association with the Archives of American Art, Smithsonian Institution, and the Fine Arts Museums of San Francisco, 1996.

Orr-Cahall, Christina, ed. *The Art of California: Selected Works from the Collection of The Oakland Museum.* Oakland: The Oakland Museum and Chronicle Books, San Francisco, 1984.

Slivka, Rose, and Karen Tsujimoto. *The Art of Peter Voulkos.* New York: Kodansha International Ltd. in collaboration with the Oakland Museum, 1995.

Trapp, Kenneth R., ed. *The Arts and Crafts Movement in California: Living the Good Life.* Oakland: The Oakland Museum and Abbeville Press, New York, 1993.

Chapter Five: Chinatown Roots

Ah-Tye, Howard. *Resourceful Chinese.* Oakland: Chinese Presbyterian Church of Oakland, 1999.

Ah-Tye, Howard. "The evolution of a Chinatown." *Asian Week,* April 23, 1981.

Chen, Jack. *The Chinese of America: From the Beginnings to the Present.* San Francisco: Harper & Row, 1982.

Chinn, Thomas W., ed. Him Mark Lai and Philip P. Choy eds. *A History of The Chinese in California.* San Francisco: Chinese Historical Society of America, 1969.

Ma, Eve Armentrout, and Huei Ma Jeong. *The Chinese of Oakland: Unsung Builders.* Oakland: Oakland Chinese History Research Committee, 1982.

Takaki, Ronald. *Strangers from a Different Shore: A History of Asian Americans.* Boston, Toronto, London: Little, Brown and Company, 1989.

Yabuki, Dean. "The Japanese in Oakland: Identity and Historical Experience." *Oakland Heritage Alliance News,* Fall 1983, pp. 1-2.

Sher, Sandra. "How Do You Spell Relief? O-A-K-L-A-N-D." *The Museum of California.* Vol. 10, No. 5, March/April 1987.

Oakland Herald. "Ask Restriction of Chinatown." June 19, 1906.

Oakland Herald. "Chinese Crowding into Fashionable District." April 27, 1906.

Oakland Herald. "Orientals Seek New City." May 12, 1906.

Oakland Herald. "White People Protest Against Chinese Influx." June 13, 1906.

Oakland Herald. "It's a Chinese Empire in Miniature." February 2, 1907.

Yokomizo, Motomi (Tony). *A History of the Oakland Buddhist Church.* Unpublished manuscript.

Yokomizo, Motomi and Nobuye. Interview by Abby Wasserman. Oakland, February 18, 2000.

Saito, Leo and Margaret. Interview by Abby Wasserman. Oakland, March 2, 2000.

Utsumi, Bob and Yasuko. Interview by Abby Wasserman. Oakland, February 28, 2000.

Chapter Six: Wheels and Wings

Beardsley, Roger. "The Durant Mark in Oakland." *Durant Standard,* Vol. 8, Issue 3. Green Bay: Durant Family Registry, November 1983.

Durant, R.C. "Why Chevrolet Motor Company Located in Oakland." Oakland: *Oakland Tribune Yearbook,* 1921.

Fort, James H. "Great Oakland Manufacturing Plant is Pioneer in Production." Oakland: *Oakland Tribune Yearbook,* 1928.

Dutart, Samuel W. "The Automobile Astounded Oaklanders 'way Back in '98." *Oakland Tribune*, May 4, 1952.

Forden, Lesley. "The Dole Race." *American Aviation Historical Society*, Winter 1955.

Hamlen, Joseph R. *Flight Fever*. New York: Doubleday & Co., Inc., 1971.

Jones, DeWitt, ed. *The Port of Oakland*. Oakland: State Emergency Relief Administration, 1934.

Minor, Woodruff. *Pacific Gateway: An Illustrated History of the Port of Oakland*. Oakland: Port of Oakland, 2000.

Oakland Tribune. Tribune Centennial Edition — Automotive Section, October 17, 1974.

Oakland Tribune Yearbook, Oakland, 1927-1947.

Port of Oakland Compass, 1932-1942. Oakland: Oakland Board of Port Commissioners.

Port Progress, 1975-1977. Oakland: Oakland Board of Port Commissioners.

Roseberry, C.R. *The Challenging Skies: The Colorful Story of Aviation's Most Exciting Years, 1919-1939*. New York: Doubleday & Co., Inc., 1966.

Sturm, William. "California Motor Car Company." *Oakland Heritage Alliance News*, Spring 1988.

Talbot, David, "GM to Oakland: Drop Dead." *East Bay Voice*, November-December 1978.

Chapter Seven: Grace Under Pressure

Birt, Rodger. "African Americans in the Gold Rush." *The Museum of California*, Vol. 22, No. 2, Spring 1998.

Butler, Mary Ellen. *Oakland Welcomes the World*. Montgomery: Community Communications, 1996.

Collins, Willie R. "Putting on the Big Hat: Labor and Lore Among Oakland's Redcaps." CalTrans brochure, 1997.

Crouchett, Lawrence P., *William Byron Rumford: The Life and Public Service of a California Legislator*. El Cerrito, California: Downey Place Publishing House, Inc., 1984.

Dellums, C.L. Interviewed by Joyce Henderson for Earl Warren Oral History Project. Regents of the University of California, 1973.

Hausler, Donald. "The Black Y's of Oakland." *Oakland Heritage Alliance News*, Vol. 7, No. 4, Winter 1987-88.

Hausler, Donald. "Mary Sanderson and the Brooklyn School." *Oakland Heritage Alliance News*, Vol. 13 No. 3-4, Winter-Spring 1994.

Hazard, Ben. Interview by Mary Perry Smith. Oakland, March 2000.

Lavoie, Steven. "NAACP's roots in Oakland run deep." *Oakland Tribune*, Jan. 7, 1996.

Lemke-Santangelo, Gretchen. *Abiding Courage: African American Migrant Women and the East Bay Community*. University of North Carolina Press, 1996.

Payton, Brenda. "Black History Series." *Oakland Tribune*, January 1, 1993.

Wollenberg, Charles M. *All Deliberate Speed: Segregation and Exclusion in California Schools, 1855-1975*. Berkeley: University of California Press, 1976.

Chapter Eight: Safe at Home

Brodie, John. Interview by Phil Mumma. Palo Alto, California, January 1983.

Cohn, Howard. "All America Family (Zoe Ann Olsen and Jackie Jensen)" *Collier's*, June 21, 1952 p. 24.

Dobbins, Dick. *The Grand Minor League: An Oral History of the Old Pacific Coast League*. San Francisco: Woodford Press, 1999.

Dobbins, Dick, and Jon Twichell. *Nuggets on the Diamond: A History of Baseball in the Bay Area*. San Francisco: Woodford Press, 1994.

Hession, Joseph, and Steve Cassady. *Raiders*. San Francisco: Foghorn Press, 1987.

Morgan, Joe. Interview by Phil Mumma. Oakland, January 1983.

Norton, Ray. Interview by Phil Mumma. Berkeley, March 2000.

Post Enquirer. "Zoe Ann Wins Olympic Berth." July 10, 1948.

Pollard, Jim. Interview by Phil Mumma. Lodi, California, January 1983.

Powles, George. Interview by Phil Mumma. Walnut Creek, California, January 1983.

Rayman, Graham. "At Ringside." *The Museum of California,* Vol. 15, No. 1, Summer 1991.

Robinson, Frank. Interview by Phil Mumma. San Francisco, January 1983.

Zingg, Paul J., and Mark Medeiros. *Runs, Hits and an Era: A History of the Pacific Coast League.* Urbana and Chicago: Published for the Oakland Museum by the University of Illinois Press, 1994.

Chapter Nine: For the People

Abe, Patricia. Interview by Erika Mailman. Oakland, March 2000.

Bamford, Georgia Loring. *The Mystery of Jack London.* Oakland: Georgia Loring Bamford, 1931.

Batoon, Rene. Interview by Erika Mailman. March 1999 and March 2000.

"California Spring Garden Show, a brief history." *Business Men's Garden Club* pamphlet, 1933.

Coburn, William P. "Rose Garden Renaissance." *Oakland Heritage Alliance News,* Vol. 16, No. 1, Summer 1966.

Colombo, Rena. Interview by Eleanor Swent. Oakland, March 23, 1983. *Dunsmuir House & Gardens, Inc.* Vol. 7.

Conmy, Peter Thomas. *Oakland Library Association: 1868-1878.* Oakland: Oakland Public Library, 1968.

Covell, Dr. Charles B. "The Oakland Municipal Rose-Garden." *American Rose Annual,* 1946.

Elliott, W.W. *Oakland and Surroundings.* Oakland: W.W. Elliott, 1885.

Ferguson, Charles Arthur. Interview by Erika Mailman. Oakland, April 2000.

Golden State Bonsai Collection — North: Bonsai & Suiseki Display Garden. Pamphlet, n.d.

Greenberg, Joan, et al., eds. "Dunsmuir House and Gardens." Oakland: *Dunmuir House & Gardens, Inc.,* September 1994.

Greene, Charles S. *Library History in Oakland.* Oakland: Oakland Public Library, 1925.

Held, Ray E. *The Rise of the Public Library in Califorma.* Chicago: American Library Association, 1973.

Hillenbrand, Ron. Interview by Erika Mailman. Oakland, March 2000.

"History of Hellman family." *Dunsmuir House & Gardens, Inc.,* Vol. 6.

Hoysradt, Paul. "Paul Ecke: the Christmas Flower King." *Horticulture,* December, 1961, reprinted in *Dunsmuir House & Gardens, Inc.* Vol. 7.

McGinty, Brian. "Poinsettias by the Acre." *Americana,* November/December, 1980, repinted in *Dunsmuir House & Gardens, Inc.* Vol. 7.

Oakland Public Library. *Annual Report, 1998-1999.* Oakland: Oakland Public Library, 2000.

Oakland Public Library. *A Library for the 21st Century: Oakland Public Library Strategic Plan,* 1995-1010. Oakland: Oakland Public Library, 1995.

Oakland Times. "The Library and the Reading Room." April 7, 1878.

Oakland Transcript. "Oakland Library Association Opening of the Rooms To-day." January 1, 1869.

Oakland Tribune. "The Free Library." November 7, 1878.

Oakland Tribune. "Successful library." July 15, 1874.

Oakland Tribune. "25,000 visit Rose Garden." April 27, 1936.

Oakland Tribune. "100,000 Roses in Bloom here for Mother's Day." May 9, 1937.

Rhodehamel, Josephine DeWitt and Raymond Francis Wood. *Ina Coolbrith, Librarian and Laureate of California.* Provo: Brigham Young University Press, 1973.

Roses. Pamphlet published by Oakland Park Department, 1947.

Todd, Frank Morton. *The Story of the Exposition.* New York: G. P. Putnam's Son, 1921.

Wilkins, Teresa. Interview by Erika Mailman. Oakland, September 1999.

Wilson, Marlene. *Oakland Rose Garden, a short history.* Broadsheet. Oakland: Oakland Heritage Alliance, August, 1982.

Wood, Myron W. *History of Alameda County, California.* Oakland: M.W. Wood, 1883.

Chapter 10: Native Spirit

Bickel, Polly M. "Changing Sea Levels Along the California Coast: Anthropological Implications." *Journal of California Anthropology,* Summer 1978.

Hall, William Haynes. "The San Antonio Lagoon Shell Mound" in *Historic Sites and Landmarks of Old San Antonio and Clinton.* Berkeley: Works Progress Administration, 1937.

Lobo, Susan. "Is Urban a Person or a Place? Characteristics of Urban Indian Country." *American Indian Culture and Research Journal,* Vol. 22, No. 4, 1998.

Lobo, Susan, ed. *The American Indian Urban Experience.* Walnut Creek, California: AltaMira Press, 2001.

McCann, William E. and J. Hinkel, Director. *History of Rural Alameda County,* 2 vols. Oakland: Works Progress Administration Project, 1937.

Milliken, Randall. *A Time of Little Choice.* Menlo Park, California: Ballena Press, 1995.

Margolin, Malcolm. *The Ohlone Way: Indian Life in the San Francisco-Monterey Bay Area.* Berkeley: Heyday Books, 1978.

Moisa, Ray. "BIA Relocation Program." *News From Native California,* May/June 1988.

Nelson, N.C. "Shellmounds of the San Francisco Bay Region." University of California Publications in American Archaeology and Ethnology, December 1909.

Nelson, N.C. Annotated update of Dec. 1909 map, source unspecified. Map Room, University of California, Berkeley.

Rogoff, Ethel. Interviewed by Susan Lobo, Marilyn St. Germaine and Geraldine Lira. Oakland: Community History Project, Intertribal Friendship House, 1979.

Schenck, W. Egbert. "The Emeryville Shellmound: Final Report." University of California Publications in American Archaeology and Ethnology, 1926.

Sowers, Janet M. *Creek & Watershed Map of Oakland and Berkeley.* Oakland: Oakland Museum of California, revised 1995.

Uhle, Max. "The Emeryville Shellmound." University of California Publications in American Archaeology and Ethnology, June 1907.

Chapter 11: Permission to Dance

Beckford, Ruth. Interview by Chiori Santiago. Oakland, April 2000.

Beene, Melanie & Associates. "Autopsy of an Orchestra: An Analysis of Factors Contributing to the Bankruptcy of the Oakland Symphony Orchestra Association." January 1988.

Cavaglia, Tony. Interview by Chiori Santiago. Oakland, April 2000.

Harmon, Walt. "Documenting a Sweet period in Oakland's History," from Oakland History Room file, publication not noted, n.d.

Hildebrand, Lee. "Bay City Blues." *San Francisco Examiner Image Magazine,* May 11, 1986.

Hildebrand, Lee. "The Thrill Goes On." *The Museum of California,* Fall 1982.

Hildebrand, Lee. *Bay Area Blues.* San Francisco: Pomegranate Artbooks, 1993.

Huck, William. "Oakland Ballet: The First 25 Years." Oakland: Oakland Ballet, 1990.

Lujan, Lori. "A Short History of the Mexican-American Presence in Oakland" in *Chicano/Mexicano Traditional and Contemporary Arts and Folklife in Oakland,* Willie R. Collins, ed. Oakland: Cultural Arts Division of the City of Oakland. 1995.

Marshall, John A. Letter to the Editor. *Oakland Tribune,* December 1, 1964.

Noland, Fred. "Oakland and Sister Cities of the Eastbay Set High Standard in Realm of Music." *Oakland Tribune Yearbook,* February 26, 1936.

Oakland Bulletin. "Dance Hall Control by Municipal Dance Hall." May 24, 1922.

Oakland Tribune. "'Abolish All Rag Dances,' says Mayor." August 1, 1913.

Oakland Tribune. "1000 Frolic at Outdoor Dance." August 20, 1938.

Stone, Susannah Harris. *The Oakland Paramount.* Oakland: Oakland Paramount Theatre, 1992.

Chapter 12: Transformations

Bellman, Phil, and Betsy Yost. "Oakland's Remarkable Flatirons." *Oakland Heritage Alliance News,* Vol. 13, No. 1, Summer 1993.

Lenahan, Gaye, "The Hotel Oakland." *Oakland Heritage Alliance News,* Vol. 13, No. 2, Fall 1993.

Marvin, Betty, "Downtown Historic District." *Oakland Heritage Alliance News,* Vol. 18, No. 3, Spring 1998.

Allen, Annalee. "Landmarks" (columns on architecture). *Montclarion,* 1994-1996. *Oakland Tribune,* 1997-1998.

Douthat, Carolyn. "Economic Incentives for Historic Preservation, Oakland, CA." National Trust for Historic Preservation, Oakland City Administration Building Environmental Impact Report, July 1994.

Staniford, Edward Fawsitt, "Governor in the Middle: The Administation of George C. Pardee, Governor of California, 1903-1907." Doctoral dissertation. Berkeley: University of California, 1955.

Williams, Diana. "Historic Sites Face Wrecking Ball." *Oakland Tribune,* March 24, 1994.

Oakland Cultural Heritage Survey — Central District properties, 1979-95. City of Oakland Planning Department, Community and Economic Development Agency.

Chapter 13: A Writer's Place

Beasley, Delilah Leontium. *Negro Trailblazers of California.* Privately printed, 1919.

Christie, Alix. "The Pen's Might." *Oakland Tribune,* March 29, 1991.

Counts, Laura. "A pledge to respect Oakland's diversity," *Oakland Tribune,* January 5, 1999.

Crouchett, Lorraine J. *Delilah Leontium Beasley: Oakland's Crusading Journalist.* El Cerrito, California: Downey Place Publishing House, Inc., 1990.

George, Henry Jr. *The Life of Henry George: First and Second Periods.* Garden City, New York: Doubleday, Page & Company, 1911.

Gioia, Dana. "Fallen Western Star: San Francisco as a Literary Region." *Hungry Mind Review.* Winter 1999-2000.

Hendricks, King and Shepard, Irving, eds. *Letters From Jack London.* New York: Odyssey Press, 1965.

Herron, Don. "Points East." *The Literary World of San Francisco & Its Environs.* San Francisco: City Lights Books, 1985. Kingston, Maxine Hong. *Tripmaster Monkey: His Fake Book.* New York: Alfred A. Knopf, 1989.

London, Joan. *Jack London and His Times.* Seattle: University of Washington Press, 1939.

Markham, Edwin. "The Man With the Hoe," *San Francisco Examiner,* January 15, 1899.

O'Connor, Richard. *Jack London: A Biography.* Boston: Little, Brown and Company, 1964.

Oliver, Myrna. "Exposé writer Jessica Mitford dies at age 78." *Los Angeles Times,* July 24, 1996.

"The Poetry of Joaquin Miller," Central California Poetry Journal, Volume 96, Number 1 (online version). Santa Cruz, California: Solo Publications, 1996.

Reed, Ishmael. "Money Can't Buy You Love," in *Airing Dirty Laundry.* Reading, Massachusetts: Addison-Wesley Publishing Company, 1993.

Rosenbaum, Fred. *Free To Choose: The Making of a Jewish Community in the American West.* Berkeley: The Judah L. Magnes Memorial Museum, 1976.

Salamo, Lin, and Harriet Elinor Smith. *Mark Twain's Letters: Volume 5 1872-1873.* Berkeley: University of California Press, 1997.

Salas, Floyd. *Buffalo Nickel: A Memoir.* Houston: Arte Publico, 1992.

Salas, Floyd. *To Build a Fire: A commemorative anthology of 77 writers in, from & about a geographical place known as Oakland, California. For the Celebration, November 6, 1976.* Oakland: California Syllabus, 1976.

The Neighborhoods

Neighborhood Profiles. Series of informational brochures. Oakland: Oakland Citizens Committee for Urban Renewal (OCCUR), 1997.

Index

The Spirit of Oakland

294

295

Partners & Web Site Index